Power BI Tools Volume 2:
Learning Power Pivot For Excel Made Easy

By Indera E. Murphy

Tolana Publishing
Teaneck, New Jersey

Power BI Tools Volume 2: Learning Power Pivot For Excel Made Easy

Published By:
Tolana Publishing
PO Box 719
Teaneck, NJ 07666 USA

Find us online at www.tolanapublishing.com
Inquiries may be sent to the publisher: tolanapub@yahoo.com

Our books are available online at www.barnesandnoble.com. They can also be ordered from Ingram.

ISBN-13: 978-1-935208-27-3
ISBN-10: 1-935208-27-6

Library of Congress Control Number: 2016910217

Printed and bound in the United States Of America

Notice of Liability
The information in this book is distributed on as "as is" basis, without warranty. Every effort has been made to ensure that this book contains accurate and current information. However, the publisher and author shall not be liable to any person or entity with respect to any loss or damage caused or alleged to be caused directly or indirectly, as a result of any information contained herein or by the computer software and hardware products described in it.

Trademarks
All companies and product names are trademarks or registered trademarks of their respective companies. They are used in this book in an editorial fashion only. No use of any trademark is intended to convey endorsement or other affiliation with this book.

About The Series

Power BI Tools Volume 2: Learning Power Pivot For Excel Made Easy, is part of the growing series of computer software books that are designed to be used as a self-paced learning tool, in a classroom setting or in an online class. The books in this series contain an abundance of step-by-step instructions and screen shots to help reduce the "stress" often associated with learning new software. Some of the titles in the series are shown below.

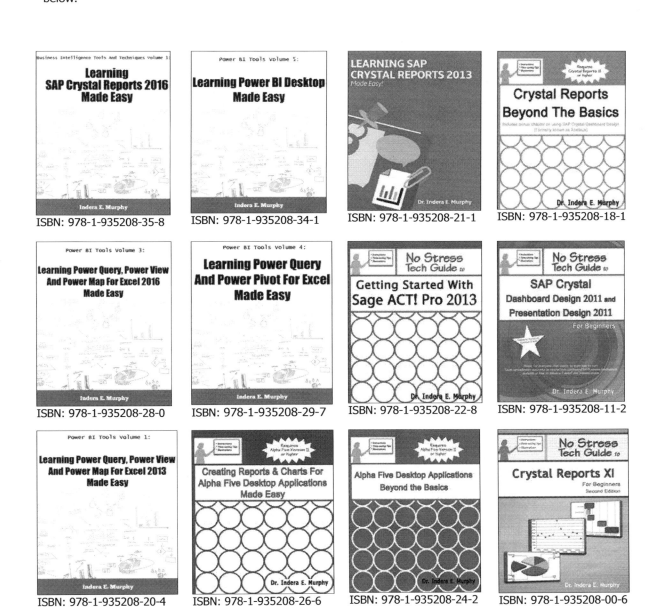

ISBN: 978-1-935208-35-8

ISBN: 978-1-935208-34-1

ISBN: 978-1-935208-21-1

ISBN: 978-1-935208-18-1

ISBN: 978-1-935208-28-0

ISBN: 978-1-935208-29-7

ISBN: 978-1-935208-22-8

ISBN: 978-1-935208-11-2

ISBN: 978-1-935208-20-4

ISBN: 978-1-935208-26-6

ISBN: 978-1-935208-24-2

ISBN: 978-1-935208-00-6

Visit us online at www.tolanapublishing.com for more information

Who This Book Is For

This book is primarily for people that have not used Power Pivot for Excel and want to learn what functionality Power Pivot adds to pivot tables and pivot charts. Business Intelligence consultants and professionals will find this book helpful in terms of how they can incorporate Power Pivot into the projects that they work on. It is also for people that are somewhat familiar with Power Pivot and are now looking for step-by-step instructions.

I know that many books claim to have "step-by-step instructions". If you have tried to follow books that make this claim and you got lost or could not complete a task as instructed, it may not have been your fault. When I decided to write computer books, I vowed to really have step-by-step instructions that actually included every step, even though some people claim that it is annoying. This includes steps like which file to open, which option to select and more. In my opinion, it is this level of detail that makes a computer book easy to follow. I hope that you feel the same way. If not, this is probably not the book for you.

About The Author

Dr. Indera E. Murphy is an author, educator and IT professional that has over 20 years experience in the Information Technology field. She has held a variety of positions including technical writer, programmer, consultant, web designer, course developer and project leader. Indera has designed and developed software applications and web sites, as well as, manage technology driven projects in several industries. In addition to being an Executive Director and consultant, as an online adjunct professor, she taught courses in a variety of areas including project management, technical writing, information processing, Access, HTML, Windows, Excel, Dreamweaver and critical thinking.

Thank you for purchasing this book!

CONTENTS

After reading this chapter and completing the exercises you will:

☑ Know what Power Pivot is and what it can be used for
☑ Understand the difference between the 32 and 64-bit versions of Excel
☑ Have downloaded the practice files used in this book
☑ Understand terms related to Power Pivot

CHAPTER 1

Welcome To Power Pivot!

There are several types of people that have an interest in learning Power Pivot because it can be used across an organization. The fact that the software is included with some versions of Excel, will definitely increase the number of users. When I first heard about Power Pivot, I was concerned about how seriously the software be taken because at the time, it was a separate add-on and it was free. Not so long ago, free software was not taken seriously and was often deemed inferior on one level or another. Thankfully, there have been some very successful software packages that have helped remove the stigma of free software automatically being considered inferior, and Power Pivot has risen to the challenge.

What I do know is that traditional business intelligence tools, self-service or otherwise, are in demand, even if they have a steep learning curve. I know that there are millions of Excel users around the world. I also know from having taught Introduction to Excel college level courses, that creating pivot tables and pivot charts give a lot of people, a lot of trouble.

What intrigued me was that this software was brand new when I wrote my first Power Pivot book. I knew that I wanted to be part of this new venture from Microsoft. I am happy that I took a "walk out on faith", as it opened up a whole new category of software for me to show people how to use.

The goal of Power Pivot is to allow people to create their own data sets and reports (with all of the slicing and dicing of data they want) without having to rely on the IT department build or help them build the data set.

There is a broad spectrum of people that could benefit from using Power Pivot. There are regular Excel users like me and probably, you too. There are Excel power users that have spent countless hours pushing Excel past its intended limits <smile>. I suspect that business analysts will use it as a prototype tool for a business intelligence solution. Hopefully, you feel that this book is the right fit for your hands-on introduction to Power Pivot.

One thing that intrigued me about Power Pivot (well actually all of the Power BI toolset), was that data from a variety of data sources could be imported into it. And with the amount of data being created online and then analyzed offline, I was sure that these tools for Excel would be helpful.

This book is a visual guide that has over 500 illustrations that practically eliminates the guess work. I don't know about you, but it can be frustrating when you need to emulate something that you have "read" is possible, for a software package to do, and you try it on your own and it doesn't work! It is at that very moment that you realize how helpful it would be to have step-by-step instructions.

Learning tips and shortcuts will let you work faster and smarter. The more that you know about Power Pivot, the easier your day to day data analysis experiences will be, which will make you more productive.

Sit back and lets get started!

Business Intelligence is often called BI for short. Even though the concept of business intelligence has been around for over a decade, there are still different schools of thought in the business community on what it is, what it isn't and how it should be implemented.

BI is the first topic discussed in this book because it is a primary reason that people use tools like Power Pivot, Tableau and Power BI Desktop. All of these tools allow you to perform some, if not all, of the analysis needed to make business decisions.

BI, in the broad sense, is a collection of technology and applications that are used to gather, store, access and analyze data, often in an enterprise environment. Generally speaking, business intelligence is the process of analyzing data, raw or otherwise and converting the analysis into knowledge. This process is usually used to make business decisions or track business trends and changes. This decision making process requires the raw data to be transformed, so that it can be presented accurately and usually in real-time. The typical business intelligence process includes querying, reporting, forecasting, data mining and statistical analysis.

In the beginning, BI solutions were primarily built by the IT department. These solutions took months to build and were often complex. One goal was to bring data from all over the company and place it in what came to be known as a "data warehouse". This repository of data, should be accurate and not redundant.

Some of the goals of BI analysis include being able to easily find new business opportunities, making decisions on existing processes, looking for ways to save money, having the ability to recognize where improvement is needed and to be able to respond to change, as quickly as possible.

BI, especially self-service or personal (do it yourself) business intelligence, is gaining a lot of momentum because companies are looking to bring more decision making tools to their employees. This allows employees at several levels in the company to gain access to data that will help them make more accurate business decisions in a timely manner. And yes, a major goal is to make a company more profitable.

While giving users more tools to get their jobs done more efficiently is a good strategy, users can also make mistakes that can do the opposite of what the tools were intended to do. I am not saying this to rain on your enthusiasm of learning Power Pivot. I just want you to be aware of the fact that if you do not have a very good understanding of the data that you work with, the chances of displaying the data incorrectly are high. This means that decisions will be made based on incorrect data.

Power BI Tools For Excel

I think that the two main reasons people that use Excel on a regular basis, start using any of the Power BI Tools for Excel are:

① They are looking for another or easier way to complete tasks.
② Excel cannot handle all of their needs.

The Power BI tools are a collection of enhancements for Excel. The tools are briefly explained below.

POWER QUERY In Excel 2016, Microsoft stopped using the name "Power Query". The Power Query functionality is built into Excel and does not have a separate update process. It no longer has it's own tab. The **GET & TRANSFORM** section on the Data tab in Excel, contains the Power Query options. This tool is used to "discover" and consolidate data from a variety of sources. This is done by importing, merging, shaping and cleansing data. The data can then be added to an Excel workbook. A better solution is to load the data into the data model, so that it can be used by Power Pivot, Power View and 3D Maps. You will still see people referring to the Get & Transform options as Power Query.

POWER PIVOT Is used to manage the data model in the workbook, join tables, create calculated fields, KPI's and more. While Power View and Power Map reports and maps can be created from Excel data tables, it is easier for Power View and Power Map to use data in the data model.

Each Excel workbook only has one data model. While data can be added to the data model and relationships can be created in Excel, without Power Pivot, Power Pivot is the only tool that has direct access to the data model. By direct access, I mean that you can view the data, create calculations and more. This is what makes Power Pivot important. In addition to calling it the "data model", it is also referred to as the Power Pivot data model or the Excel data model.

POWER VIEW Is the report writer, if you will, in the Power BI toolset for Excel. Like Power Pivot, slicers and filters can be added to reports (or presentations, as some people like to say). Because Power View connects directly to the data model, some of the features that can be tweaked to enhance the data model to be used with Power View are included in this book. I tried to point out Power Pivot options, that you should be aware of or that will enhance using the data model to create reports in Power View. [See Power View Tips, in the index]

POWER MAP In Excel 2016, this tool was renamed to **3D MAPS**. As its name suggests, this tool is used to display geographical data on a map. I, like many people, still refer to it as Power Map.

Based on the order that the Power BI tools were listed above, it may seem like data must be loaded into Power Query first and then into Power Pivot. That is not true. The reason that I listed Power Query first is because it can be used to clean data, which is something that Power Pivot cannot do. As you will see, data can be imported straight into the data model. Having said that, many people import data into Power Query first to clean it, then load it into the data model.

Power Pivot is at the center of Microsoft's BI toolset for Excel, because it is used as the foundation for data analysis. The data model can also be used by the other software packages in the Power BI toolset. I have covered as many features as I could in this book. Not to overwhelm you, but to let you see what the possibilities are. I understand that it would be rare to use every topic covered in this book, for every pivot table or pivot chart that you create, but hopefully, when the time comes to use a feature, this book will also be a great reference guide.

Power Query, Power View and Power Map sit on top of the data model. Hopefully, this brief introduction of the Power BI toolset for Excel, brings some clarity to what each tool brings to the table.

While the tools discussed here may sound like the end all, be all, they were not designed to replace corporate reports. That is not a bad thing! One reason they should not replace corporate reports is because users can wind up with duplicate (redundant) data and/or something less than the most recent copy of the data. The Power BI tools for Excel are designed to provide more interactive reports, especially for data that changes all the time. The good news is that these tools and the people that know how to use them are in great demand in companies of all sizes, in all types of industries. The other three tools discussed above, are covered in Volume 3 of my Power BI Tools book series. (See ISBN 978-1-935208-28-0)

Unlike the four tools discussed above, the two newcomers to the Power BI toolset, discussed below, do not require Excel:

① **POWER BI DESKTOP** This software contains Power Pivot, Power Query and Power View, in one interface. It was officially released in July 2015. What I like a lot about this software is that it is updated monthly. Power BI Desktop is covered in my Volume 5 book. (See ISBN 978-1-935208-34-1) So, stay tuned <smile>.

② **POWER BI** This is a cloud-based solution for sharing data via dashboards, reports and more. It also has functionality built-in to create reports and dashboards.

How This Book Is Organized

Topics and exercises in one chapter build on ones covered in previous chapters. Working through the exercises in the order that they are presented in this book will provide a better understanding of the concepts, because you can see first hand what Power Pivot is capable of, instead of just reading about the concepts.

To get the most out of this book, it is not advised that you skip around. The first reason is because some of the workbooks used in later chapters are created in exercises earlier in the book. The other reason is that a topic or option may have been covered in more detail earlier in the book. If you decide to skip around and cannot complete an exercise because there is something that you do not understand, you will have to go back and find the section that covers the topic in question. Below is an overview of what is covered in each chapter.

Chapter 1, Getting Started With Power Pivot covers background information on Power Pivot, different versions of Excel, what Power Pivot can be used for, Power Pivot workbooks vs Excel workbooks and Power Pivot terminology.

Chapter 2, Quick Tour Of Power Pivot walks you through the steps needed to connect to a data source, import data into Power Pivot and use the Pivot Table Fields list to create a pivot table, using data in the data model.

Chapter 3, Exploring The Power Pivot Workspace covers Power Pivot options, including the Power Pivot tab on the Excel ribbon and the Power Pivot workspace.

Chapter 4, Using The Table Import Wizard covers the Table Import Wizard and the types of data sources that Power Pivot can import data from.

Chapter 5, Import Data From Databases covers importing data from databases, views and queries.

Chapter 6, Import Data From Non Database Sources covers a variety of data sources that can be used to import data into Power Pivot, including importing data from a text file, spreadsheet and data feed.

Chapter 7, Linking Tables, Pasting And Appending Data covers linking tables in Excel spreadsheets, pasting and appending data to tables in the data model.

Chapter 8, Using Filters And Sorting Data covers filter options and sorting data in the Power Pivot window. Other topics covered include changing the data type of columns, formatting data and creating custom filters in the data model.

Chapter 9, Creating Relationships covers creating relationships between tables in the data model. Managing relationships is also covered.

Chapter 10, Creating Pivot Tables covers building pivot tables. The options on the Pivot Table Tools contextual tab and Pivot Table Fields list are also covered.

Chapter 11, Creating Pivot Charts covers building pivot charts. Chart types and the options on the Pivot Chart Tools contextual tab are also covered.

Chapter 12, Using Slicers covers adding slicers to pivot tables and charts.

Chapter 13, Enhancing Pivot Tables And Charts Part 1 covers features that can take your pivot tables and charts to the next level.

Chapter 14, Enhancing Pivot Tables And Charts Part 2 continues from the previous chapter and covers additional features that can take your pivot tables and charts to the next level.

Chapter 15, Timelines, Sparklines And Conditional Formatting covers how these Excel options can be used with data in the data model.

Conventions Used In This Book

I designed the following conventions to make it easier for you to follow the instructions in this book.

- ☑ The Courier font is used to indicate what you should type.
- ☑ **Drag** means to press and hold down the left mouse button while moving the mouse.
- ☑ **Click** means to press the left mouse button once, then release it immediately.
- ☑ **Right-click** means to press the right mouse button once, which will open a shortcut menu.
- ☑ Click **OK** means to click the OK button on the dialog box.
- ☑ Press **Enter** means to press the Enter key on your keyboard.
- ☑ SMALL CAPS are used to indicate an option to click on or to bring something to your attention.
- ☑ 💡 This icon indicates a shortcut or another way to complete the task that is being discussed. It can also indicate a tip or additional information about the topic that is being discussed.
- ☑ 💣 This icon indicates a warning, like a feature that has been removed or information that you need to be aware of. This icon can also represent what I call a quirk, meaning a feature that did not work as I expected it to.
- ☑ ⁝ This icon indicates that some of the screen shot has been removed because it does not provide any value.
- ☑ [Text in brackets] references a section, table or figure, that has more information about the topic being discussed. If the reference is in a different chapter, the chapter number is included, like this. [See Chapter 2, Update Options]
- ☑ When you see the phrase "YOU SHOULD HAVE THE OPTIONS SHOWN IN FIGURE X-X", or something similar in the exercises, check to make sure that your screen does look like the figure. If it does, continue with the next set of instructions. If your screen does not look like the figure, redo the steps that you just completed so that your screen does match the figure. Not doing so may cause problems when trying to complete exercises later in the book.
- ☑ Many of the dialog boxes in Excel and Power Pivot have OK, Cancel and Help buttons. Viewing these buttons on all of the figures adds no value, so for the most part, they are not shown.
- ☑ Some toolbars or ribbons have a lot of options. When displayed, it can be hard to see each option on the toolbar or ribbon. When that is the case, I split the toolbar into two, so that it is easier to see all of the options.
- ☑ The section heading **EXERCISE X.Y:** (where X equals the chapter number and Y equals the exercise number) represents exercises that have step-by-step instructions that you should complete. You will also see sections that have step-by-step instructions that are not an exercise. They are not meant to be completed as you go through the book. They are for future reference.
- ☑ **PAGE LAYOUT TAB** ⇒ **PAGE SETUP GROUP** ⇒ **ORIENTATION**, means to click on the **PAGE LAYOUT** tab in Excel, look in the **PAGE SETUP** group (on the Page Layout tab), then click the **ORIENTATION** button, shown in Figure 1-1.

Figure 1-1 Navigation technique

☑ "E2.4 File Name" is the file naming convention for the workbooks that you will create. E2.4 stands for Chapter 2, Exercise 4. You may consider some of the file names long. I did this on purpose, so that it will be easier to know what topic the workbook covers. If you do not want to type the entire file name, type E2.4, as the workbook name.

Assumptions

Yes, I know one should never assume anything, but the following assumptions have been made.
It is assumed that . . . .

☑ You know that this book covers Power Pivot for Excel 2016.

☑ You have a version of Excel 2016 for Windows (32 or 64-bit) installed on your computer, that has Power Pivot. The book has not been tested with any other version of Excel.

☑ You know that the operating system used to write this book is Windows 8.1. If you are using a different version of Windows, some of the screen shots may have a slightly different look.

☑ You know to click OK or the appropriate button to close a dialog box and know to save the changes (to the workbook) before going to the next section or exercise. Instructions like these are omitted, as much as possible.

☑ You know that when I discuss a topic and reference pivot tables, the topic also applies to pivot charts, unless stated otherwise.

☑ When you see <smile>, you know that signifies my attempt of adding humor to the learning process.

☑ You know that the phrase "end user" refers to the person that will use the pivot tables that you create. If you will create and use the pivot tables, in the context of this book, you are also the end user.

☑ You know that in Excel 2010, formulas were called Measures. In Excel 2013, Measures were renamed to Calculated Fields. In Excel 2016, formulas were renamed back to Measures. When you see "formulas", "measures" or "calculated field", know that they are one in the same.

☑ You understand that for a reason that I can't explain, I use the words "spreadsheet" and "worksheet" interchangeably when referring to the data on a tab in Excel. I also use the words "field" and "column" interchangeably because the data is in a field in the database that you import data from and then it's called a column in Excel and Power Pivot.

☑ You understand that when I refer to "data", "a table" or "importing data", that I am referring to data in the data model, unless stated otherwise.

☑ You understand that when I refer to Power Pivot, I am referring to the window shown in Chapter 2, Figure 2-8. This keeps me from having to say something like "in the Power Pivot window", over and over again <smile>.

☑ You understand that some topics or concepts are repeated on purpose, in this book because they are important and I want you to remember them when you are using Power Pivot on your own.

☑ You know that the end of each chapter in this book has a summary section. In addition to providing a recap of the topics covered, some summaries contain new information, like explaining another way to accomplish a task that was already covered. I did this to not interrupt the flow of the chapter.

☑ You know that the links (to other web sites) in this book worked when the book went to print and that I have no control over when or if the web site owners change or remove web pages.

☑ You know the difference between the **SAVE** option (saves the file with the same file name) and the **SAVE AS** option (saves the file with a different file name or the same file name in a different folder). Excel has buttons for both of these options above the ribbon on the **QUICK ACCESS TOOLBAR**, as illustrated in Figure 1-2. The Save options are also on the File button in Power Pivot. [See Chapter 3, Figure 3-13] Keep in mind that when you save a file, changes in the Excel workbook and the data model are saved, regardless of which window you clicked the Save button in. Many exercises instruct you to save an existing workbook with a new file name.

This is when you would use the Save As button. If you want to use the Save As button, but it is not currently displayed on your Quick Access Toolbar, you will learn how to add it later in this chapter.

Figure 1-2 Save and Save As options illustrated

☑ You know that right-clicking on an Excel workbook or Power Pivot icon on the Windows taskbar, displays the shortcut menu shown in Figure 1-3.

If you need or want to display more files on this shortcut menu, right-click on a blank space on the Windows Taskbar and select Properties.

On the **JUMP LISTS** tab, change the Recent items option to a larger number.

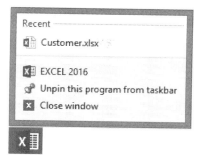

Figure 1-3 Excel shortcut menu on the Windows Taskbar

What Is The Difference Between The 32 And 64-Bit Versions Of Excel?

The list below provides an overview of the differences between the versions of Excel.

① The 32 and 64-bit versions of Excel cannot be installed on the same hard drive on a computer.

② The 32-bit version of Excel can be installed on a computer that has an older version of Excel installed and will not modify the older version of Excel. This means that you can have the 2013 and 2016, 32-bit versions of Excel installed on the same computer. The 64-bit version of Excel does not allow prior versions of Excel to be installed on the same hard drive.

③ The 64-bit version of Excel can handle larger file sizes and no longer has a maximum file size limitation.

 If you know that you will be working with large data sets (millions of records in a table), you should consider installing the 64-bit version of Excel.

Excel Pivot Tables

Pivot tables have been part of Excel for as long as I can remember. As great as they are and as easy as they are to use, there are some limitations of pivot tables created in Excel, that there is no work around for. Some of these limitations are briefly explained below.

① Creating the queries to get the data from a data source requires a skill set that many Excel users do not have. This is because the data needed for the pivot table is usually stored in multiple tables in a database or stored in multiple data sources. For example, some data may be stored in a database and other data that is needed to create the pivot table is stored in an Excel workbook.

② Pivot tables in Excel can only be created from one table on a worksheet, unless you use the **VLOOKUP FUNCTION**.

③ If the data needs to be analyzed several ways, multiple queries may be needed to get the data in a format that can be used to create a pivot table, for each way the data needs to be analyzed.

④ Excel worksheets have a row limitation. If the data source has more than one million rows, all of the query writing in the world will not let you add more rows of data to the worksheet.

What Is Power Pivot And What Can I Use It For?

Power Pivot is a tool that is used to import data from multiple sources into one database (called the **DATA MODEL**) that is part of and stored in an Excel workbook. You may see the terms "Power Pivot data model", "internal data model" and "data model" used interchangeably. They are one in the same. This functionality is used to enhance data analysis created in pivot tables and pivot charts and other tools in Excel. Technical people often refer to Power Pivot as the "front end" of the data model. Power Pivot workbooks, as I call them, can also be shared in real-time with other users if the workbook is published on a SharePoint server. Power Pivot workbooks can also be uploaded and shared on an Analysis Services server. Starting in Excel 2016, Power Pivot is built into Excel. In previous versions of Excel, Power Pivot was an add-in.

The standard business intelligence approach to data is to place the data in a data warehouse for staging and then import the data into an Online Analytical Processing (OLAP) database. Power Pivot allows the data to bypass the data warehouse staging area step and be imported directly into the software (Excel, in this case) that will be used to analyze the data.

One reason that Power Pivot is growing in popularity, is because it empowers an Excel user to create and analyze data in pivot tables. For business analysts, Power Pivot will become an asset because they can connect to external data sources and import data into Excel, without having to get the IT staff to help, once access to the data has been granted. In my opinion, the primary reasons to use Power Pivot are discussed below.

① You need the ability to create a pivot table or another type of report, with data from more than one data source.
② You need to create pivot tables that currently cannot be created in Excel.
③ You need to analyze a data set that has more than 1,048,576 rows of data, which is the maximum number of rows that an Excel worksheet supports.

One purpose of Power Pivot is to help Excel users access data in multi-dimensional databases without having extensive training and knowledge of this type of data modeling. Usually, only IT staff has the data modeling knowledge to access this type of data. To me, a big advantage that Power Pivot brings to the table is that it allows you to perform data analysis without knowing how to use SQL or MDX, even though these tools can be used with Power Pivot.

The primary functionality that Power Pivot adds to Excel is that it brings self-service business intelligence to the desktop. This means that the data that you use to create pivot tables in Excel, that use data in the data model, can actually be saved on your computers hard drive, opposed to having to be saved on a server.

The data model is a repository that stores data. Data in cells, in a table in the data model, cannot be changed like cells can be changed in Excel. Power Pivot cannot be used to modify the source data. If the actual data needs to be changed, it has to be done at the source, or in Power Query, before it is imported into Power Pivot.

As I mentioned earlier, Power Pivot can be used to analyze millions of records. The Table Import Wizard is the primary tool used to import data into Power Pivot. The data is imported into the data model and saved in tables and displayed on separate tabs in the Power Pivot window. Believe it or not, data can also be pasted into a Power Pivot table. Really? That's what I thought when I first found that out. Power Pivot stores the data that is imported in a database (aka, the data model) that is saved in the Excel workbook. The local (database) engine, in Excel, is used to load, query, and update the data model, in the workbook.

Sometimes I get the feeling that some people think that Power Pivot "does" something to pivot tables. The truth is the Power Pivot does not do anything to pivot tables. What it does, is provide a way to connect to many more data sources, including tables that have millions of rows of data.

Power Pivot is a **DATA MODELING TOOL** that is used to put data in a format (loading, structuring, creating relationships and defining data types, to name a few), if you will, that allows the data to be used by what are known as **CLIENT TOOLS**, that these tools could not otherwise access. Additionally, Power Pivot has its own programming language (DAX) that is used to create formulas that client tools do not have the ability to create. The formulas that are created are saved in the data model.

Benefits Of Using Power Pivot

Below are some of the benefits of using Power Pivot, to access enterprise data, to create business intelligence solutions.

① Data from several sources can be imported into the same data model.
② One table can handle millions of rows of data.
③ Linking to data sources provides the ability to refresh the data in the data model easily.
④ Because the data model is read only, data security is increased.
⑤ Power Pivot allows you to use Excel, which you are already familiar with, to create enhanced pivot tables and pivot charts.
⑥ Power Pivot comes with the **DATA ANALYSIS EXPRESSIONS (DAX)** language.
⑦ This data analysis tool adds a lot of functionality to Excel's pivot tables, charts and other analysis tools. Once the data is imported into the data model, relationships between the tables of data can be created, even if the data in the tables come from different data sources.

Power Pivot Workbooks vs Excel Workbooks

In addition to how Power Pivot and Excel handle data differently, there are other differences between workbooks that have data in the data model and those that don't, that you should be aware of, as discussed below.

① Workbooks with data in the data model can only be saved by using one of the following file types: **.XLSX** (Excel workbook), **.XLSM** (Macro enabled workbook) and **.XLSB** (Excel Binary workbook).

② Power Pivot provides direct access to the data model, whether the data comes from one data source or 20 data sources.

③ The biggest difference between these workbooks is that a Power Pivot workbook stores data in the data model that is embedded in the workbook. Keep in mind that Power Pivot is part of Excel, not a stand alone application (like Power BI Desktop), which means that Power Pivot, cannot run on its own.

④ The second biggest difference is that tables in the data model can store more than one million rows of data, which is the maximum in Excel. While one million rows may sound like a lot of data, in BI analysis, one is often working with tens of millions of rows of data. One scenario that comes to mind is the number of transactions for a major credit card company over the last year.

⑤ Power Pivot does not support **VISUAL BASIC FOR APPLICATIONS (VBA)**, but VBA can be used on the Excel side of a Power Pivot workbook to enhance pivot tables, if needed.

⑥ The **GROUP** option (on the Pivot Table Tools Analyze tab) is not available in pivot tables that use Power Pivot data. **MEASURES** in Power Pivot provides similar functionality.

⑦ Power Pivot supports moving and copying spreadsheets in an existing workbook, but does not support moving and copying worksheets that have pivot tables or pivot charts, to a different workbook.

Using The Data Model vs Excel's VLOOKUP Function

The biggest difference between these two options becomes evident when working with millions of rows of data in a table. Large datasets is what the data model was designed to be able to handle. Using the VLOOKUP function with millions of rows of data in one table can bring the computer to a grinding halt and potentially make the computer unstable. This is because of the amount of processing power that VLOOKUP requires to work with large amounts of data. Other differences include:

① It is easier to create a relationship (a link) between tables in the data model, then it is to use VLOOKUP in Excel.

② Relationships also allow for more robust analysis of the data then VLOOKUP provides.

③ Some relationships are created automatically, when the data is imported into the data model. You can also create relationships as needed.

④ As if that is not enough reasons to use Power Pivot, don't forget the data models ability to store millions of rows of data <smile>.

Power Pivot Forum

You can post questions and learn how other people are using the software. The forum is also a great way to keep current on the latest Power Pivot and DAX trends and for getting ideas on how to enhance your pivot table and pivot charts. The name of the forum is SQL Server Power Pivot. The web site is https://social.msdn.microsoft.com/Forums/sqlserver/en-US/home?forum= sqlkjpowerpivotforexcel.

Exercise 1.1: Create A Folder For Your Files

Many of the topics discussed in this book have step-by-step exercises. If you want to follow along, you can download the files used in this book. Some of the files used in this book are in a zip file named powerpivot.zip on our web site. Obtaining the other files used in this book is covered in Exercise 1.2.

1. To obtain the zip file, send an email to powerpivotv2@tolanapublishing.com. If you do not receive an email in a few minutes with the subject line Power Pivot Book Files, check the spam folder in your email software. When you receive the email, follow the steps below.

2. Open Windows Explorer ⇒ Right-click on the C drive or the letter of the primary hard drive that you save files on ⇒ New ⇒ Folder. Type `Power Pivot Book` as the folder name. I will refer to this folder as **YOUR FOLDER** throughout this book.

3. Open the web page listed in the email that you received and download the zip file into your Folder ⇒ Once the zip file is downloaded, extract the files to your folder.

Vol 2 Links.txt File
This file is in the zip file that you just downloaded. When you go through this book, there are links that you may need to type in. In case you do not want to type them in, you can copy and paste them from this file into your web browser. You're welcome! <smile>

If you are going to complete the exercises in this book and plan to use the File menu in Excel to open workbooks, you may want to change the **SHOW THIS NUMBER OF RECENT WORKBOOKS** option on the Advanced panel, on the Excel Options dialog box (shown below in Figure 1-4) to at least 20, so that many of the workbooks that you work on will be displayed on the Recent Workbook List on the File menu.

Change The Default Folder Location

The folder that you just created will also be used to save the workbooks in that you create in this book. Therefore, it may be useful to set it as the default folder that Excel uses. If you want to change the default folder, follow the steps below. Doing this is optional. When you are finished working on the exercises in this book, you can change the default folder to the one that you will use most.

1. Open Excel ⇒ File tab ⇒ Options ⇒ Save panel.

2. In the **DEFAULT LOCAL FILE LOCATION** field, type `C:\Power Pivot Book\`, as illustrated Figure 1-4.

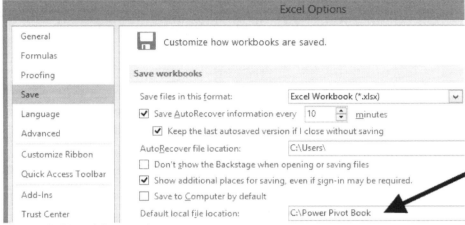

Figure 1-4 Excel Save options

 On the Advanced panel, if checked, the **QUICKLY ACCESS THIS NUMBER OF RECENT WORKBOOKS** option, will display the number of workbooks selected at the bottom of the File menu in Excel, as shown in Figure 1-5. The File menu is also referred to as **BACKSTAGE.**

Figure 1-5 Bottom of the File menu with workbooks displayed

Exercise 1.2: Download More Files

In addition to the practice files that you downloaded from the books web site in the previous exercise, there are additional files that are used in this book. The steps below show you where to get the files from.

Contoso Data Files These files are for a fictitious company named Contoso. They sell a variety of products in their stores around the world. The zip file that you will download, has the files explained in Table 1-1. To download the zip file, follow the steps below.

1. Go to http://powerpivotsdr.codeplex.com.

2. On the right side of the web page, you should see a link for the Power Pivot for Excel Tutorial Sample Data v2 file. The file date is June 10, 2010. Click the Download button. The file name is **CONTOSOV2.**

3. Download this file to your folder, then extract the files into your folder.

File Name	Description
Contoso Sales	This Access database contains tables for company store locations, products, product subcategories, promotions that stores have and sales information.
Geography	This spreadsheet contains information about the continents and countries that the company does business in.
Product Categories	This Access database has one table that lists the categories of products that the company has.
SQL Query	This text file contains a query that is used to select the records that will be imported from a database.
Stores	This spreadsheet contains contact information for all of the stores.

Table 1-1 Contoso data files explained

Adventure Works Database This database is for a fictitious company named Adventure Works. This global company makes and sells bicycles. The version that you will download is the Microsoft Access version of the popular SQL database by the same name, that has been around for years. The database has 67 tables.

I decided to use the Access version of the database for this book because I did not want readers to have to download and install SQL Server or upgrade the version that you may already have installed. If something went wrong with the installation or your computer is not powerful enough to support it, you would be stuck. The Access version does not require you to install any other software, not even Microsoft Access.

1. Go to http://adventureworksaccess.codeplex.com/releases/view/44496.

2. Click on the **ADVENTURE WORKS IN ACCESS 2010 FORMAT (ZIPPED)** link.

3. Download this file to your folder, then extract the database into your folder.

Exercise 1.3: Enable Power Pivot

If you do not see the Power Pivot tab on the Excel ribbon and you have a version of Excel that supports Power Pivot, follow the steps below.

1. Open Excel ⇒ File tab ⇒ Options ⇒ Add-Ins panel.

2. At the bottom of the Excel Options dialog box, open the **MANAGE** drop-down list (shown later at the bottom of Figure 1-7) ⇒ Select **COM ADD-INS** ⇒ Click Go.

3. On the dialog box shown in Figure 1-6, check the Power Pivot For Excel option.

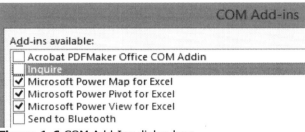

Figure 1-6 COM Add-Ins dialog box

4. Reopen the Excel Options dialog box. You should see an option for Power Pivot, in the Active Application section, illustrated in Figure 1-7.

Once Excel is open, you should see the Power Pivot tab on the Excel ribbon. Click on this tab, then click the Manage button. An empty Power Pivot window will open. Seeing this window lets you know that Power Pivot is enabled correctly.

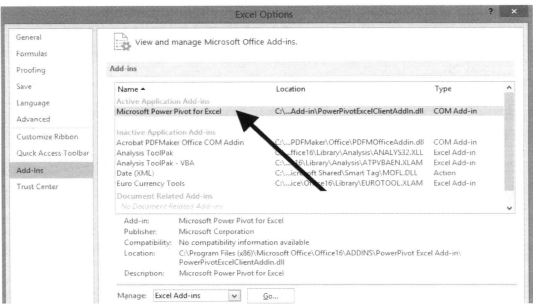

Figure 1-7 Excel Add-Ins options

Displaying File Extensions

Going through this book you will open a variety of file types. Some of the file names are the same, even though they have different file extensions, as illustrated in Figure 1-8. The arrows point to the file extensions. If you do not see file extensions on your computer, in Windows Explorer, but want to see them, do this: (Doing this is optional) In Windows, open Windows Explorer ⇒ View tab ⇒ Check the **FILE NAME EXTENSIONS** option, illustrated in Figure 1-9.

Figure 1-8 File extensions illustrated

Figure 1-9 View menu

Resolution To An Issue That I Had Using Power Pivot

While writing this book, I came across this issue that presented a problem for me. The problem and solution are listed below. It is not a requirement that you make these changes now. I included this information in case you have the same issue.

Security Warning Message

Depending on the options that you have selected on the Trust Center tab on the Excel Options dialog box in Excel, you may see the warning shown in Figure 1-10.

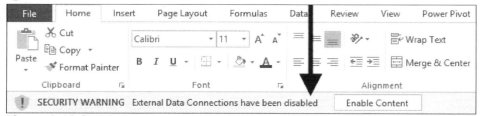

Figure 1-10 Security Warning message illustrated

Opening an Excel workbook with a pivot table that is connected to an external data source, displayed the warning.

Solution Modify the Excel Trust Center options to include the location of the data source files. The steps below show you how to make the changes for the files used in this book.

1. In Excel ⇒ File tab ⇒ Options ⇒ On the Excel Options dialog box, select the **TRUST CENTER** panel.

2. Click the **TRUST CENTER SETTINGS** button ⇒ Select the **TRUSTED LOCATIONS** panel ⇒ Clear the check mark for the **DISABLE ALL TRUSTED LOCATIONS** option, at the bottom of the screen, if it is selected.

3. Click the **ADD NEW LOCATION** button.

   Click the **BROWSE** button and select the folder for this book. All of the files used in this book are in one folder.

   Check the Subfolders option, shown in Figure 1-11.

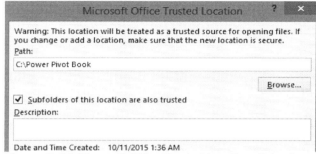

Figure 1-11 Microsoft Office Trusted Location dialog box

4. Select the **EXTERNAL CONTENT** panel ⇒ In the Data Connections section, select the **ENABLE ALL DATA CONNECTIONS** option, shown at the top of Figure 1-12.

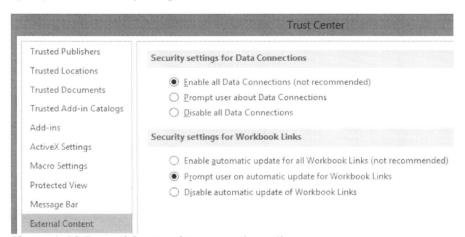

Figure 1-12 External Content data connection options

5. Click OK twice to close both dialog boxes. Now, you will not be prompted with the warning message, shown earlier in Figure 1-10.

Data Concepts

There are some data concepts that you need to be aware of. Having an understanding of these concepts is helpful to utilize Power Pivot effectively.

Dashboards The intended goal is to display large amounts of data in a clear, consolidated and meaningful way. A dashboard should allow the person viewing it to see the information at a glance. Sadly, out in the workplace, you will see dashboards that have animation and gauges that are hard to figure out what the data represents. Try not to join this group <smile>.

Data Dictionary A data dictionary contains detailed information about the database and includes the following types of information: Database and table names, field names, field types, field sizes, indexes and related files. A data dictionary can be handwritten or typed. It can also be generated by some database software packages. When using Power Pivot, this document or file is very helpful if you are not familiar with the data.

Data Source A data source is what the data is stored in. Examples of data sources are databases, text files, OLAP cubes and spreadsheets.

SQL Stands for **STRUCTURED QUERY LANGUAGE**. It is the language that is most used to interact with databases. It is used to create and populate tables with data, modify data and retrieve data from a database. This is also known as a **QUERY**. Before you start to frown, the answer is no, you do not have to write SQL code to retrieve the data that you need for the reports that you create in this book. At some point, you may have the need for functionality that Power Pivot or Power Query can't provide, in terms of retrieving data to import, which means that you will have to write code to get the data that you need.

MDX Stands for **MULTIDIMENSIONAL EXPRESSIONS**. It is a language used to work with data in a multidimensional data source, like an OLAP cube. Like DAX (explained later in this chapter), MDX can be used to create measures in Power Pivot.

Database Terminology

Below are key terms that you should understand about databases in order to work with them efficiently.

Field A field contains one piece of information and is stored in a record. Examples of fields include customer name and customer address. A column in a Power Pivot table is the same as a field in a database.

Record A record has one or more fields. Each of the fields in a record are related. A record looks like a row of data in a spreadsheet.

Table A table is stored in a database and is a collection of records. Most databases have more than one table. Tables are linked on fields. Tables may remind you of a spreadsheet, because SQL databases have rows and columns. Each table contains information about a specific topic. For example, a well designed customer table would only contain information about customers. The customer table would not contain information about products.

Primary Key is a unique identifier for each row of data in the table. Primary keys are usually numeric and system generated, sequentially. They are usually used to create relationships between tables.

Database A database is a collection of information that is stored in one or more tables in the database. It is important to note that there are different types of physical database structures.

Relational Database A relational database is a collection of **RELATED** information that is stored in one or more tables in the database.

Relationship A relationship is a connection between two tables. It is how two or more tables are joined (linked). This relationship is based on a field in each table that has the same value. Tables can have more than one relationship. Tables can be joined when they have at least one field that is the same in each table. For example, an invoice table can be joined to a products table because each invoice will have at least one item from the products table.

Power Pivot Terminology

Before you go any further, there are some terms that you need to understand to get a better idea of how Power Pivot can aid in the decision making process, display trends in data and much more. These terms will also help you start to understand how powerful Power Pivot is. These are terms that you may have heard before, but are not exactly sure what they mean. The goal of this section is to briefly explain them and their relationship to Power Pivot.

Data Analysis Expressions (DAX) Is a programming language that Power Pivot supports. It contains a collection of functions that are used to create formulas. These formulas are used to manipulate data in tables in the data model.

Data Model Is a collection of tables and their relationships. Power Pivots database, is the data model. [See Chapter 9, What Is A Data Model?]

Data Refresh This feature is used to bring (re-import) the most recent version of data into a Power Pivot table from the original data source.

Data Source Connection Contains instructions that Power Pivot uses to connect to a data source, so that data can be imported into Power Pivot.

In-Memory Processing Engine In my opinion, there would be no Power Pivot without the **XVELOCITY** processing engine. This engine allows millions of rows of data to be processed quickly because the processing of data in Power Pivot tables is done in the computers memory, instead of processing data on a hard drive.

. . . .

Power Pivot uses a **COLUMNAR DATABASE** that compresses the data, thus using less space than Excel tables would use for the same amount of data. This is why millions and millions of rows of data can be imported into Power Pivot tables.

Power Pivot Data Is data that has been imported, appended or added to the data model.

Power Pivot Table A table is one tab of data in the Power Pivot window. A Power Pivot workbook can have as many tables as needed.

Slicers Are used to filter data in pivot tables and pivot charts.

Customize The Quick Access Toolbar In Excel

Throughout this book you will create a lot of workbooks, open a lot of existing workbooks and save the existing workbook with a new file name. You may find it easier and faster to have options for these "File saving" tasks on the Quick Access Toolbar. The steps below show you how to add the Save options to the toolbar. Customizing the Quick Access Toolbar in Excel is not required to complete the exercises in this book.

1. Open Excel ⇒ Click on the Customize Quick Access Toolbar button, illustrated at the top of Figure 1-13.

   You can select any of the options shown in the figure that are currently not checked on your computer, if you want to add them to the toolbar.

   The **MORE COMMANDS** option, illustrated at the bottom of the figure, opens the Excel Options dialog box.

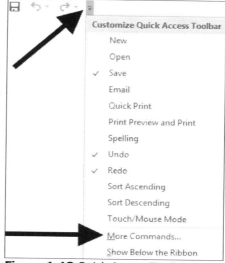

Figure 1-13 Quick Access Toolbar button options

2. Select the More Commands option ⇒ In the list of commands in the left column, click on the **SAVE AS** option ⇒ Click the Add button.

3. Rearrange the items in the Customize column on the right, so that they are in the order, from left to right, that you want them to appear in, on the Quick Access Toolbar. To move an option, click on it, then click the Move Up or Move Down button to place the item where you want it. Figure 1-14 shows how I have the options arranged on the toolbar, but you can put the options in the order that works best for you.

If there is an option (command) that you want to add, (from any tab on the Ribbon), but do not see it in the list of Popular Commands, shown in Figure 1-14, open the **CHOOSE COMMANDS FROM** drop-down list and select **ALL COMMANDS**. This will display all of the built-in commands that you can add to the toolbar.

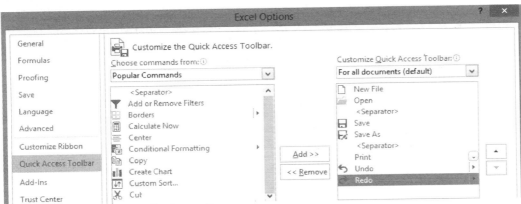

Figure 1-14 Quick Access Toolbar options

Summary

This chapter discussed Business Intelligence and how companies are implementing it. The Power BI toolset was introduced. An overview of what Power Pivot does, what it can be used for and how it works with the other software in the toolset was covered. The intention was to paint a picture of what Power Pivots role is, in the Power BI stack.

Concepts and terminology that will help you become familiar with Power Pivot, BI and data were covered. Hopefully, you downloaded the practice files, so that you can dive right in to the next chapter. I think that once you take the tour of Power Pivot, you will start to see the potential of what you can create in Power Pivot.

Active vs Passive Learning

An example of passive learning would be sitting on the beach and reading this book. This learning style is helpful when you need to add skills to an existing knowledge set. In the context of this book, that would mean that you have already used Power Pivot and now want to see "What's New". If you are new to Power Pivot and select this learning style, more than likely, the first time that you try to use Power Pivot on your own, it will not be smooth sailing.

As a former technology professor, I believe in the concept of "learning by doing". This is known as active learning. In the context of this book, that would mean using a computer to work on the exercises in this book. Just like classroom technology courses have hands-on exercises, so does this book. Completing these exercises will not only show you how to use the software, they will hopefully get you to see data from a different perspective. Understanding raw data, is one of the best skills that you can have, when you have the need to create reports.

QUICK TOUR OF POWER PIVOT

This chapter will take you on a quick tour of Power Pivot, by going step-by-step through the process of creating a pivot table using data that you import into the data model. This will provide an overview of the features and steps used to create pivot tables using data in the data model.

 Keep in mind that even though this chapter is a quick tour covering creating a pivot table, that the majority of options and features, also apply to creating pivot charts.

CHAPTER 2

Overview

Since the 1990's when pivot table and pivot chart functionality was added to Excel, these tools have been used to analyze data. Hopefully, as you go through the quick tour of Power Pivot in this chapter, you will see the benefit of being able to work with data from multiple external (to Excel) data sources seamlessly.

Once the data is imported, some relationships between the tables may automatically be created. Any relationships that are automatically created can be changed or deleted. You also have the ability to create additional relationships, as needed. After the data is imported, formulas can also be created, if needed.

Excel is used to create pivot tables with data that is stored in the Power Pivot database (aka the data model). As you will see, Power Pivot has two components, as explained below.

① The **POWER PIVOT WINDOW** (shown later in Figure 2-8) is used to import data, create relationships and to create measures.

② The **PIVOT TABLE FIELDS LIST** is used to select the fields to create a pivot table. Measures can also be created on this panel.

Exercise 2.1: Let Me See What Power Pivot Can Do

In this exercise you will learn the basic steps of importing data into the data model and creating a pivot table using the imported data. By the end of this exercise, you will have used many of the core features of Power Pivot.

Step 1: Open Power Pivot

1. Open a new Excel workbook ⇒ Power Pivot tab ⇒ Manage button. Power Pivot may take a few seconds to open, if you have never opened it before. **Welcome To Power Pivot!**

2. Home tab ⇒ Get External Data group ⇒ From Database button ⇒ From Access option. The **TABLE IMPORT WIZARD** dialog box will open.

> **Having Several Excel Workbooks And Power Pivot Windows Open At The Same Time**
> As you can see, Power Pivot has its own window, separate from the Excel window. Behind the scenes, the Power Pivot window is connected to the Excel workbook. It is very easy to have several workbooks and Power Pivot windows open at the same time, while going through this book. The good thing is that Excel knows which Power Pivot window belongs to which Excel workbook. If you have multiple Excel workbooks and Power Pivot windows open, it can get confusing looking at the Windows taskbar or if you are copying and pasting between workbooks. It may be easier to close all but one workbook at the end of each exercise, but that is up to you.

Step 2: Select The Data Source

This step covers selecting the data source and connecting to it. Data from different sources including text files, spreadsheets and data feeds, as well as, enterprise databases can be used to get the data for your analysis needs. This process is known as **ESTABLISHING A CONNECTION TO A DATA SOURCE**. Each imported table is placed on its own tab in the Power Pivot window, like worksheets in an Excel workbook.

1. On the Table Import Wizard dialog box, in the Friendly connection name field, type First Power Pivot Project.

> **Using The Friendly Connection Name Field**
> It is not a requirement to use this field. By default, the type of database and database file name will automatically be filled in this field, once data is imported from the data source, if you leave the field empty. It will be helpful to enter a name for the connection if you are going to import data from more than one data source into the same workbook. For example, if you are going to import data from different databases of the same type (like SQL or Access), using a descriptive name in this field will help you know which type of database or which database the tables of data came from. Power Pivot displays all of the connections in the workbook, as shown in Figure 2-1. The name entered in the Friendly connection name field is also displayed on this dialog box, as illustrated in Figure 2-1. Both of the database data sources (in the Power Pivot Data Connections section) in the figure are Access databases. What helps to distinguish them is the Friendly connection name.

This dialog box is accessed by clicking the **EXISTING CONNECTIONS** button on the Home tab.

Figure 2-1 Existing Connections dialog box

2. Click the Browse button.

   If necessary, navigate to your folder ⇒ Double-click on the Adventure Works database.

   You should have the options filled in, that are shown in Figure 2-2.

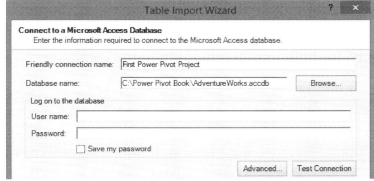

Figure 2-2 Microsoft Access database connection options

3. Click the **TEST CONNECTION** button to make sure that the Excel workbook is connected to the database.

   If connected, you will see the message shown in Figure 2-3 ⇒ Click OK ⇒ Click Next.

Figure 2-3 Successful connection message

 Importing Tips
Below are some tips that will help you import data more efficiently.
① Using the OLE DB provider for the data source can provide faster performance, especially for large databases.
② The rule of thumb is to import tables with the largest number of rows first. The order that tables are imported into Power Pivot is only important if you have really large tables and are worried about performance during the import process. Doing this is optional.

Step 3: Select The Data To Import

Databases, often have a lot of tables. There will be times that you do not need all of the tables in a database. The steps below show you how to select the tables that you need to import. All of the tables and views in the database are displayed on the Select Tables and Views screen on the Table Import Wizard dialog box. Only importing the columns and rows in the tables that you will use, will keep the size of the data model small, which is a good thing <smile>.

For example, if a database has tables in the following categories; employees, products, financial, orders, car leases and retail stores and your goal is to create reports on product sales, you can skip importing the financial and car leases tables. Remember that there is a workbook file size limitation, depending on where the workbook will be placed. For example, online options, like Power BI, have a workbook size limit of 250 MB.

1. Select the first option on the screen shown in Figure 2-4 ⇒ Click Next.

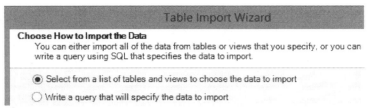

Choose How to Import the Data
You can either import all of the data from tables or views that you specify, or you can write a query using SQL that specifies the data to import.

◉ Select from a list of tables and views to choose the data to import

○ Write a query that will specify the data to import

Figure 2-4 Import options

Resizing Columns On The Table Import Wizard
If you need to see more of the Source Table name then is visible, the columns on the Table Import Wizard dialog box, shown in Figure 2-5, can be resized by placing the mouse pointer on the vertical line after the column heading that you need to resize and dragging the vertical line to the right, just like resizing a column in Excel.

Selecting Records To Import
If you do not need to import all of the records and fields in a table, click the **PREVIEW & FILTER** button on the screen shown in Figure 2-5. This is where you would create a filter to select the records and fields that you do not want to import.

2. On the Select Tables and Views screen, click in the box in front of the following tables, to select them: HumanResources_Employee, Person_Contact, Sales_SalesOrder Header, Sales_SalesPerson and Sales_SalesTerritory, as shown in Figure 2-5. These are the tables that will be imported and added to the data model.

Figure 2-5 Tables selected to import

3. Click Finish. The data will now be imported from the Access database into tables in the data model.

Step 4: Save The Power Pivot Workbook

The data is imported into what is known as the **POWER PIVOT DATA MODEL** or **DATA MODEL** for short. The import process creates a table in the data model for each table or dataset that is imported. The imported data is displayed on tabs in the workbook. The data should be saved before you modify it, because it is currently stored in the RAM (the memory) on your computer.

1. You will see the screen shown in Figure 2-6, while the data is being imported. When the import is finished, click the Close button.

Clicking the DETAILS link, on this screen, opens the dialog box shown in Figure 2-7.

It shows the relationships that are in the data source that were imported with the tables.

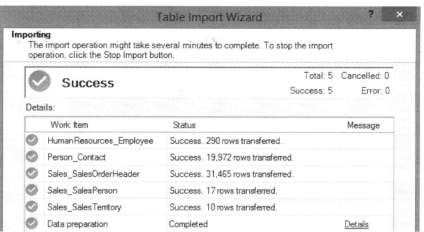

Figure 2-6 Importing screen

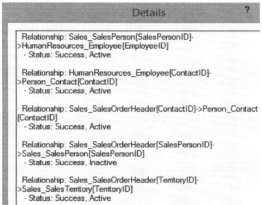

Figure 2-7 Details dialog box

2. When you see the five tables of data that you just imported, in Power Pivot, as illustrated in Figure 2-8, click the Save button on the Quick Access Toolbar (upper left corner of the window) ⇒ Navigate to your folder if necessary ⇒ Type E2.1 First Power Pivot Workbook as the file name.

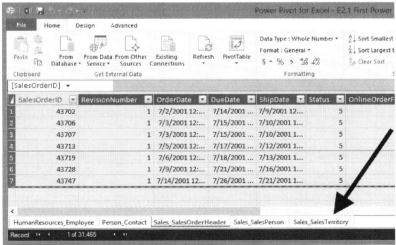

Figure 2-8 Power Pivot window with five tables of data

Creating Formulas (Measures) In Power Pivot
If you need to create formulas, you would create them in Power Pivot. Formulas can also be created by using the Measures button on the Power Pivot tab or the **EDIT MEASURE** option on the Pivot Table Fields list (Values area) or the **ADD MEASURE** option, when you right-click on the table name, in the Pivot Table Fields list.

Power Pivot Window Views

Figure 2-9 shows the lower right corner of the Power Pivot window. The buttons are explained below.

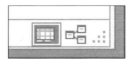

The first button displays the **GRID VIEW**. This is the default view and is shown earlier in Figure 2-8.

Figure 2-9 Power Pivot window buttons

The second button displays the **DIAGRAM VIEW**, shown in Figure 2-10.

Step 5: Create Or Edit The Relationships

If you were to create a pivot table based on the relationships that came from the relationships in the database, the output may not be correct. Relationships are covered in detail later in this book. For the purposes of this quick tour chapter, follow the steps below Figure 2-10.

Figure 2-10 shows the relationships that came with the tables that were imported. These relationships were created in the database that the tables were imported from. As shown in the figure, it is difficult to know which fields some of the relationships are based on. To be sure, I use the Manage Relationships dialog box, shown in Figure 2-11.

The lines indicate the relationships between the tables. If you look closely, you will see that each line is actually pointing to a specific field in the table. It is the data in those fields that allow you to be able to select fields from different tables on the Pivot Table Fields list to create pivot tables.

The arrow points to what some call the "Lookup Table", meaning it has the values that another table needs to reference. I prefer to create relationships on the Diagram View (because I like using drop and drag) instead of the Create Relationship dialog box.

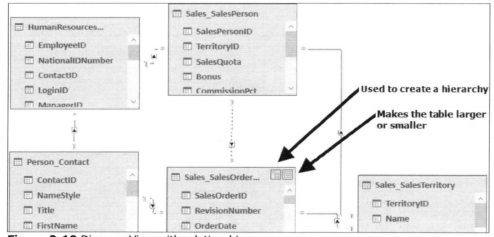

Figure 2-10 Diagram View with relationships

1. Design tab ⇒ Click the Manage Relationships button ⇒ Delete all of the relationships on the **MANAGE RELATIONSHIPS** dialog box, by selecting all of them and clicking the Delete button.

2. Display the Diagram View.

3. In the Sales Order Header table, drag the Territory ID field to the Territory ID field in the Sales Territory table.

4. Create the following relationship: Sales Order Header table - Sales Person ID ⇒ Sales Person table - Sales Person ID.

5. Click the Manage Relationships button. You should have the relationships shown in Figure 2-11.

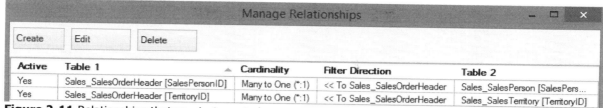

Figure 2-11 Relationships that you just created

Step 6: Create The Pivot Table

In this step you will learn how to create a pivot table using the data that you imported into Power Pivot. The pivot table that you create will show the total sales amount, by region, for each sales rep. I call what other people refer to as the "Fields list", the Pivot Table Fields list because that is what is displayed at the top of the panel, as shown later in Figure 2-13.

1. In the Excel window, Insert tab ⇒ PivotTable button ⇒ Select the Use this workbook's Data Model option ⇒ Select the **EXISTING WORKSHEET** option on the Create Pivot Table dialog box ⇒ Click OK.

   The place holder shown in Figure 2-12 is added to the worksheet.

   This is how you add fields to create the pivot table.

   The Pivot Table Fields list, should be displayed on the right side of the Excel worksheet.

Figure 2-12 Pivot table place holder

The **ALL** option displays all of the tables in the workbook, whether or not they are currently be used in the selected pivot table or chart.

The **SEARCH** field, on the Pivot Table Fields list, is helpful when you do not know what table a field is in that you need to use.

Type in some or all of the field name, as illustrated at the top of Figure 2-13. The fields that match, will be shown below the Search field, listed under the table that the field is in.

Figure 2-13 Search field illustrated

2. In the Pivot Table Fields list, display the fields for the Sales_SalesOrderHeader table ⇒ Right-click on the SalesPersonID field ⇒ Select **ADD TO ROW LABELS**, as illustrated in Figure 2-14.

   This option will create the row of data in the left most column in the pivot table.

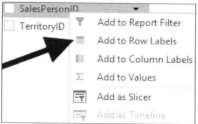

Figure 2-14 Pivot Table Fields list shortcut menu

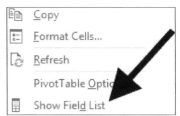

> 💡 **How To Display The Pivot Table Fields List**
> If you close the Pivot Table Fields list by mistake, right-click on the pivot table on the worksheet and select **SHOW FIELD LIST**, as illustrated in Figure 2-15. Depending on the part of the pivot table that you right-click on, you may see more options on the shortcut menu.

Figure 2-15 Cell shortcut menu

3. In the Sales_SalesTerritory table, right-click on the Name field ⇒ Select Add to Column Labels. This will create the column headings across the top of the pivot table.

4. In the Sales_SalesOrderHeader table, right-click on the SubTotal field ⇒ Select Add to Values. This will calculate the values that will be displayed in the middle of the pivot table.

The drop zone area of the Pivot Table Fields list should look like the one shown in Figure 2-16. Figure 2-17 shows the first few columns of the pivot table.

Did you notice that you used fields from more than one table to create the pivot table without writing a formula or selecting any additional options? That is one of the features that makes Power Pivot rock, in my opinion.

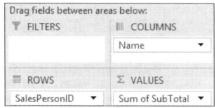

Figure 2-16 Pivot Table Fields list drop zone area

Sum of SubTotal	Column Labels					
Row Labels	Australia	Canada	Central	France	Germany	Northeast
(blank)	$9,061,000.58	$1,977,844.86	$3,000.83	$2,644,017.71	$2,894,312.34	$6,532.47
268		$264,867.01	$43,824.02			$100,165.04
275			$3,127,053.03			$3,547,034.40
276			$2,225,871.15			
277			$3,543,660.98			$4,735,174.26
278		$4,380,714.26				
290	$1,758,385.93					
Grand Total	$11,038,475.39	$19,458,653.72	$9,564,668.95	$8,268,510.78	$5,375,351.52	$8,388,906.16

Figure 2-17 Pivot table created from data in the data model

Creating Measures From The Pivot Table Fields List

To create a measure from the Power Pivot Table Fields list, right-click on the table name that you want the measure saved in and select **ADD MEASURE**.

You will see the dialog box shown in Figure 2-18.

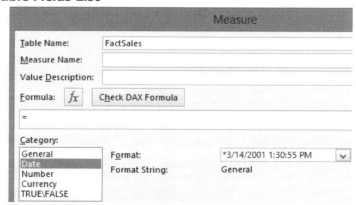

Figure 2-18 Measure dialog box

Using The Pivot Table

At this point, Power Pivots job is finished, unless more data needs to be added to the pivot table or you need to create more measures.

From this point on, you primarily use the Pivot Table Fields list and the options on the Power Pivot tab to create pivot tables. The pivot table that is using data from the data model can be used just like the pivot tables that are created from data in an Excel worksheet. That means that the Excel filter options, shown in Figure 2-19, can be used.

If you find that you are using the same filter options over and over, you can add the (fields) to the **FILTERS** area on the Pivot Table Fields list. That is what you will do in the next exercise.

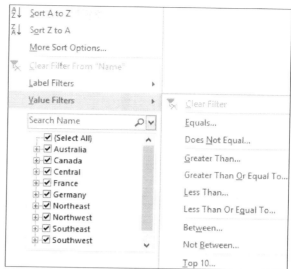

Figure 2-19 Excel filter options

Exercise 2.2: Modify A Pivot Table

In this exercise you will modify the pivot table that you created, in the previous exercise, to have a report filter. The filter that you add, will allow the pivot table to display the sales data by shipping method.

If you look in the Sales_SalesOrderHeader table, you will see the ShipMethodID field. While you can use this ID field (which is a number) for the shipping method filter, it may be difficult for people using the pivot table to remember what each number means. None of the tables that you imported in Exercise 2.1 have the field with the shipping method names. These values are stored in the Purchasing_ShipMethod table.

This is when it is helpful to have the data dictionary that I discussed in Chapter 1 or a print out of all of the fields in each table in the database. On your own, having that document would make it easier to find the field that you need. As you read in Chapter 1, the Adventure Works database has 67 tables. This is the database that has the field to create the filter for. Aren't you happy that this book has step-by-step instructions? <smile>

Step 1: Add More Data To The Data Model

In this step you will import the table that has the shipping method names that will be used for the report filter.

1. Save the E2.1 workbook as E2.2 Modified pivot table.

2. Power Pivot tab ⇒ Manage button ⇒ Home tab ⇒ Existing Connections button.

3. Select the First Power Pivot Project connection (in the Power Pivot Data Connections section) ⇒ Click the Open button.

4. Click Next on the Import Data screen.

5. Check the Purchasing_ShipMethod table ⇒ Click Finish. The table will now be imported ⇒ Click Close after the data has been imported.

6. On the Diagram View, create a relationship between the Ship Method ID field in the Sales Order Header table and the same field in the Ship Method table.

7. Refresh button ⇒ Refresh All.

Step 2: Create The Report Filter

1. Display the pivot table in Excel.

2. Select the **ALL** option at the top of the Pivot Table Fields list ⇒ Display the fields in the Purchasing_ShipMethod table ⇒ Add the Name field from this table to the Filters area by selecting **ADD TO REPORT FILTER** on the shortcut menu.

Relationship Detection And Creation

Sometimes you may see a message, at the top of the Pivot Table Fields list, that a relationship may need to be created, as shown in Figure 2-20.

Power Pivot will display the message shown in Figure 2-20 because there may be a relationship that needs to be created between tables, based on the data that was modified in the workbook or fields that were added to the Drop Zone area to create a pivot table.

Figure 2-20 Pivot Table relationship message

This can happen for a few reasons, including column names in tables that have been renamed. You will also see this warning message when you add a field from a table that was imported after the pivot table in the workbook had already been created. In this exercise, you see the message because you are now adding a field from the new table that was imported.

I have found that more times than not, that this warning is not true. I tend to click the X in the upper right corner of the message and keep working. Your mileage may vary <smile>.

The **AUTO-DETECT** button will try and find relationship(s) and create them. Keep in mind that relationships that are created using this option may not be what you need. You also will not know which relationships were created, by using this option.

The **CREATE** button is used to manually create a relationship on the dialog box shown in Figure 2-21.

If you do not create a relationship for the table that was imported before getting to this point, you would have to create it now, by following the steps below. Don't complete these steps now because you already created this relationship. Go to the next section.

Create A Relationship From The Pivot Table Fields List

Being able to create a relationship from the Pivot Table Fields list, saves a little time because you do not have to switch to the Power Pivot window.

1. Click the Create button shown above in Figure 2-20.

2. Open the Table drop-down list and select the Sales_SalesOrderHeader table ⇒ Select the Ship Method ID field in the Column drop-down list.

3. Select the Related Table options shown in Figure 2-21, then click OK.

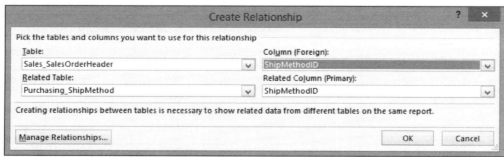

Figure 2-21 Create Relationship dialog box

The **MANAGE RELATIONSHIPS** button (shown above in Figure 2-21), opens the dialog box shown in Figure 2-22.

It displays the relationships for the tables in the data model.

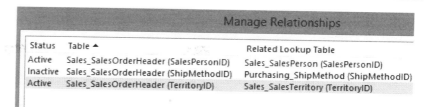

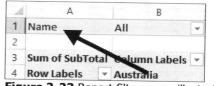

Figure 2-22 Manage Relationships dialog box

How To Rename And Use A Report Filter

By default, when a field is added to the (Report) Filters area, the filters field name is displayed above the pivot table, as illustrated in Figure 2-23.

Sometimes, this name is not the best option to be displayed with the pivot table. When that is the case, you can rename the filter.

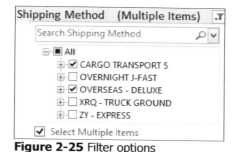

Figure 2-23 Report filter name illustrated

The steps below show you how. Later in this book, you will see that not all report filters can be renamed. Fortunately, there is a workaround.

1. Right-click in cell A1 ⇒ Select the **FIELD SETTINGS** option on the shortcut menu.

2. In the Custom Name field type `Shipping Method`, as shown in Figure 2-24. You will see that the filters name, in the upper left corner of the worksheet, changed from "Name" to "Shipping Method", once you click OK.

If you select two shipping methods from the filter drop-down list, shown in Figure 2-25, the data in the pivot table will only display rows of data for orders that were shipped with the shipping methods that you selected, as shown in Figure 2-26. Being able to use a field in one table as the filter for data in multiple other tables should demonstrate how powerful Power Pivot is.

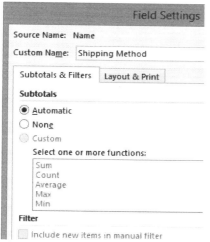

Figure 2-24 Field Settings dialog box

Figure 2-25 Filter options

	A	B	C	D	E	F	G
1	Shipping Method	(Multiple Items)					
2							
3	Sum of SubTotal	Column Labels					
4	Row Labels	Australia	Canada	Central	France	Germany	Northeast
5	268		$264,867.01	$43,824.02			$100,165.04
6	275			$3,127,053.03			$3,547,034.40
7	276			$2,225,871.15			
8	277			$3,543,660.98			$4,735,174.26
9	278		$4,380,714.26				

Figure 2-26 Pivot table with filtered data

If the tables used in this exercise did not have relationships created between them in the database, you could still use the same fields to create a pivot table. Power Pivot would prompt you to create relationships, as shown earlier in Figure 2-20.

Interestingly enough, if you do not create the relationships, Power Pivot will create the pivot table anyway. However, it will not display the data correctly, as shown in Figure 2-27. This happens because without relationships, Power Pivot has no way of knowing which territory each order is from, in this exercise.

Hopefully, the difference between the pivot tables in Figures 2-26 and 2-27 convinces you to complete the rest of the exercises in this book, because you can do much more with pivot tables created from tables in the data model, then pivot tables in Excel <smile>.

	A	B	C	D	E	F	G
1	Shipping Method	All					
2							
3	Sum of SubTotal	Column Labels					
4	Row Labels	Australia	Canada	Central	France	Germany	Northeast
5		29358677.22	29358677.22	29358677.22	29358677.22	29358677.22	29358677.22
6	268	1369624.649	1369624.649	1369624.649	1369624.649	1369624.649	1369624.649
7	275	11252038.77	11252038.77	11252038.77	11252038.77	11252038.77	11252038.77
20	288	219088.8836	219088.8836	219088.8836	219088.8836	219088.8836	219088.8836
21	289	2241204.042	2241204.042	2241204.042	2241204.042	2241204.042	2241204.042
22	290	1758385.926	1758385.926	1758385.926	1758385.926	1758385.926	1758385.926
23	Grand Total	127337180.1	127337180.1	127337180.1	127337180.1	127337180.1	127337180.1

Figure 2-27 Pivot table without relationships

Quick Tour Wrap Up

This section is in lieu of the normal summary at the end of each chapter. Yes, I realize that you probably feel that you were rushed through the exercises in this chapter, with all of the "Do this" and "Click that" instructions, without a lot of explanation of why. Lengthy explanations are not the goal of this chapter because that is what is covered in the rest of the book <smile>. The goal of this chapter is to briefly demonstrate some of the functionality that Power Pivot adds to Excel, in particular, what using data in the data model adds to pivot tables.

As I stated at the beginning of this chapter, Power Pivot can be used to import data from a variety of database types and other data sources. Once the data is imported into the data model, it can be used to create a single pivot table or pivot chart, as well as, multiple pivot tables on multiple worksheets in the workbook. You are not limited to only using one worksheet in the workbook to create pivot tables. One thing that I hope is clear is that Power Pivot is used to manage the data model and Excel is used to create and maintain pivot tables and charts.

As you saw in the exercises in this chapter, you used data from different tables in the data model, to create one pivot table. This alone is worth the price of admission, as some people say. If you stick with it and learn how to use the DAX programming language, as well as, the pivot table functionality, you will be able to create extensive and elaborate pivot tables for analysis and reporting needs, without needing the IT department to help you. That is what self-service BI tools are designed to do.

What Are Pivot Tables?

Pivot tables are used to summarize data by displaying different types of totals. The goal is to present data (large datasets are definitely welcome) in an easy to understand format. The data presented in a pivot table should answer at least one question.

EXPLORING THE POWER PIVOT WORKSPACE

 Overview

In this chapter you will learn about the Power Pivot workspace.
This includes the options on the Power Pivot tab on the Excel ribbon
and the options on the Power Pivot workspace.

CHAPTER 3

Power Pivot Tab On The Excel Ribbon

The Power Pivot tab on the Excel ribbon is used to interact with the data model, using Power Pivot.

Figure 3-1 shows the Power Pivot tab. The buttons are explained in Table 3-1.

Figure 3-1 Power Pivot tab on the Excel ribbon

Button	Description
Manage	Opens Power Pivot, which is where you have access to the data model. This button is also on the Data tab (in the Data Tools section).
Measures	[See Measure Options]
KPI's	[See Chapter 14, KPI's]
Add to Data Model	Is used to add an Excel table to the data model and create a linked table from data in an Excel table.
Update All	Is used to update the data in all of the tables in the data model, that are linked to Excel tables.
Detect	[See Relationship Options]
Settings	Opens the dialog box shown in Figure 3-6. The options on this dialog box are used to collect information about your Power Pivot environment.

Table 3-1 Power Pivot tab buttons explained

Measure Options

Measures are more powerful than calculations that can be created in Excel. Figure 3-2 shows the shortcut menu for this button. The options are explained below.

The **NEW MEASURE** option opens the Measure dialog box. It is used as a shortcut to creating measures, so that you do not have to open the Power Pivot window.

The **MANAGE MEASURES** option opens the dialog box shown in Figure 3-3. It is used to create a new measure, as well as, edit or delete an existing measure.

Figure 3-2 Measures button options

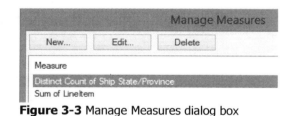

Figure 3-3 Manage Measures dialog box

Relationship Options

Clicking the **DETECT** button displays the dialog box shown in Figure 3-4. The dialog box is used to view relationships that were created for the tables in the data model.

If you click either of the **DETAILS** links, on the Relationship dialog box, you will see the dialog box shown in Figure 3-5. You will see the relationships, if any, that were detected.

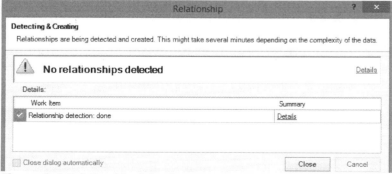

Figure 3-4 Relationship dialog box

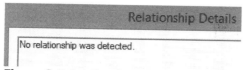

No relationship was detected.

Figure 3-5 Relationship Details dialog box for the relationship detection option

Power Pivot Settings Dialog Box

The options on the **SUPPORT & DIAGNOSTICS** tab are used to enable tracing, which is used for troubleshooting Power Pivot issues.

The options on the **LANGUAGE** tab are used to select a different language for the text that is displayed on the Power Pivot window.

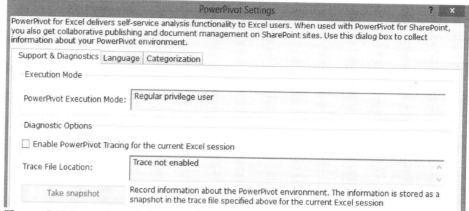

Figure 3-6 Power Pivot Settings dialog box

Power Pivot Window

The Power Pivot window is used to import data into tables, from a single source or multiple sources. The imported data is displayed on tabs. Each tab has data from a different table, query or view in a database or a different data source. This is how the relational data model is built. This window is also used to create and manage relationships, create DAX calculations and more.

When you click the **MANAGE** button shown earlier in Figure 3-1, you will see the window shown in Figure 3-7. This is where you import data and customize the data in the data model. Table 3-2 explains the illustrated parts of the Power Pivot window.

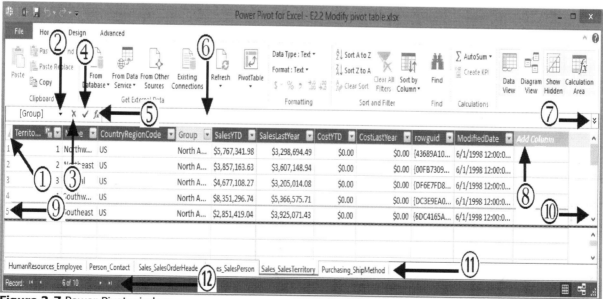

Figure 3-7 Power Pivot window

Option	Description
1	Clicking on this square selects the entire table.
2	Opens a drop-down list that displays a list of the fields that are in the table. Select the column that you want displayed. This option is useful if the table has more columns than can be displayed on the screen. It keeps you from having to scroll to the right, to find the field that you want to view.
3	Is used to delete the formula on the formula bar. (1)
4	Is used to apply the formula after you type it in. (1)
5	Displays the dialog box shown in Figure 3-8. The options on the dialog box are used to add a function to the calculated column to create a formula. (1)
6	Is used to type in the formula to create a calculated column.
7	This button expands the formula bar, as shown in Figure 3-9. Doing this is helpful if the formula is long.
8	The column **ADD COLUMN**, is a calculated column that is used to create a DAX formula. This adds a new column of data to the table. The data for the column comes from the formula that you create. You can create as many calculated columns in a table as needed.
9	Click on the row number to select the entire row. This option is often used to select data that you want to copy. More than one row can be selected at the same time.
10	When right-clicked on, the **VERTICAL SCROLLBAR** displays the shortcut menu shown in Figure 3-10. The options are used to move around the table vertically.
11	Displays the tables in the data model. Click on a tab to display the data from a different table.
12	The **STATUS BAR** displays the row (record) number that is currently selected and how many rows (records) are in the table. There are also four navigation buttons that are used to select a different row of data in the table.

Table 3-2 Parts of the Power Pivot window explained

(1)   This option is only available when a calculated column (the Add Column) or cell in a calculated column is selected.

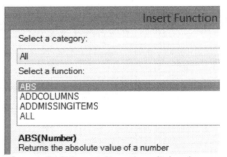

Figure 3-9 Expanded formula bar

Figure 3-10 Vertical scrollbar shortcut menu

Figure 3-8 Insert Function dialog box

Quick Access Toolbar

As shown earlier in Figure 3-7, the Power Pivot window has its own Quick Access Toolbar, in the upper left corner of the window.

The customization options are shown in Figure 3-11. This toolbar does not have all of the customization options that the Quick Access Toolbar in Excel has.

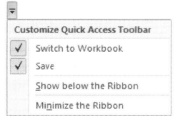

Figure 3-11 Power Pivot Quick Access Toolbar options

Adding Buttons To The Toolbar

If there are options that you want to add to the Quick Access Toolbar, right-click on the button (on any tab in the Power Pivot window) and select **ADD TO QUICK ACCESS TOOLBAR**, as shown in Figure 3-12.

Figure 3-12 Toolbar button shortcut menu

Power Pivot Window Ribbon

The File button to the left of the Home tab displays the options shown in Figure 3-13. The options are links to a feature in Excel. When one of the options is selected, the Power Pivot window is minimized and the Excel window and option that you select is displayed or executed.

CLOSE Closes Power Pivot, then displays the Excel window.

SWITCH TO NORMAL (OR ADVANCED) MODE Displays or hides the Advanced tab. If you do not see the Advanced tab on your computer, select the Switch option shown above in Figure 3-13. I personally do not understand why this option is necessary. [See Advanced Tab, later in this chapter]

Figure 3-13 File button options

Home Tab

The options on the tab shown in Figure 3-14 are used to import data, add formatting to the imported data, sort and filter the data, if needed. The options in each group are explained below.

If the buttons on the tabs disappear, clear the check mark for the **MINIMIZE THE RIBBON** option, shown earlier in Figure 3-11.

Figure 3-14 Home tab

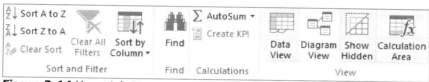

Figure 3-14 Home tab (Continued)

Clipboard Group

The options in this group are used to paste data from the Windows clipboard into a table in the data model or copy data from a table in the data model to the clipboard. The table-like data that you paste into a table in the data model, can come from another software package like Microsoft Word. The options in this group are explained in Table 3-3.

Option	Description
Paste	Pastes the copied data into a new table in the data model.
Paste Append	Pastes the copied data as additional rows to the bottom of an existing table in the data model. (2)
Paste Replace	Overwrites the data in the table with the data that you copied to the clipboard. The current column header names will not be changed. If the table already has relationships defined, they are not overwritten when the data is replaced. (2)
Copy	Copies data to the clipboard, so that it can be pasted into another application. This option works the same as using **CTRL+C**.

Table 3-3 Clipboard group options explained

(2)   This option is only available when a table in the data model was initially created by using the Paste command. The data that you want to paste has to have the same number of fields (columns) as the table in the data model has, that you want to paste the data to.

Get External Data Group

The first three options in this group, shown above in Figure 3-14, are used to import data into the data model. In order to import the data, you have to create a connection to the data source. The data connection options are covered in Chapter 4.

Existing Connections Button

Clicking the button displays the dialog box shown in Figure 3-15. This dialog box shows all of the connections that have been created in the workbook.

One option is used to import data using an existing data connection. Another option is used to modify the data source for a table.

Examples of when you would need to change the connection information is if the location or name of the data source has changed.

The **BROWSE FOR MORE** button opens a dialog box that is used to select a file that has connections, that you want to use.

The **OPEN** button opens the Table Import Wizard, so that you can import another table from the data source in the connection, create filter options for a table that will be imported or change anything about a table of data that has already been imported.

Figure 3-15 Existing Connections dialog box

To me, it is easier to import tables or columns using this option, then it is to start from scratch. And even better, this option bypasses some of the beginning screens on the wizard.

The **EDIT** button opens the **EDIT CONNECTION** dialog box. It is used to modify the connection information, like the data source name or location of the data source file. The Edit Connection dialog box has the same options that the Connect to screen on the Table Import Wizard has.

REFRESH button [See Refreshing Data]

The **DELETE** button deletes the selected connection from the workbook.

While a new connection can be created for each table in a data source, it is best to create one connection per data source, for the reasons listed below.

① If the data source name or location changes, you only have to change the information in one connection.
② If all of the tables in a database are in the same connection, they can be refreshed at the same time.
③ The chances of importing the same table more than once is reduced, because all tables that have already been imported from the data source, are in the same connection.

Refreshing Data

Initially, the pivot tables that you create are based on tables in the data model, at the time the data was first imported. After the pivot tables are initially created, more than likely, the data in the underlying data sources has changed.

This means that the data in the data model is out of sync and that the data displayed in the pivot tables and charts that use the data, are not displaying current data.

The frequency that data is refreshed depends on how volatile the data is (how often the data changes). If the data source is updated all day (think credit card transactions), the tables in the data model need to be refreshed frequently. The Refresh button option cannot be used for tables that have linked or pasted data. To keep us from trying, the button is not enabled when a linked table is displayed. Keep in mind that updating or refreshing data also updates the tables in the Pivot Table Fields list.

Refreshing Data vs Recalculating Formulas
Refreshing data is different then recalculating formulas. Refreshing data replaces the existing data in the data model, with an updated copy of the data from the data source. Recalculating formulas does not update data. The recalculation process reruns the DAX formulas (that you created) against the data that is currently in the data model. To have the most current information in the data model, refresh the data, then recalculate the formulas.

Refreshing Data Options

As you will see, there are several places where data can be refreshed from, as explained below.

① The **REFRESH** button on the Home tab in Power Pivot, displays the options shown in Figure 3-16. They are used to refresh one table at a time or all tables in the workbook at one time.

② Pivot table shortcut menu [See Chapter 13, Figures 13-1 and 13-2].

③ The **REFRESH** button on the Existing Connections dialog box, shown earlier in Figure 3-15. This option is used to refresh all of the tables in the connection. Select the connection that has the tables that you want to refresh, then click the **REFRESH** button. The benefit of using this option instead of the Refresh All option, covered below, is that it only refreshes data from one data source in the workbook, instead of refreshing all of the tables, in all of the connections, in the workbook.

④ Pivot Table Tools ⇒ Analyze tab ⇒ Refresh button, as shown in Figure 3-18. The **CONNECTION PROPERTIES** option (on the Refresh button) opens the dialog box shown in Figure 3-19.

⑤ The **REFRESH** button shown in Figure 3-19, is used to update the data in the selected connection or all connections.

⑥ Excel Data tab ⇒ Refresh All button, displays the options shown in Figure 3-18.

⑦ Excel Data tab ⇒ Connections button, opens the dialog box shown in Figure 3-19. The difference is that this version of the dialog box also displays the **THIS WORKBOOK DATA MODEL** file and will show when the model was last refreshed.

This button is used to refresh the data from an external data source.

To refresh the data for the table that is currently displayed, select the **REFRESH** option shown in Figure 3-16.

To refresh all of the tables in the data model, select the **REFRESH ALL** option. This could take a while, if the workbook has a lot of tables or if several tables have millions of rows of data.

Figure 3-16 Refresh button options (Home tab)

When either of the refresh options shown above in Figure 3-16 is selected, the dialog box shown in Figure 3-17 is displayed.

This dialog box shows the progress of the data refresh.

If there are any problems with the refresh, you will see a link in the Message column.

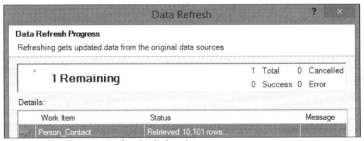

Figure 3-17 Data Refresh dialog box

If you click the **STOP REFRESH** button at the bottom of the dialog box (the button is not shown above in Figure 3-17), data that was updated or imported is removed from the table and the original data in the table is restored.

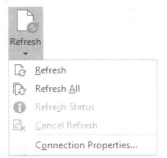

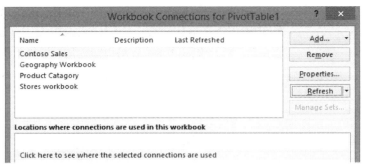

Figure 3-18 Refresh button options
(Analyze tab)

Figure 3-19 Workbook Connections dialog box

Pivot Table Button

The layout options shown in Figure 3-20 are used to create a pivot table or pivot chart, that uses tables in the data model.

Pivot tables and pivot charts can be placed on an existing or new worksheet in the workbook.

The options are explained in Table 3-4.

The data in the pivot tables and pivot charts are independent of each other.

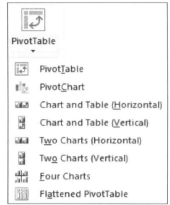

Figure 3-20 Pivot Table button options

Layout Option	Is Used To Create . . .
PivotTable	One pivot table.
PivotChart	One pivot chart.
Chart and Table (Horizontal)	A pivot chart and pivot table side by side.
Chart and Table (Vertical)	A pivot chart and pivot table with the pivot table placed below the chart.
Two Charts (Horizontal)	Two pivot charts, side by side.
Two Charts (Vertical)	Two pivot charts, one placed below the other.
Four Charts	Four pivot charts.
Flattened Pivot Table	A pivot table. [See Chapter 10, Flattened Pivot Table]

Table 3-4 Pivot Table button options explained

Formatting Group

The options in this group are used to change the data type and to format the data. Select the column of data that you want to apply the formatting to or change the data type of, before selecting an option in this group. The options in this group change, depending on the data type of the selected column. The options are explained in Table 3-5.

 Formatting Options
Keep the following in mind when using the options in the Formatting group. The options are only for formatting the data in Power Pivot. The formatting applied to the data is not carried over to Excel, where the pivot table is created from the data. However, the formatting is applied when the data is used to create reports in **POWER VIEW**.

Option	Description
Data Type	Displays the data type of the selected column. The options available to change the data type to, depend on the existing data type of the selected column. For example, Figure 3-21 shows the text data type options. Figure 3-22 shows the data type options that dates can be changed to.
Format	Is used to select a format for the data in the selected column, as shown in Figure 3-23. The **FORMAT OPTIONS** that are available, depend on the data type of the selected column.
Apply Currency Format	This option is only enabled for columns that have numeric data. The default currency formatting comes from the computer that you are using. Select one of the options shown in Figure 3-24 to display the data in currency format. The **MORE FORMATS** option, opens the dialog box shown in Figure 3-25. It contains the currency formatting options.
Apply Percentage Format	Displays the numbers in percent format.
Thousands Separator	Displays the numbers with a comma.
Increase Decimal	Moves the decimal point in the number one digit to the left. (3)
Decrease Decimal	Moves the decimal point in the number one digit to the right. (3)

Table 3-5 Formatting group options explained

(3) This option does not change the actual data, it only changes how the data is displayed.

Data Type Options

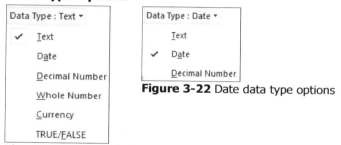

Figure 3-22 Date data type options

Figure 3-21 Text data type options

Format Options

Figure 3-23 Whole Number format options

Figure 3-24 Currency format options

Figure 3-25 Currency Format dialog box

Sort And Filter Group

To use the options in this group, a column of data has to be selected first. The options are explained in Table 3-6.

 The names of the two sort options at the top of the Sort and Filter group change slightly, based on the data type of the selected column. Regardless of the name, the sort order functionality is the same. Figure 3-26 shows the sort option names when text data is selected.

Figure 3-26 Text data sort options

Option	Description
Sort A to Z	Sorts the data in ascending (low to high, A-Z or 0-9) order.
Sort Z to A	Sorts the data in descending (high to low, Z-A or 9-0) order.
Clear Sort	Removes the sort. (4)
Clear All Filters	Removes all filters from the table. (4)
Sort by Column	[See Chapter 8, Use The Sort By Column Option]

Table 3-6 Sort And Filter group options explained

(4)   After selecting this option, the data is displayed the way it was, when it was imported.

Find Group

The **FIND BUTTON** opens the dialog box shown in Figure 3-27.

It is used to search for metadata like column names, a hierarchy or KPI in a table.

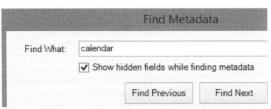

Figure 3-27 Find Metadata dialog box

Calculations Group

The **AUTO SUM** button displays the options shown in Figure 3-28.

Sum is the default Auto Sum option. The options are used to create a summary (aggregated) calculated field for the selected column. The calculated field is placed in the **CALCULATION AREA** on the window.

Calculated fields can be used to create a pivot table, chart or KPI. What's cool is that this option creates the DAX formula for you.

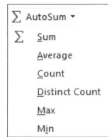

Figure 3-28 Auto Sum options

The **CREATE KPI** button is only enabled when a measure is selected. This option opens the **KEY PERFORMANCE INDICATOR** dialog box, to convert (change) the selected measure into a KPI. Once converted, the KPI icon will be displayed next to the measure in the calculation area, at the bottom of the Power Pivot window.

View Group

The options in this group are used to change how the columns are displayed. The options are explained in Table 3-7.

Option	Description
Data View	This is the default view that was shown earlier in Figure 3-7. This view displays the data in the tables and the **CALCULATION AREA**. It is also used to create measures. This is the same view as clicking the **GRID** button in the lower right corner of the window.
Diagram View	[See Diagram View]
Show Hidden	Displays objects (columns) that have been hidden from the **CLIENT TOOLS** (Excel pivot tables, third party tools and **POWER VIEW** are some examples). Hidden objects are displayed in a disabled state. This option works in the Data and Diagram views.
Calculation Area	Displays or hides the grid that is below the table of data. This area is used to create and display measures and KPI's. This section can be resized as needed. If you do not see the section, click the Calculation Area button.

Table 3-7 View group options explained

Diagram View

This view displays the data model (the tables, fields and relationships) in the workbook. This is the same view as clicking the **DIAGRAM** button, in the lower right corner of the window.

Figure 3-29 shows the options at the bottom of the Diagram View.

They are used to change how the tables are displayed in this view. The buttons are explained in Table 3-8.

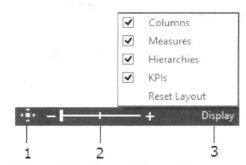

Figure 3-29 Diagram View options

Button	Description
1	The **FIT TO SCREEN** button resizes the tables, so that all of the tables are displayed in the window. The larger the window size, the larger the table size will be.
2	The **ZOOM SLIDER** button increases or decreases the size of the tables.
3	The **DISPLAY** button displays the menu shown above in Figure 3-29. The menu is used to select whether the option is displayed in the table or calculation area. The **RESET LAYOUT** option displays the tables as they were before the layout was changed from using the other options on the menu.

Table 3-8 Diagram View buttons explained

Design Tab

The options on the tab shown in Figure 3-30 are used to add columns to a table, manage table properties, modify existing data source connections and create relationships between tables. The options in each group are explained below.

Figure 3-30 Design tab

Columns Group

The options in this group are used to hide, add, freeze and delete columns. The options are explained in Table 3-9.

Option	Description
Add	Is used to create a DAX calculated column.
Delete	Is used to permanently delete columns and any calculations that use the column, from the table. Ctrl+Click does not allow multiple columns to be selected, so that they can be deleted at the same time.
Freeze	Select the Freeze option, shown in Figure 3-31, to move the selected columns to the left. The columns that this option is applied to will always be visible when you scroll to the right. The option is similar to the Freeze Panes option in Excel. The difference is that the columns that this option is applied to, are physically moved to the left most columns in the table. This means that you could move the 29th and 30th columns, to the far left of a table.
Width	Is used to change the width of the selected columns by typing the new width in the dialog box shown in Figure 3-32. (5)

Table 3-9 Columns group options explained

Figure 3-31 Freeze column options

Figure 3-32 Column Width dialog box

(5) Unlike Excel, Power Pivot does not display pound signs (####) in a cell when a column is not wide enough to display the data. Instead, an ellipsis is displayed at the end of the cell, as illustrated in Figure 3-33. This indicates that all of the data in the cell is not displayed.

Figure 3-33 Narrow column indicator illustrated

Calculations Group

The **INSERT FUNCTION** button opens the Insert Function dialog box shown earlier in Figure 3-8.

The **CALCULATION OPTIONS** button displays the options shown in Figure 3-34.

The options are used to select how and when formulas are calculated. The options are explained in Table 3-10.

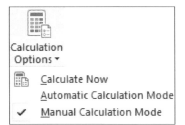

Figure 3-34 Calculation Options

Option	Description
Calculate Now	Recalculates all of the formulas in the workbook immediately.
Automatic Calculation Mode	When a formula is changed or any change in the workbook is made, the formulas are recalculated. While helpful, this option can cause the workbook to run slow, if changes (like pivot tables or formulas are created) are made to the workbook frequently.
Manual Calculation Mode	Disables automatic calculation. If this option is currently selected, select the Calculate Now option to recalculate the formulas, when needed.

Table 3-10 Calculation options explained (Design tab)

Relationships Group

The options in this group are used to link tables based on related data in at least one column in each table. The relationship is what allows data from different tables to be displayed, in the same pivot table or pivot chart. The options are explained in Table 3-11.

Option	Description
Create Relationship	Is used to create a relationship (a link) between tables, on the dialog box shown in Figure 3-35.
Manage Relationships	Opens the Manage Relationships dialog box. The options are used to create, edit, view and delete relationships.

Table 3-11 Relationships group options explained

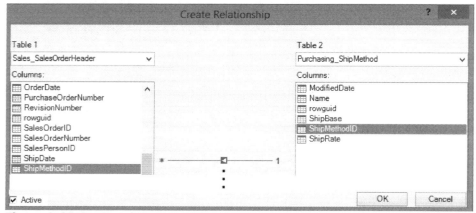

Figure 3-35 Create Relationship dialog box

Table Properties Button

As its name suggests, this button is used to display information about the selected table and to modify the query that was created when the data was imported via the Table Import Wizard. There are two views of the properties, on the Edit Tables Properties dialog box, as explained below.

① **TABLE PREVIEW** This view is shown in Figure 3-36. Filters can be created on this screen to remove rows or columns of data in the table. Columns in a table that were not already imported can be selected now to be imported. The options are explained in Table 3-12.

② **QUERY EDITOR** This view is shown in Figure 3-37. It displays the SQL query used to select the data for the table. If you edit the query, click the Save button. The **VALIDATE** and **DESIGN** buttons are explained in the next chapter. [See Chapter 4, Import By Query]

The table properties of linked tables or tables that have pasted data cannot be edited on the Edit Table Properties dialog box. The Table Properties button is not enabled for these types of tables.

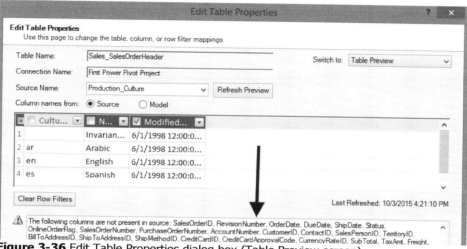

Figure 3-36 Edit Table Properties dialog box (Table Preview screen)

Option	Description
Table Name	Displays the table name of the data displayed in the middle of the dialog box.
Switch To	Toggles between the Table Preview and Query Editor views, explained earlier.
Connection Name	Displays the name of the connection for the table in the Table Name field.
Source Name	Displays the selected table by default. If the data source of the connection has more than one table, the drop-down list is enabled on this field. This allows you to select a different table that you want to replace the current table with. If you select a table that has a different structure then the current table, you will see a message similar to the one illustrated above in Figure 3-36. This lets you know that the columns are different. You can select to add all of the fields from the new table, by clicking in the box in the upper left corner of the grid or individually select fields. Once you have made the changes, click the Save button.
Refresh Preview button	Displays an updated version of the data in the selected source table.
Column names from	Is used to select where the column names that are displayed come from.
Check box	(Before each column name) If checked, the column will be imported.
Clear Row Filters button	Click this button to remove filters that you have created on this dialog box.

Table 3-12 Edit Table Properties dialog box options explained

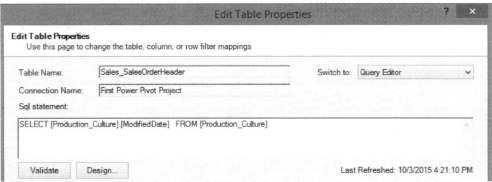

Figure 3-37 Edit Table Properties dialog box (Query Editor screen)

Calendars Group

The options in this group are used to create a table that is based on dates or change an existing table to be used as a date table. The options are explained in Table 3-13.

Option	This Option . . .
Mark as Date Table	Marks the currently displayed table as a date table, if the table has a column that has unique date values.
Date Table	[See Chapter 14, Date Table Button Options]

Table 3-13 Calendars group options explained

What Is A Date Table?

This type of table contains dates in many formats. Usually, the full date (month, day and year) are separated and placed in many columns. Month number, month name, year and week of year, are some examples of columns that would be in a date table. Date tables have a continuous set of dates. These tables are used to aggregate and group data by a date range, like second quarter of last year.

The data contained in this table is a contiguous (no gaps in the series of dates in the table) list of dates that are used to see how data (in other tables) changes over time. Power Pivot refers to this as **ADDING TIME INTELLIGENCE** to a data set.

Each row of data in the table is for a specific date. Each column contains all or part of the date for that row, in a specific format. For example, Figure 3-38 shows the Date Key column. It contains the full date. The Year column contains the year of the date in the Date Key column. The Quarter Full column contains which quarter the date is in.

The table should contain all of the date variations needed to create all of the reports that you need. That way, you only need to create and maintain one table and use it as much as needed. The number of dates to include in the table is up to you. Over time, you may have the need to add more date variations to the table, which is fine.

DateKey	Year	MonthNum	MonthFull	MonthAbbr	QuarterNum	QuarterFull	QuarterAbbr
12/29/2013	2013	12	December	Dec	4	Quarter 4	Q4
12/30/2013	2013	12	December	Dec	4	Quarter 4	Q4
12/31/2013	2013	12	December	Dec	4	Quarter 4	Q4
01/01/2014	2014	1	January	Jan	1	Quarter 1	Q1
01/02/2014	2014	1	January	Jan	1	Quarter 1	Q1
01/03/2014	2014	1	January	Jan	1	Quarter 1	Q1

Figure 3-38 Portion of a Date table

Edit Group

The options in this group are used to add or remove features that have been applied to a table. The options are explained in Table 3-14.

Option	Description
Undo	Undoes the last action. This is the same as using **CTRL+Z**. (6)
Redo	Reapplies the last action. This is the same as using **CTRL+Y**. (6)

Table 3-14 Edit group options explained

(6) In addition to clicking the button, you can open the Undo drop-down list shown in Figure 3-39 or the Redo drop-down list shown in Figure 3-40, and select the options that you want to undo or redo. The drop-down list only displays the options that can be undone or reapplied.

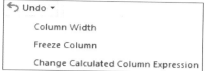

Figure 3-39 Undo drop-down list options   **Figure 3-40** Redo drop-down list options

 Undo Tip
I know this will be hard to believe, but sometimes I get carried away making changes to a table. When I want to undo all of the changes I made, since the last time I saved the workbook, I close the workbook, but don't save the changes and reopen it. To me, that is easier then clicking the Undo button 25 times <smile>.

Advanced Tab

The options on the tab shown in Figure 3-41 are used to create Perspectives, change the default aggregate function from SUM to something else and select options for reports that will be created using **POWER VIEW**.

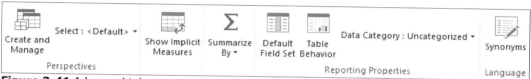

Figure 3-41 Advanced tab

Perspectives Group

The options in this group are used to create and manage custom views of the tables in the data model. The columns, including KPI's and measures can be included in a perspective.

The **CREATE AND MANAGE** button opens the dialog box shown in Figure 3-42. Perspectives are created on this dialog box. The data for the view can come from any table in the data model.

The **SELECT** button displays the perspectives that you have created, as shown in Figure 3-43. The Multi Table View perspective that I created, displays data from several tables in one view. To view the columns in a perspective, select the perspective from this drop-down list.

When a perspective is selected, the columns in the view are displayed and the other columns in the tables are hidden. Perspectives can be viewed on the Grid or Diagram View.

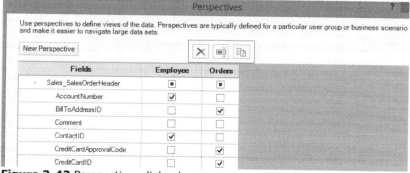

Figure 3-43 Select button (Perspectives)

Figure 3-42 Perspectives dialog box

Show Implicit Measures Button

Clicking this button displays the implicit measures. They are in the Calculation area, below the column that they were created from, as shown at the bottom of Figure 3-44. This is the same area that KPI measures are placed in.

Implicit measures are the measures that are automatically created when you add a field to the Values area on the Pivot Table Fields list.

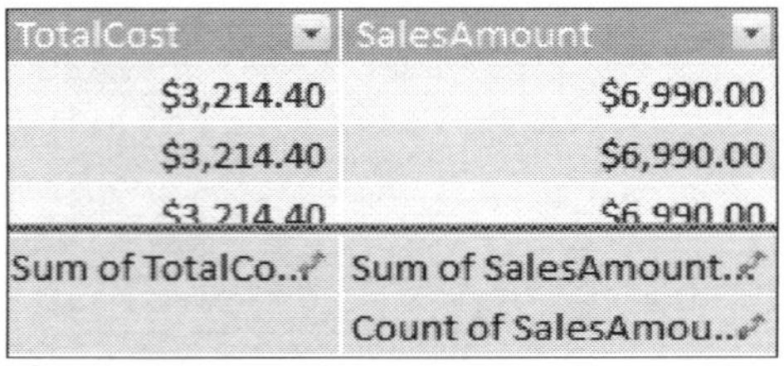

Figure 3-44 Implicit measures

Notice that the icon next to the implicit measure fields is the same as the one on the Show Implicit Measures button on the Advanced tab. The icon lets you know what type of measure the field is. KPI's have their own icon.

Summarize By Button

This button is only enabled for numeric and currency columns. The options shown in Figure 3-45 are used to change the default aggregate Auto Sum option. The default aggregate is Sum.

Use these options when you want something other than a total amount of the values displayed in the column to be used as the default option.

For example, if you know that most of the time, you need to calculate more average amount values then sum values for the pivot tables that you will create, you would select the Average function on this drop-down list. Then, when you are creating a calculated field and click the Auto Sum button, the formula will automatically be created using the Average function.

Figure 3-45 Summarize By button options

Reporting Properties Group

The options in this group are used to select default settings for reports that will be created using **POWER VIEW**.

The **DEFAULT FIELD SET** button opens the dialog box shown in Figure 3-46. It is used to select which fields and measures in a table are available and the order that they will be displayed in, when the table is viewed in Power View. The fields added to the set can be added to a report in Power View at one time. Fields not selected for the set can be used to query the table. This is helpful when you do not want people to have access to certain columns of data.

The **TABLE BEHAVIOR** button opens the dialog box shown in Figure 3-47. The options are used to change the grouping behavior of detail rows of data, when the fields are used in Power View. The options are also used to select a different default placement of identifying information, like names and images.

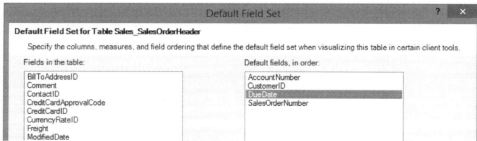

Figure 3-46 Default Field Set dialog box

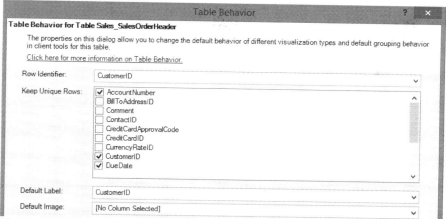

Figure 3-47 Table Behavior dialog box

The **DATA CATEGORY** button is used to select a category from the ones shown in Figure 3-48, for the selected column. As needed, these category options are used to better define the data in a table.

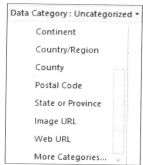

This option is especially helpful in Power Pivot for fields that have a URL, because URL's are normally stored in a text field.

Selecting the Web URL category will cause the web site address to be displayed as a link instead of plain text.

The **MORE CATEGORIES** option opens the dialog box shown in Figure 3-49. It has more options that can be used to categorize the data.

Figure 3-48 Data Category options

Data categories are more important if the workbook will be used with **POWER VIEW** or **3D MAPS** for several reasons including:
1) Displaying data geographically (maps) and
2) Displaying images. Power Pivot does not support either of these features.

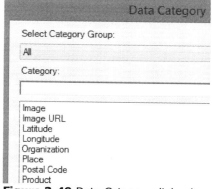

Figure 3-49 Data Category dialog box

Linked Table Contextual Tab

This tab is only available when a table in the data model is displayed that is linked to an Excel table. Unlike the other tabs on the Power Pivot ribbon, the Linked Table contextual tab is part of the Table Tools.

The options on the tab shown in Figure 3-50 are used to refresh data that is linked to an Excel table and select how the data should be refreshed.

The options are explained in Table 3-15.

Figure 3-50 Linked Table contextual tab

Option	Description
Update All	Updates all tables that are linked to an Excel table. This option works the same as the Update All option on the Power Pivot tab.
Update Selected	Updates the table that is currently displayed.
Excel Table	Displays the name of the Excel table that the selected Power Pivot table is linked to. The Excel table names in the list come from the Table Name field on the Table Tools Design tab in Excel. [See Chapter 7, Figure 7-2] This may be different then the name of the tab that the data is on. The drop-down list on this button only displays the Excel tables that are linked to a table in the data model. If the Excel table name is changed, the new name is automatically displayed in the Excel Table field if the **UPDATE MODE** option is set to Automatic.
Go to Excel Table	Is used to display the Excel table that is linked to the currently displayed table.
Update Mode	Is used to select how the data in the linked table is updated. Select the **MANUAL** option if you only want the data to be updated when you click the Update All or Update Selected button. **AUTOMATIC** is the default option, which means that the update will happen without your intervention, each time the workbook is opened. This option can make the workbook run slow and/or take longer for Power Pivot to open. If the workbook has a lot of data, it is best not to have the data updated automatically each time Power Pivot is opened.

Table 3-15 Linked Table contextual tab options explained

Shortcut Menus

The grid in the Power Pivot workspace has two shortcut menus: One for cells and one for columns. The options on these shortcut menus are explained below.

Cell Shortcut Menu

The shortcut menu shown in Figure 3-51 is displayed when you right-click on a cell in a table.

The options are explained in Table 3-16.

Figure 3-51 Cell shortcut menu

Option	Description
Copy	Is used to copy the data in the selected cell(s) and paste it into a new table.
Filter	The options on the submenu shown on the right of Figure 3-51 above, are used to only display rows of data in the table that have the value in the cell that you select. The **CLEAR FILTER FROM** option, removes the filter. These filter options are a subset of the filter options for the column. [See Chapter 5, Using The Preview & Filter Button Options]

Table 3-16 Cell shortcut menu options explained

Create A Table From Data In The Data Model

As you read above in Table 3-16, the Copy option on the cell shortcut menu is used to create a new table from data in an existing table. You do not have to use all of the columns in the existing table to create a new table. If you need to create a table this way, the steps below show you how to create a new table using the Copy option.

1. Open the workbook that has the data that you want to use to create a new table.

2. Power Pivot window ⇒ Click on the tab that has the data that you want to copy to a new table.

3. Select the cells that you want to copy to a new table.

4. Home tab ⇒ Clipboard group ⇒ Copy button.
   Home tab ⇒ Clipboard group ⇒ Paste button. You will see the dialog box shown in Figure 3-52.

This dialog box displays the name of the table that you copied the cells from and the data that you selected to paste into the new table.

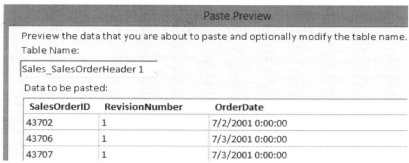

Figure 3-52 Paste Preview dialog box

5. More than likely, you want this data on a new tab. In the Table Name field, type in a name for the new table ⇒ Click OK. A new table will be created that has the data that you copied ⇒ Save the changes to the workbook.

Column Shortcut Menu

Some of the options on the shortcut menu shown in Figure 3-53 are shortcuts to options on the tabs in Power Pivot.

Right-click on a column heading to display this shortcut menu.

The options are explained in Table 3-17.

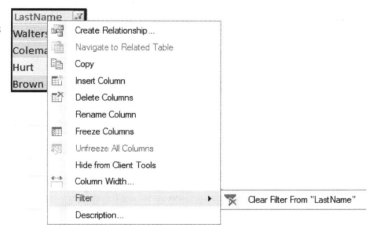

Figure 3-53 Column shortcut menu

Option	Description
Create Relationship	Is used to join two tables, so that data from both tables can be used in the same pivot table or pivot chart.
Navigate to Related Table	This option is only enabled for a column in a **CHILD TABLE** that has been used to create a relationship. When this option is selected, the table that the column is linked to is displayed. The lookup column in the related tabled is selected.
Copy	[See Table 3-16]
Insert Column	Is used to add a calculated column to the table.
Delete Columns	Deletes the selected column(s) from the table.
Rename Column	[See Renaming Tables And Columns]
Freeze Columns	[See Table 3-9, Freeze]
Unfreeze All Columns	Removes the freeze option, but does not move the columns that were frozen, back to where they were before the freeze option was applied.
Hide from Client Tools	This option is used to hide columns and fields. Once enabled, this option changes to **UNHIDE FROM CLIENT TOOLS** on the shortcut menu. [See Chapter 8, Hiding And Unhiding Columns]
Column Width	[See Table 3-9, Width]
Filter	Displays the Clear Filter From option, explained earlier in Table 3-16. It is enabled when a filter has been applied to a cell in the selected column. (7)
Description	Opens the dialog box shown in Figure 3-54. It is used to add a description to the selected column.

Table 3-17 Column shortcut menu options explained

(7) **How To Remove Some Filters And Leave Others**
If you only want to remove some filters, right-click on the column that has a filter that you want to remove ⇒ Select Filter ⇒ Clear Filter From, as shown above in Figure 3-53, on the right.

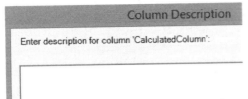

Enter description for column 'CalculatedColumn':

Figure 3-54 Column Description dialog box

Renaming Tables And Columns

Once the data has been imported, there may be a need to change the table or column name. The good thing is that when a table or column is renamed, it is renamed every place it is used in the workbook, including in formulas.

Rename A Table

To rename a table, right-click on the tab for the table and select **RENAME**, as shown in Figure 3-55.

Type in a new table name, then press Enter.

During the import process, a table can be renamed by using the Friendly Name column on the Table Import Wizard.

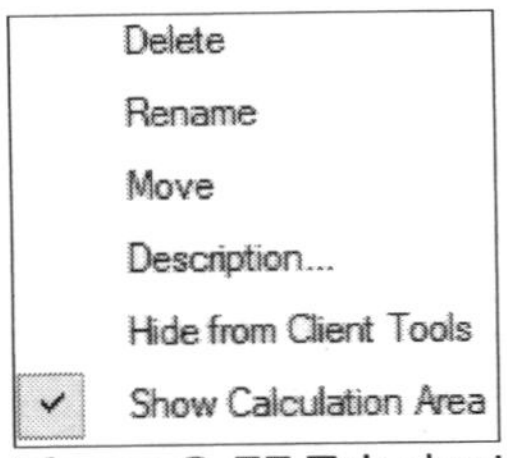

| Delete |
| Rename |
| Move |
| Description... |
| Hide from Client Tools |
| ✓ Show Calculation Area |

Figure 3-55 Tab shortcut menu

Rename A Column

To rename a column, right-click on the column heading and select **RENAME COLUMN**. Type in the new name, then press Enter.

Column Filter And Sort Options

Clicking on the arrow at the end of the column name will display the filter and sort options. Figure 3-56 shows the filter and sort options for a currency field.

The **(BLANKS)** option is used as a group for rows of data that do not have a value in the selected column.

Notice the icon to the right of the Sales Quota column heading that is illustrated in the figure. It indicates that the column has a filter applied.

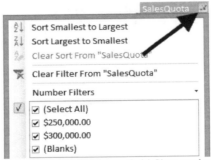

Figure 3-56 Currency field filter and sort options

If you see the **NOT ALL ITEMS SHOWING** link below the filter options, it means that there is more data in the column that is not being displayed. [See Chapter 5, Figure 5-8 for an example of the link]

Changing The Grid Background Color

If you do not like the default background color of the Power Pivot grid, you can change it by following the steps below.

1. Display an Excel worksheet in the workbook that you want to change the background color of.

2. Page Layout tab ⇒ Themes group ⇒ Themes. You should see the options shown in Figure 3-57.

   Select a different theme from the list or click on the Browse for Themes link, at the bottom of the list, to select a theme that is on your hard drive or in another location.

Figure 3-57 Theme options

3. Save the changes, then close the Power Pivot window and reopen it to see the new theme color.

Summary

This chapter presented a tour of the Power Pivot workspace. At the beginning of the chapter, the Power Pivot tab in Excel was covered. This tab is helpful because it provides options for adding functionality to the pivot tables that you create, without having to open the Power Pivot window. Power Pivot has a lot of options that are designed to help you get the data ready to be used to create pivot tables and charts.

 Overview

In this chapter you will probably learn more than you want to about the Table Import Wizard <smile>.

CHAPTER 4

Importing Data

Importing data is the most important part of the process of being able to use Power Pivot. Without data, Power Pivot can't be used. A benefit that Power Pivot has over traditional BI tools is that the data comes straight into Power Pivot, instead of having to be stored in a data warehouse for staging and then imported into the BI tool. Because of its flexibility, Power Pivot can import data from a rather impressive list of data sources.

My Import Data Advice

The best advice that I can give you is **Do Not Import Data That You Will Not Use**. While you have the option of importing as much data as you want, keep in mind that the import can fail if your computer does not have enough RAM to support the amount of data in the import. The second best piece of advice that I have is to rename tables and columns, so that they are meaningful.

One way to reduce the chance of the import failing, is to not import columns or rows of data that you will not use to create pivot tables, pivot charts or other types of reports. Power Pivot provides filter and query options on the Table Import Wizard that can be used to reduce the number of records and number of columns of data that are imported. Unless you are using Copy and Paste, you can import a column later, if you need it.

Table Import Wizard

The Table Import Wizard takes you step-by-step through the process of setting up a connection to a data source and selecting the data to import. Data can be imported from a variety of sources into one Power Pivot workbook. Data is imported in table format, regardless of the source. As you have seen, each table is automatically placed on its own tab, just like tabs in an Excel worksheet.

Unlike some wizards in other software packages that I have used, I am happy to say that the Table Import Wizard is very straight forward. What I like is that each screen on the wizard has a sentence or two that explains in non technical terms what task needs to be completed.

If you are asking yourself why would you have the need to import data from a variety of sources into one workbook, the most common answer is because you want to perform analysis on all data that is relevant, regardless of the location or format that the data is stored in.

Behind the scenes, the Table Import Wizard is creating a query, based on the options that you select. This query can be saved, which is known as a **CONNECTION**. The connection can be used over and over again. What I think would be cool is to be able to view all of the options selected on the Table Import Wizard. It would be helpful if you are expecting to see data, but didn't because you accidentally created a filter that prevented the data that you are expecting to be imported.

Maybe this is my IT background kicking in, but another reason being able to see all of the import options that were selected, would be to compare data from different data sources, to confirm accuracy or remove redundant data.

Because an important aspect of Power Pivot is importing data and the Table Import Wizard is the tool used to import data, I felt that it deserved its own chapter.

Figure 4-1 Get External Data group

In Step 1 below, you will learn about the options in the Get External Data group, shown in Figure 4-1, which is on the Home tab in Power Pivot.

Step 1: Select The Data Source

In this step, the database, text file, spreadsheet, data feed or other data source that you want to import data from is selected. The data source options are explained below.

Figure 4-2 From Database options

FROM DATABASE Displays the options shown in Figure 4-2. The options are used to import data from different Microsoft databases. The options are explained in Table 4-1.

Option	Select This Option To Connect To A . . .
From SQL Server	SQL Server database. The options shown in Figure 4-3 are used to connect to this type of database.
From Access	Access database. This database software comes with some editions of Microsoft Office or it can be purchased as a stand alone product. Access databases can reside on your computers hard drive or on a server. This is the data source option that was used in the Quick Tour in Chapter 2.
From Analysis Services or Power Pivot	SQL Server Analysis Services database, which is similar to connecting to a SQL Server database. As shown in Figure 4-4, the connection options are similar to the SQL Server database connection options. The difference is that an **MDX QUERY** is used for the Analysis Services database, instead of an SQL query to retrieve the data. This option is also used to connect to and import data from a Power Pivot workbook that has been published to a SharePoint server.

Table 4-1 From Database options explained

When you open the Server name drop-down list, Power Pivot will automatically search for servers that the computer is connected to.

If the search takes a while, your computer may not be connected to any servers.

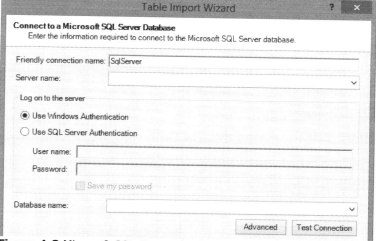

Figure 4-3 Microsoft SQL Server database connection options

 Microsoft Access databases that have already been published to a SharePoint server cannot be imported into Power Pivot.

Unlike the Server Name field in an SQL Server connection, the Server or File Name field on the SQL Server Analysis Services screen shown in Figure 4-4, does not have a drop-down list that you can select a server from.

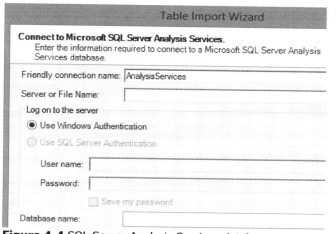

Figure 4-4 SQL Server Analysis Services database connection options

 Importing SQL Server Analysis Services OLAP Cubes
Select the From Analysis Services or Power Pivot option when you want to import data from an Analysis Services OLAP cube. Because OLAP cube files do not contain tables, an MDX query must be used to import the data. Power Pivot has an MDX editor that you can use to create queries for OLAP data. [See Chapter 13, Figure 13-17]

FROM DATA SERVICE Displays the options shown in Figure 4-5. They are used to import data from an enterprise system or an online source. These options are used to connect to web sites that provide data that can be imported into Power Pivot. Figure 4-6 shows some of the free data sources available in the **MICROSOFT AZURE MARKETPLACE**.

Once enabled, the **SUGGEST RELATED DATA** option also searches the Azure Marketplace for data sources. It searches for datasets that match data in the data model, in the workbook that is currently being used.

Figure 4-5 From Data Service options

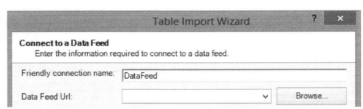

Figure 4-6 Azure Marketplace

FROM ODATA DATA FEED Is used to import data from an **ATOM DATA FEED** or from an online data source (corporate or public), by using the options shown in Figure 4-7.

RSS DATA FEEDS are not supported.

Figure 4-7 Data Feed connection options

FROM OTHER SOURCES displays the options shown in Figure 4-8.

This screen can be used to import data from every data source type that Power Pivot supports.

Usually, this option is selected when the data source is not one of the options already explained above.

Data source connections are Power Pivot workbook specific, meaning that if workbook 1 is connected to database 1 and workbook 2 needs to import data from database 1, a connection to database 1 will have to be created in workbook 2.

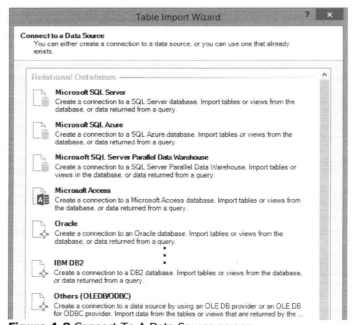

Figure 4-8 Connect To A Data Source screen

 If you need to connect to a database, the drivers for the type of database that you are using, have to be installed on your computer. Microsoft Access and SQL Server drivers are probably already installed on your computer. If you do not see the driver that you need for other databases, you will have to install the driver.

Relational Databases

Earlier in this chapter you learned about the database connections that have their own option in the Get External Data group section on the Home tab. This section discusses some of the relational database options on the Connect to a Data Source screen, shown above in Figure 4-8.

Microsoft SQL Server Parallel Data Warehouse is a scalable data warehouse solution that is capable of storing hundreds of terabytes of data. Data can be imported from tables, views or from a query.

Oracle, **Teradata**, **Sybase**, **Informix** and **IBM DB2** are all enterprise level relational database management systems, owned by different companies. Drivers for these databases do not come with Power Pivot.

Many of these databases use the connection options shown in Figure 4-9.

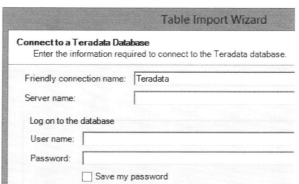

Figure 4-9 Enterprise database connection options

Others (OLEDB/ODBC) Select this option if the database that you want to connect to is not in the list of databases discussed above, as long as it is OLE DB or ODBC compliant. The OLE DB provider may already be installed on your computer, if SQL Server is installed. An example of this type of database is dBASE.

When the Others (OLEDB/ODBC) option is selected and the Next button is clicked, the screen shown in Figure 4-10 is displayed.

The options on this screen are used to add the information needed to connect to the database that you want to import data from.

Figure 4-10 OLEDB/ODBC connection options

If you have no idea how to create a connection string, click the **BUILD** button, shown above in Figure 4-10, to display the dialog box shown in Figure 4-11. The options on this dialog box are used to create the connection by selecting the appropriate provider. If you want to see a connection string, see Chapter 6, Figure 6-11.

If you have never created a connection string, you will probably find using this dialog box easier then creating the connection string on your own.

More than likely, you will select the **ODBC DRIVERS** option on this screen, if you do not see the database type that you want to connect to in the list and then click Next to select the data source.

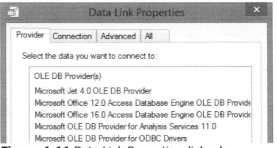

Figure 4-11 Data Link Properties dialog box

Multidimensional Sources

MICROSOFT ANALYSIS SERVICES This data source option is used to connect to a Microsoft Analysis Services cube. Select this option when the data that you want to import will be retrieved from a **MULTI DIMENSIONAL EXPRESSIONS (MDX)** query. The data retrieved from an MDX query is in cube format.

If you have created reports in Crystal Reports™ and used an **OLAP CUBE**, you are familiar with the cube data format. Usually, data in cube format is data that has been summarized. Cube data is not in table format, which Power Pivot requires. Fortunately, you do not have to manipulate the data in the cube before importing it into Power Pivot. During the import process, Power Pivot will import the data in a cube from the Analysis Services query, into table format.

Data Feeds

If you have seen the icon shown in Figure 4-12 on a web site and clicked on it, you were subscribing to a data feed.

Figure 4-12 Data Feed icon

What Is A Data Feed?

A data feed is a way to exchange data. They provide the data via web services. To connect to a web service, type in the web site address of the web service. Data feeds allow people to receive updates to data on a web site when the source data changes. Figure 4-13 shows the types of data feeds that Power Pivot supports.

GENERIC DATA FEEDS are the type of data feed that you may have already subscribed to or are already familiar with.

Select the From OData Feed option shown earlier in Figure 4-5 or one of the Data Feed options shown in Figure 4-13.

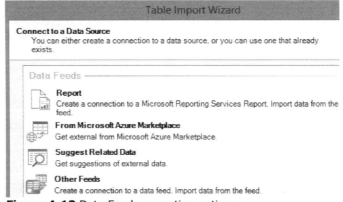

Figure 4-13 Data Feed connection options

REPORT DATA FEED Is used to import data from a Microsoft Reporting Services report, by using the options on the dialog box shown in Figure 4-14.

The data from a report is imported into Power Pivot via a data feed.

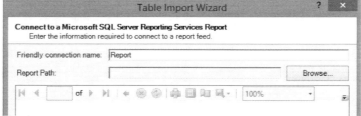

Figure 4-14 Microsoft SQL Server Reporting Services Report connection options

There are two data feed formats: **ATOM** and **RSS**. Power Pivot only supports Atom data feeds.

There are two **DATA FEED ACCESS TYPES**: Those that require a logon account to access the data feed or a public data feed, which does not require a logon account.

Using .Atomsvc Documents

In addition to typing in the URL for the data feed, you can use an .atomsvc document, which is the Microsoft Data Feed Provider for Power Pivot. This is an XML file that defines one or more data feeds. This type of document contains pointers (connections) to at least one data feed or service that provides data feeds. You can point the OData connection to the URL of the .atomsvc file or use a URL address in the .atomsvc document to connect to the web service.

Text Files

Text files do not have any formatting like bold, italic or font size options. To be used in Excel, this file type has to have rows of data, as shown in Figure 4-15. Each row of data has fields (columns). The fields are usually separated by commas. An advantage of text files is that they can handle millions of rows of data.

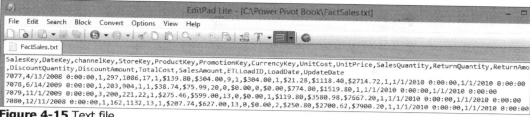

Figure 4-15 Text file

The Text file option is used to import data from a file that is in one of these formats: .txt, .tab or .csv, by using the options shown in Figure 4-16.

These file types are known as **FLAT FILES**.

Files with the **.TAB** extension are Tab Separated files, meaning that the data in the file is separated by tabs.

Files with the **.CSV** extension are Comma Separated files.

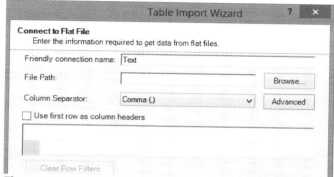

Figure 4-16 Flat File (text) connection options screen

> -💡- **Table Import Wizard Tips**
> ① If you want the column headers to be imported, but forget to select the **USE FIRST ROW AS COLUMN HEADERS** option before selecting the file to import, you can select the option after the preview records from the data source are displayed at the bottom of the screen shown above in Figure 4-16.
> ② The Table Import Wizard does not display all of the data that will be imported. 50 rows of data are displayed as a preview, on the screen shown above in Figure 4-16.

The options in the **COLUMN SEPARATOR** drop-down list, on the screen shown above in Figure 4-16, are used to select what character is used in the file, to separate the fields that will be imported.

The separator character is in parenthesis, as shown in Figure 4-17. If you are not sure which character is used, view the data in the file before starting the import process.

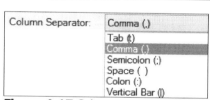

Figure 4-17 Column separator options

The **ADVANCED** button on the screen shown earlier in Figure 4-16, opens the dialog box shown in Figure 4-18. The options on this dialog box are used to select a different encoding option.

ENCODING is a way to format data.

LOCALE is used to select a language that will be used for ordering (sorting) the records and for the date and time formats.

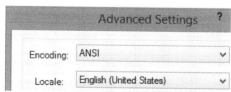

Figure 4-18 Advanced Settings dialog box

Database Providers

All of the database connection screens, including the Report Data Feed and From Data Feed options have an **ADVANCED** button. This button opens a dialog box that displays the supported database providers for the data source that you selected. The providers are in the drop-down list, at the top of the dialog box.

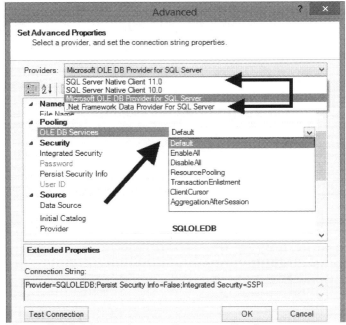

Figure 4-19 shows the advanced properties for an SQL Server database.

The order that the **PROVIDERS** are listed in the drop-down list is the preferred order of use.

For example, as illustrated at the top of Figure 4-19, the most preferred provider is the SQL Server Native Client 11.0. The least preferred provider for this type of database is the .NET framework. If multiple providers are supported, Power Pivot will select the best one, based on the providers that are installed.

Power Pivot does not install the providers that are in the drop-down list. Installing providers are beyond the scope of this book.

Figure 4-19 Advanced connection properties for an SQL Server database

As shown, the SQL Server database has multiple providers that Power Pivot supports. Other databases may not.

What may not be obvious is that many of the advanced property options, on the Advanced dialog box, can be changed. When you click in the column on the right of some options, you can type in the setting that you want. For other options, when you click in the column on the right, you will see a drop-down list of options that you can select from, as illustrated in the middle of Figure 4-19.

Figure 4-20 shows the advanced properties for a Microsoft Access database.

Some of the providers may already be installed on your computer because of other software that you have installed.

For example, the provider for Access will already be installed if Access is installed on your computer.

Figure 4-20 Advanced connection properties for a Microsoft Access database

Power Pivot will warn you if it cannot find the drivers needed for the database type that you want to use. If the Next button is clicked, you will see a message similar to the one illustrated in Figure 4-21. You will see the message shown at the bottom of Figure 4-21, when the Test Connection button is clicked. This message will let you know what driver needs to be installed.

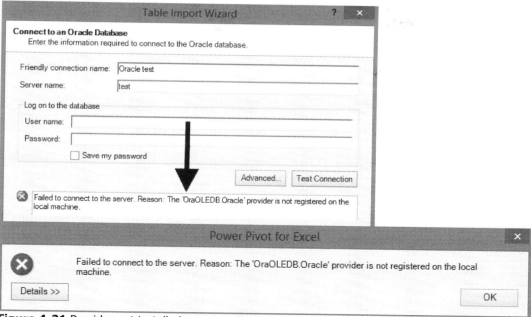

Figure 4-21 Provider not installed message illustrated

Step 2: Select How To Import The Data

As the name of the screen suggests, the options are used to select how the data will be imported. This step is only for a database connection, which includes data feeds. This step is not used for text or spreadsheet files.

Figure 4-22 shows the table and query import options.

The options are used to select how the data should be imported. The options are explained below.

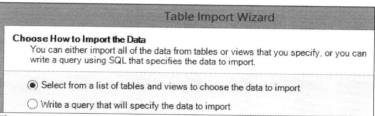

Figure 4-22 Database import options

① **Select The Tables And Views** Select this option if you want to import all or some of the tables and records in the data source. Behind the scenes, this option creates a query based on the options that you select on the Table Import Wizard. The query is sent to the database to retrieve the tables, rows and columns that you select. This process is explained below, in the Import Tables section.

② **Use A Query To Select The Data** This option requires you to create an SQL query or to select an existing SQL query to import records. This process is explained below, in the Import By Query section.

Step 3: Select And Filter The Data That Will Be Imported

This step requires you to select the tables that will be imported. If there are rows or columns of data that you do not need (in the data source), you should remove them before the data is imported into the data model. If you are not going to import all of the fields in the data source, make sure that the fields that you are not going to import are not key fields, because a relationship needs to be created for the table.

Import Tables

After selecting the Tables and Views option on the Import Data screen, you will see the screen shown in Figure 4-23.

Above the tables, you will see the name of the database that the tables are in.

If you want to select all of the tables, click in the box to the left of the Source Table column heading.

The second column has icons to denote what the source is, like a table or view.

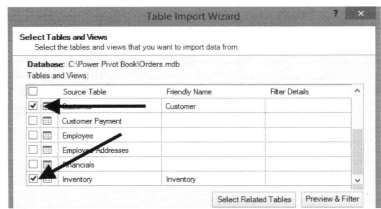

Figure 4-23 Select Tables and Views screen

The **SOURCE TABLE** column lists the tables and views in the data source.

To select specific tables or views, click in the box to the far left of the table name, as illustrated.

Import By Query

After selecting the query option on the Import Data screen, you will see the **SPECIFY A SQL QUERY SCREEN**. The options on this screen are used to create or select the query that will retrieve the records that will be imported.
[See Chapter 5, Specify A SQL Query Screen]

Depending on the type of database that you are using, you will see a different query editor when the **DESIGN** button is clicked. The query editor options are shown in Figures 4-25 and 4-26.

Creating Queries To Import Data From Access Databases
If you have used Access to create a database, you know that it allows you to create queries. If you know how to create a query in Access, the SQL code is automatically created. You can paste the SQL code into a text file and use it by selecting the query option shown earlier in Figure 4-22 to select the query that you create.

Figure 4-24 shows the query editor for a non SQL Server database. This editor (also known as the **RELATIONAL QUERY DESIGNER**) has more functionality for creating a query then the SQL query screen has.

The **EDIT AS TEXT** button (at the top of Figure 4-24) is used to switch between the text based editor (Figure 4-24) and the graphical editor (Figure 4-25).

If the data source supports graphical query designers, this button will be enabled.

Figure 4-24 Non SQL Server query editor (text based)

Figure 4-25 shows the query editor for an SQL Server database. This editor (also known as the **GRAPHICAL QUERY DESIGNER**) will be familiar if you have used the Microsoft SQL Server Report Builder software. Notice that you can create relationships on the **SQL SERVER QUERY EDITOR**.

The **AUTO DETECT** button (in the Relationships section of Figure 4-25) if clicked, will specify whether relationships are automatically detected from foreign keys in the database tables that are selected.

> **Applied Filters Parameter Option**
> The Parameter check box, in the Applied Filters section of the SQL Server query editor, (which is illustrated in Figure 4-25), does not work because parameters are not supported in Power Pivot.

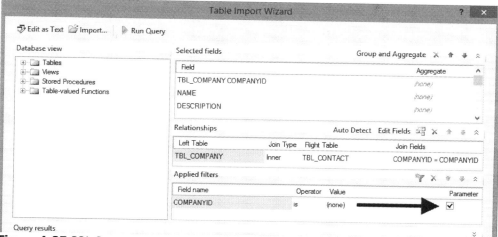

Figure 4-25 SQL Server query editor (graphical based)

Step 4: Finish The Import Process

The Finish button is not enabled on the Import Data screen. The Finish button is only enabled on the Select Tables and Views screen or the Specify a SQL Query screen.

Clicking the Finish button on either of these screens starts the data import process shown in Figure 4-26.

I stopped the import shown in the figure because I know that the Fact Sales table has a few million records.

This screen displays the status of each table or view that is being imported.

The **WORK ITEM** column lists the imported tables.

The **STATUS** column displays how many rows of data (records) were imported from each table.

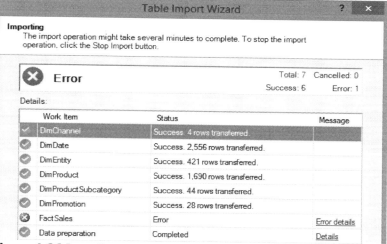

Figure 4-26 Importing screen

If there are any problems during the import, you will see a **ERROR DETAILS** link in the Message column. Clicking on the links opens a dialog box that will display what the problem is.

The **DATA PREPARATION** Work Item is not a table that is imported. It is always the last entry in the list on the Importing screen. It informs you if relationships were detected and whether or not the relationships were created. During the import process, Power Pivot will try to recreate the relationships that are already set up between the tables in the database. Clicking the Details link opens the dialog box shown in Figure 4-27.

The dialog box shown in Figure 4-27 displays relationships that Power Pivot could and could not recreate.

As you can see, the first relationship that was attempted to be created, failed. The second relationship that was attempted, was successful.

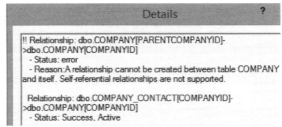

Figure 4-27 Details dialog box

Benefits Of Importing Data

Below are some of the benefits of importing data into the data model.

① Fewer people need direct access to the live data, which is good from a security perspective.

② The data model can be shared with people that do not have database experience.

③ The live data cannot be changed.

Summary

This chapter covered the Table Import Wizard in detail. The reason that I devoted an entire chapter to this tool is because if you cannot get the data into Power Pivot, it's a wrap! Power Pivot needs data to be able to work. If Power Pivot does not support the data source that you need to use, try Power Query. Enough said! Let's move on to the next chapter, which includes more details about the Table Import Wizard.

IMPORT DATA FROM DATABASES

Overview

In this chapter you will learn how to import data from databases. You will also learn about the following:

☑ Power Pivot supported data types
☑ Using a query to import and filter data
☑ Filtering data during the import process

CHAPTER 5

Overview

Chapter 3 briefly covered the options for importing data into the data model. Chapter 4 covered the Table Import Wizard in detail. This chapter and the next one will show you how to import data from a variety of data sources into the data model. As the title of this chapter indicates, this chapter is devoted to importing data from a database.

Power Pivot Supported Data Types

Power Pivot (the data model) supports the data types listed in the first column in Table 5-1. The first column in the table is how Power Pivot "classifies" data. The second column in the table is how DAX classifies data. Keep in mind that Excel does not have data types. Instead, numeric data is formatted to match the data types in the first column in the table.

Once imported, each column in the table has a specific data type and all values in the column have to be the same data type. If all of the data in a column is not defined as text and does not have the same data type, you will see an error that the column is not defined as the Text data type.

Power Pivot does not support all of the data types that some databases use. This means that some columns of data may not be displayed on the Preview Selected Table screen on the Table Import Wizard and that they may not be imported.

While some databases support more than one variation of a data type listed in the first column, Power Pivot does not. If the original data type for the field is similar to one in the table, it will be mapped to a data type in the first column in Table 5-1.

Power Pivot Data Type	DAX Data Type	Description
Text	String	Usually contains regular text. Dates and numbers are displayed as text in this data type. If all of the data in a column cannot be converted to any of the other data types in this table, the column defaults to text.
Decimal Number	64-bit real number	Positive and negative numbers with or without a decimal point. Zero is also a decimal number.
Whole Number	64-bit integer	Positive and negative numbers without a decimal point.
Date	Date/Time	DAX only supports dates and times on or after January 1, 1900.
Currency	Currency	Currency values are imported into the currency format that the computer is set to use. This could produce different or unexpected results from one computer to another.
True/False	Boolean	A true or false value.
(Not available)	Blank	In DAX, this data type replaces SQL null values.

Table 5-1 Power Pivot supported data types explained

Importing Data From A Database

Importing data from a database is a popular way to add data to the data model. In addition to tables, databases can use queries to add data to a table. Views and stored procedures are other ways to import data from a database. Queries, views and stored procedures retrieve a subset of the data that is in the tables in the database, instead of retrieving all of the records in all of the tables in the database.

For example, there could be a query that only retrieves orders from specific states. **UNLIKE TABLES, QUERIES, VIEWS AND STORED PROCEDURES DO NOT STORE DATA.** They contain code that specifies which records in the table should be retrieved or in the case of Power Pivot, which records should be imported. If you find that you are using the same criteria over and over to retrieve records or you are always applying the same filters to the same data, each time you import the data, you can create a query that has all of the options that you need. Using a query, view or stored procedure will save you time when importing data from a database because you do not have to manually select the criteria on the Table Import Wizard dialog box. Views and stored procedures are discussed in more detail in the next two sections.

Views

Views are usually created by a Database Administrator, report designer or someone that has administrator rights to the database. Views allow one to gather data from a variety of tables and databases and combine the data into a "view". This makes it easier for end users to access just the data that they need.

A view is a **RECORDSET** (the result) of a query. Views usually display a subset of the data in a data source. Views are stored in the database and are like tables, but they do not have the physical characteristics of a table. For example, records cannot be added to or deleted from a view. Fields cannot be added to a view unless the view is modified to include more fields. The field length cannot be changed in a view, like it can in a table.

Views are useful if you use the sorting, grouping and data selection (filter) options in Power Pivot. Views are created when the same recordset, calculation or query needs to be used in several reports or in the case of Power Pivot, several pivot tables or pivot charts. If you know that you will create several of these items in Power Pivot that use the same sorting, grouping or data selection options, you could create and save a view in the database, if you have the appropriate administrator rights to do so. Doing this means that you would not have to select the same options over and over again, on the Preview & Filter screen on the Table Import Wizard dialog box, each time that you import data from the same database.

Instead of selecting all of the tables, fields and options in Power Pivot, select the view in the database when importing the data. If you do not have access to do this at the database level, the **PERSPECTIVE** options in Power Pivot are used to create views. Keep in mind though, that Perspectives do not have all of the functionality discussed above.

Tables vs Views

When possible, using views is preferred over using tables. There are some differences between importing tables and views, as described below.

① Tables already have relationships that Power Pivot recognizes, when the tables are imported.
② In views, the tables have already been joined for you.
③ Power Pivot cannot automatically create relationships on views. If the view has all of the fields you need, this should not be a problem.
④ Once a view is imported, you can see how the tables are linked (or not linked), as well as, the actual data, if you have the rights to open a view in design mode.
⑤ Imported views usually have cleaner data because they only include the fields that are needed, because the data was already filtered.

Stored Procedures

Stored Procedures contain queries that are more complex then views, but less complex than commands.

The majority of the time, stored procedures are created by a DBA or programmer. Figure 5-1 shows the views and stored procedures in a database.

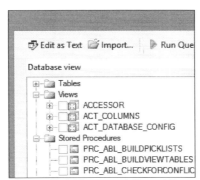

Figure 5-1 Views and Stored Procedures in a database

 Importing Comment And Note Fields
At some point, you will come across a table or file that has a comment or note field. As these fields are not used to create a pivot table, you should not import them because this type of field will take up unnecessary space in the data model. This field type also prohibits the engine behind the data model from doing the job that it was intended to do.

 Check The Data Type After The Import
It is a good idea to check the data type of the fields after the import, as data that "looks" like it is a certain data type, may not actually be defined as that. If all of the values in a field are not the same type, for example, a field of numeric values that has been defined as text, should have the data type changed in the table, if the field will be used in a formula.

Importing Exercises
Unless stated otherwise, before starting an importing exercise, open a new Excel workbook. Then, on the Power Pivot tab, click the Manage button to open Power Pivot.

Exercise 5.1: Import Data From A Microsoft Access Database

This exercise will show you how to import data from an Access database into the data model.

1. Home tab ⇒ Get External Data group ⇒ From Database ⇒ From Access.

2. In the Friendly connection name field, type `Contoso Product Table`.

3. Click the Browse button ⇒ In your folder, double-click on the Contoso Sales database. You should have the options shown in Figure 5-2. If the database required a logon and password, you would enter the information on this dialog box ⇒ Click Next.

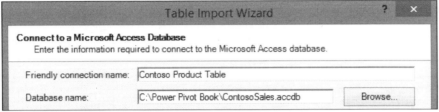

Figure 5-2 Connect to a Microsoft Access database screen

 Keep in mind that databases can be renamed, moved or deleted. Also remember that connections in Power Pivot are hard coded, so if any of the changes mentioned above occur, the connection will have to be updated to reflect the changes.

4. Select the first import option ⇒ Click Next.

Source Table Name Prefixes

It is very common for table names in a database to have a prefix.

The prefixes are used by IT people to make it easier to identify the type of table it is. As shown in Figure 5-3, the first two tables have the prefix **DIM**, which is short for **DIMENSION TABLE**.

From an Excel perspective, dimension tables are lookup tables. I have seen transaction tables, like the Fact Sales table have the prefix **FCT**.

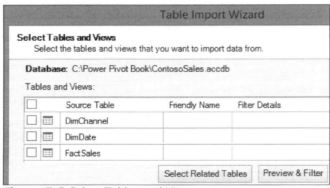

Figure 5-3 Select Tables and Views screen

Depending on who will be using these tables once they are imported into the data model, you may want to remove the prefixes from the table name on the screen shown above in Figure 5-3. Doing so will make the table names easier for end users to understand.

 Using The Friendly Name Column To Rename A Table During The Import
The **FRIENDLY NAME** column, shown above in Figure 5-3, displays the name of the table by default. If you want to use a different name for the table, type it in this column. The name in this column overrides the Source Table name and will be the table name in Power Pivot, once the data is imported. If you click on this column heading, you can change the sort order of the Tables and Views to be displayed in ascending or descending order by the Friendly Name, instead of sorting on the Source Table name.

The **FILTER DETAILS** column will display a link, if filter criteria was created on the Preview Selected Table screen, shown later in Figure 5-6, for the table.

The **SELECT RELATED TABLES** button retrieves and displays the related tables for the tables that are checked. The related tables have a link (relationship) to one of the tables that was already selected.

The **PREVIEW & FILTER** button is used to create filters and view data in the selected table. The preview and filter options are very useful because they are used to reduce the amount of data that will be imported.

5. Check the DimProduct source table. You will see that the Friendly Name field was automatically filled in with the Source Table name.

6. Double-click in the Friendly Name column across from the DimProduct table ⇒ Type `Products` in the cell.

Preview The Related Tables

Now that you have selected a table, you can check to see if the table has any related tables in the database. Related tables are often referred to as **CHILD TABLES**.

1. Click the Select Related Tables button.

    Notice in Figure 5-4, that the DimProduct Subcategory and Fact Sales tables are now checked.

    At the bottom of the dialog box you will see a message indicating how many related tables were found and selected.

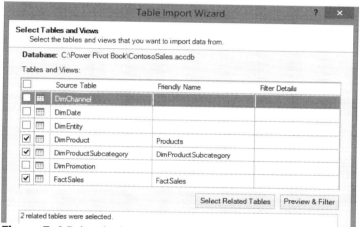

Figure 5-4 Related tables found

Don't do the instruction below. This is just a demonstration.

If you clicked the Select Related Tables button again, three more tables would be selected, as shown in Figure 5-5.

That is because all of the tables checked above in Figure 5-4 are now used as the tables to find related tables for.

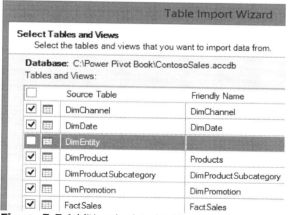

Figure 5-5 Additional related tables found

Using The Preview & Filter Button Options

The preview and filter options can be applied to each table that you import. What may not be obvious is that you have to click on the table name that you want to apply filters to before clicking the **PREVIEW & FILTER** button.

In this part of the exercise you will clear the check mark for the Manufacturer and Brand Name columns in the Products table. This will prevent the columns from being imported. Products that have a Unit Price greater than $100 will not be imported. This prevents some rows from being imported. The steps below show you how to filter the data to meet these requirements.

1. With the Products table selected, click the Preview & Filter button. Figure 5-6 displays the data in the Products table.

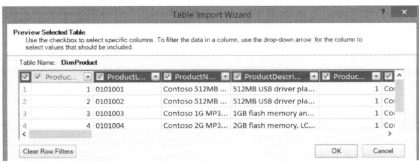

Figure 5-6 Preview Selected Table screen

On the **PREVIEW SELECTED TABLE** screen, you will see the table name that the filters will be applied to. The check box, in front of the column header, is used to select whether or not the column will be imported. Clear the check mark if you do not want to import the column of data.

The filter option (the down arrow button to the right of the column heading) on this screen works the same as it does in an Excel spreadsheet. Records that do not meet the filter requirements will not be imported. If you create filters then change your mind, click the **CLEAR ROW FILTERS** button.

2. Scroll to the right ⇒ Clear the check mark for the Manufacturer and Brand Name columns.

3. Scroll to the right until you see the Unit Price column ⇒ Click the button next to the column heading. It displays the options shown on the left of Figure 5-7.

   Click on the Number Filters option ⇒ Select the **LESS THAN OR EQUAL TO** function, shown on the right side of the figure.

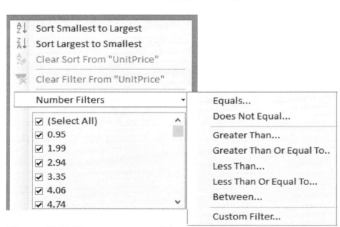

Figure 5-7 Filter options and functions

Saving Filter Options
The filter options that you select are saved with the connection in the workbook. This means that by default, when you refresh the data, the filters are automatically re-applied unless you change them.

Using The Filter Options
The filter options shown in Figure 5-8 are used to reduce the number of records (rows of data) that will be imported. If the data source has a lot of records, you will see the **NOT ALL ITEMS SHOWING** link, illustrated at the bottom of the figure. This message lets you know that all of the data for the field is not displayed in this list because there are too many items. This message will also appear in Power Pivot when you use the filter option. Clicking on the link, does not display more data. The link opens the help window in Excel. When this happens, it is best to create a custom filter to select the values that you need.

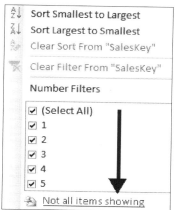

Figure 5-8 Filter with a lot of items message

4. On the dialog box shown in Figure 5-9, type 100.00 in the top field on the right ⇒ Click OK.

You will see the filter icon to the right of the Unit Price column heading, instead of the down arrow button, as illustrated in Figure 5-10. This lets you know that a filter has been applied to the column.

Figure 5-9 Custom Filter dialog box

Figure 5-10 Filter icon illustrated

5. Click OK to close the Preview Selected Table screen.

On the Select Tables and Views screen, you should see the **APPLIED FILTERS** link, in the Filter Details column, for the Products table, as shown in Figure 5-11.

If you click on this link, you will see the dialog box shown in Figure 5-12.

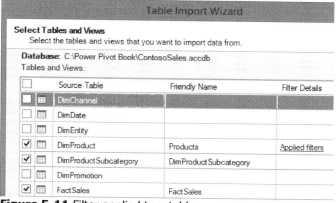

Figure 5-11 Filter applied to a table

In addition to the columns selected for the import, this dialog box displays the criteria for the filter that you created for the table.

This is part of the query that is created for the data that will be imported.

Figure 5-12 Filter Details dialog box

Finish The Import

1. Click the Finish button. The tables will be imported.

   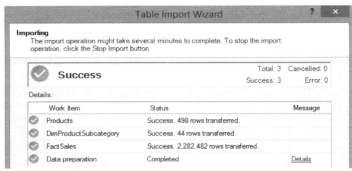

   This can take a minute because the Fact Sales table has a lot of data.

   When the import is finished, you will see the results shown in Figure 5-13.

   Notice that over 2.2 million rows of data were imported from the Fact Sales file.

Figure 5-13 Importing screen

 Large Data Files
As you saw above in Figure 5-13, Power Pivot is capable of handling data files that have millions of records (rows of data). I wanted you to see that a table with more than a million records really can be imported into Excel <smile>.

2. Click the Close button. You should see three tabs of data in the Power Pivot window.

3. Save the workbook as E5.1 Import from an Access database.

 Importing Tables With Millions Of Rows Of Data
If a table that you will import has millions of rows of data, it may take a while, especially if your computer does not have a lot of RAM or if your computer was running slow before you started using Power Pivot. If you also need to import additional tables, you may find it easier to import the table with millions of rows of data by itself, save the workbook, then import the other tables. The down side to doing this is that the relationships between tables will not be detected or imported. This means that you will have to create the relationships manually.

To import tables from an existing connection in the Power Pivot workbook, follow the steps below. You do not have to create a new connection, unless the tables are in a data source that the workbook does not already have a connection for.

1. Open the workbook that you want to import more data into.
2. Power Pivot ⇒ Home tab ⇒ Get External Data group ⇒ Existing Connections button.
3. Select the data source on the Existing Connections dialog box.
4. Click the Open button. You will see the Choose How To Import The Data screen on the Table Import Wizard dialog box. On the next screen, select the table, create the filters and rename fields as needed for the table(s) that will be imported, then import them.

 How Power Pivot Stores Data
When the data is imported into the data model, it is loaded into the memory of the computer running Excel (which is probably your computer <smile>). Power Pivot compresses the data by only storing duplicate values (in each column) once. The duplicate values are replaced with a number that points to the real value. This is how imported data can be compressed to about one-tenth of its original size in the data model.

For example, in an order table, there will (hopefully) be several orders on the same date. The order date will be stored once and each of the other orders with the same date, will have the date replaced with a number. It is this compression that removes the limitation of the number of rows that can be loaded into the data model, where Excel has a million row limitation.

Exercise 5.2: Use An SQL Query To Import Data From A Database

In the previous exercise you imported data from a database by selecting tables. You created a filter that reduced the number of rows that would be imported from a table. You also removed columns of data, which further reduced the amount of data that was imported.

In this exercise, you will use a query to select the tables and records in a database that will be imported. If you cannot write SQL code, hopefully you have access to someone that can, if you have the need to use queries. One benefit that queries provide is that they can be used over and over. Another benefit of using queries is that they can join fields from different tables to create a new table, and this new table can be imported.

1. Home tab ⇒ Get External Data group ⇒ From Database ⇒ From Access.

2. In the Friendly connection name field, type `Product Database`.

3. Click the Browse button ⇒
   In your folder, select the
   ProductCategories database ⇒
   Click the Open button.

   You should have the options shown
   in Figure 5-14 ⇒ Click Next.

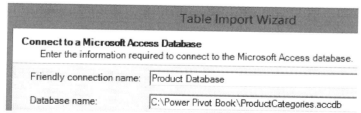

Figure 5-14 Database connection options

4. Select the second option, which allows you to select a query or create a query ⇒ Click Next.

5. Click the **DESIGN** button ⇒ Click the Import button ⇒ In your folder, click on the SQL Query file ⇒ Click the Open button. You should see the contents of the query file that you selected, at the top of the window. This is the SQL query code.

If you wanted to view the data that the query will retrieve to import, click the **RUN** button (the button with the red exclamation mark). At the bottom of the window you will see some of the records that will be imported.
[See Chapter 4, Figure 4-24]

If the query does not run, does not retrieve any records or retrieves records that you do not think should be there, you can edit the query, using the Relational Query Designer editor and re-run it.

6. Click OK.

   In the Friendly Query Name field,
   type `Find ProductsQuery`.

   The screen should look like the one
   shown in Figure 5-15.

   The **WHERE CLAUSE** in the query
   contains the filter criteria.

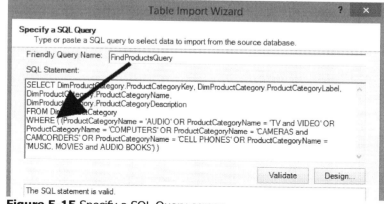

Figure 5-15 Specify a SQL Query screen

 The name that you enter in the Friendly Query Name field will be used as the table name, which is displayed on the tab in Power Pivot.

Specify A SQL Query Screen

On this screen, you have the option of typing or pasting the code in for the query or selecting the file that has the code for the query. If you typed or edited the query on this screen, instead of on the Relational Query Designer editor, click the **VALIDATE** button to make sure that the query does not have any syntax errors. At the bottom of the screen, you will see a message indicating that the SQL statement (the query) is valid or invalid.

The order that the fields are listed in the query is the order that they will be added to the table. While you can change the order of the fields (columns) after the table is created, you can change the order in the query on the screen shown above in Figure 5-15. Changing the field order in the query means that you only have to make the change once. If you change the column order in Power Pivot, you will have to do it each time the query is rerun.

. . . .

7. Click the Finish button. The records will be imported. When the import is finished, click the Close button so that you can see the data in Power Pivot.

8. Notice that the name on the tab is the query name that you entered.
Save the workbook as E5.2 Use a query to import data.

Exercise 5.3: Filter Records Before They Are Imported

In the previous exercise a query that was used to import and filter records from the database. In Exercise 5.1, you created a filter for one of the tables that was imported. This exercise will show you how to import data from a table and create filters during the import process. This will reduce the number of records that are imported.

1. Home tab ⇒ Get External Data group ⇒ From Database ⇒ From Access.

2. In the Friendly connection name field, type Filter Records.

3. Select the Import DB database ⇒ Click Next.

4. Select the first option on the Import Data screen ⇒ Click Next ⇒ Check the Customers and Orders tables.

Create The Customers Table Filter

In this part of the exercise you will create a filter to only import the records of customers in CA, NV and WI.

1. Select the Customers table ⇒ Click the Preview & Filter button.

2. Scroll to the right and open the filter list for the State/Province column.

   Change the options so that only CA, NV and WI are selected, as shown in Figure 5-16.

   Click OK twice to close both dialog boxes.

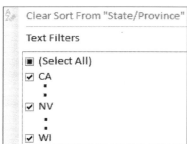

Figure 5-16 State/Province column filter options

Create The Orders Table Filter

In this part of the exercise you will create a filter to only import orders for one month.

1. Select the Orders table ⇒ Click the Preview & Filter button.

2. Open the Order Date filter ⇒ Select the four dates in June 2006 ⇒ Click OK twice.

Finish The Import

1. Click the Finish button. If you preview the data in the Customers table, you will see that all seven records, in the table, are in one of the three states selected in the filter for during the import.

2. Save the workbook as E5.3 Import Filtered Records.

Previewing Data In A View

At the beginning of this chapter, I discussed Views as being a source that data can be imported from.

At the bottom of Figure 5-17, you will see the Top Customers source table. Notice that the icon is different. This icon indicates that the data is from a view or query. When you hold the mouse pointer over the icon, it displays the word "View". When you preview the records in a View you will see, as shown in Figure 5-18, that the data looks like data from a single table. That is because the query that retrieves the data for a View can retrieve fields from multiple tables and display them together. You can also create filters for a View to limit the number of columns and records that are imported.

. . . .

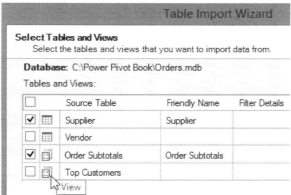

Figure 5-17 View icon on the Select Tables and Views screen

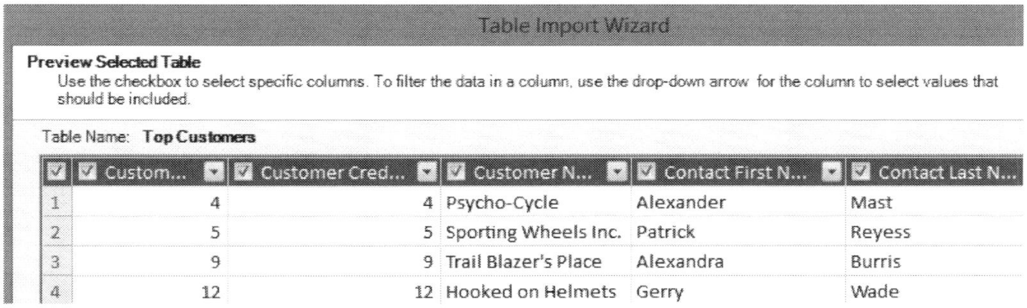

		Custom...		Customer Cred...		Customer N...		Contact First N...		Contact Last N...
1		4		4	Psycho-Cycle		Alexander		Mast
2		5		5	Sporting Wheels Inc.		Patrick		Reyess
3		9		9	Trail Blazer's Place		Alexandra		Burris
4		12		12	Hooked on Helmets		Gerry		Wade

Preview Selected Table
Use the checkbox to select specific columns. To filter the data in a column, use the drop-down arrow for the column to select values that should be included.

Table Name: **Top Customers**

Figure 5-18 Records from a view

Exercise 5.4: Orders Database Import

In this exercise you will import data from a database. The difference is that you will import the tables without the level of step-by-step instructions that the previous exercises provided. To select the database on the Open dialog box, change the File type to Access 97-2003 database.

1.   Import the following tables and views from the Orders.mdb Access database: Customer, Employee, Orders, Orders Detail, Product and Supplier tables, then select the Order Subtotals view.

2.   Use `Orders DB` as the connection name.

3.   Save the workbook as `E5.4 Orders database`.

How To View All Of The Data In The Data Model

Sometimes, all of the tabs, for all of the tables that were imported, cannot be seen in the Power Pivot window at the same time. This happens when at least one of the following is true:

   ①   The table names are long.
   ②   The Power Pivot window contains a lot of tables.

When either of these options is true, to the right of the last tab at the bottom of the Power Pivot window, you will see a button with an ellipsis and down arrow, as illustrated in Figure 5-19. Click this button to display the remaining tables, as shown in Figure 5-20.

Keep the following in mind when viewing the list of tables in the Power Pivot window.

   ①   The list shown in Figure 5-20, is in the order that the tables were imported into the workbook. They are not in alphabetical order unless that is the way that they were imported.
   ②   The only tables on the list shown in Figure 5-20 are the ones that are not displayed across the bottom of the Power Pivot window.
   ③   Notice at the top and bottom of Figure 5-20 that you see arrows. Clicking on these arrows will display more tables in the data model.

Figure 5-19 Button to show the tables that are not currently displayed across the bottom of the Power Pivot window

Figure 5-20 Additional tables in the data model

Summary

This chapter covered importing data from databases and learning how to rename tables and filter the data before it is imported. While the import process does not allow you to create a new table that uses fields from multiple tables, you can add columns to a table from another table, by creating calculated columns, if for some reason linking tables does not allow you to create the dataset that you need.

While the import exercises in this book work as expected, out in the real world, this may not always be the case, with some of the data that you need to import. Take your time to work through the issue.

IMPORT DATA FROM NON DATABASE SOURCES

In this chapter you will learn how to import data from the following types of data sources:

- ☑ Excel workbook
- ☑ .csv file
- ☑ Data feed

Importing data from multiple sources into one Power Pivot workbook, is also covered.

Overview

The previous chapter covered how to import data from databases. This chapter covers other data sources that data can be imported from.

One of the most important tasks to take care of is making sure that the data that will be imported, is in a layout that Power Pivot supports. This is more of an issue for data that will be imported from Excel or a text file, then a database.

For example, the data shown in Figure 6-1 is not in a layout that Power Pivot supports.

There are blank rows. Rows 2 and 9 would have to be deleted.

Rows 4 to 7 for example, would not have a state column.

If this spreadsheet was imported into Power Pivot, you would not get the expected results.

	A	B	C	D
1	StoreId	Store Manager	StoreName	City
2	State: WA			
3				
4	1	35	Contoso Seattle No.1 Store	Seattle
5	2	35	Contoso Seattle No.2 Store	Seattle
6	3	36	Contoso Kennewick Store	Kennewick
7	4	37	Contoso Bellevue Store	Bellevue
8				
9	State: TX			
10	66	88	Contoso Houston No.1 Store	Houston
11	67	88	Contoso Houston No.2 Store	Midland
12	68	88	Contoso Houston No.3 Store	Russellville

Figure 6-1 Incorrect import layout in Excel

Figure 6-2 shows the same data in a layout that Power Pivot supports.

The first row has the headings and the data starts in row 2.

There are no empty rows and a state column has been created.

	A	B	C	D	E
1	StoreId	Store Manager	StoreName	City	State
2	1	35	Contoso Seattle No.1 Store	Seattle	WA
3	2	35	Contoso Seattle No.2 Store	Seattle	WA
4	3	36	Contoso Kennewick Store	Kennewick	WA
5	4	37	Contoso Bellevue Store	Bellevue	WA
6	66	88	Contoso Houston No.1 Store	Houston	TX
7	67	88	Contoso Houston No.2 Store	Midland	TX
8	68	88	Contoso Houston No.3 Store	Russellville	TX

Figure 6-2 Correct layout in Excel to be imported into Power Pivot

Importing Tips For Excel And Text Files
The tips discussed below will make it easier for you to import data from Excel and text files.
① There should not be any blank rows or columns in the range of data that will be imported. There can be blank cells.
② There should only be one row of column headings.
③ The data should start on the row below the column headings.

Importing Data vs Linking Tables vs Pasting Data

In this chapter you will learn how to import data from different data sources into the same workbook. Chapter 7 covers how to link an Excel table to a table in the data model and how to paste data to a create a table in Power Pivot.

Importing Data From Excel Files

There are several Excel file types that can be used to import data from. The two that are covered in the next two exercises are the **.XLSX** and **.CSV** file formats. Many people save Excel workbooks in .csv format so that the file can be opened in other software packages.

Exercise 6.1: Import Data From An Excel File

This exercise will show you how to import data from an Excel file.

1. Home tab ⇒ Get External Data group ⇒ From Other Sources ⇒ **EXCEL FILE** option ⇒ Click Next.

2. In the Friendly connection name field, type `Import Products`.

3. Check the Use first row option ⇒ Click the Browse button.

4. In your folder, double-click on the Products workbook.

   You should have the options shown in Figure 6-3.

   Click Next.

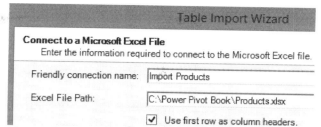

Figure 6-3 Excel file connection options

5. Check the DimProduct table ⇒ Click Finish. When the import is finished, you will see that 1,690 records were imported.

6. Save the workbook as `E6.1 Import product data from Excel`.

Handling Non Adjacent Data On A Worksheet
In the exercise that you just completed, the data on the worksheet that you used had the data in adjacent rows and columns and did not contain any charts or other objects. If the worksheet that you need to import data from looks like the one shown in Figure 6-4, the table created during the import will look like the one shown in Figure 6-5. This is probably not what you were expecting to see. Power Pivot does not automatically rearrange data before or after it is imported.

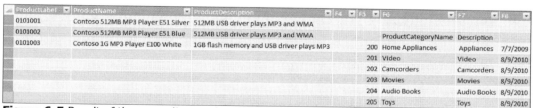

Figure 6-4 Worksheet with non adjacent data

Figure 6-5 Result of the non adjacent data imported into the data model

If you are wondering why the imported data is not on the Excel worksheet, it is because imported data is not stored in Excel worksheets. It has to be stored in the data model in to the workbook.

CSV Files

Like the text files that were covered earlier in this chapter, .csv files are also text files because they do not contain any formatting, even though they are saved in a workbook. This file type is most often created as an export file from a database or a spreadsheet. Having the ability to import data from .csv files opens up a lot of possibilities, especially if you do not have direct access to data that is stored in an enterprise system. You can get the IT department to schedule an export of the data, in an enterprise system, and save it in a .csv file for you.

Exercise 6.2: Import Data From A CSV File

This exercise will show you how to import data from a .csv file.

1. Save the E6.1 workbook as `E6.2 Import data from a csv file`.

2. Power Pivot window ⇒ From Other Sources ⇒ Text File option.

3. In the Friendly connection name field, type `CSV file`.

4. Check the Use first row option ⇒ Click the Browse button.

5. Navigate to your folder ⇒ Open the File Type drop-down list on the Open dialog box ⇒ Select the **COMMA SEPARATED FILES (*.CSV)** option, shown in Figure 6-6.

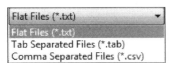

Figure 6-6 File Type drop-down list options

6. Select the Products.csv file ⇒ Click the Open button. When the import is finished, you will see a new tab of data in Power Pivot.

Exercise 6.3: Import A Range Of Data From An Excel File

In Exercise 6.1 you imported data from a spreadsheet that had over 1,500 rows of data. There may be times when you only need to import part of the data on the spreadsheet. If that is the case, you can create one or more ranges in the spreadsheet and select the range on the Tables and Views screen on the Table Import Wizard, as the data to import. This would be helpful when the data on the spreadsheet looks similar to the spreadsheet shown earlier in Figure 6-4.

In this exercise you will import data from a spreadsheet that already has the ranges set up. On your own, you may have to create the range in the spreadsheet before importing the data.

1. Power Pivot window ⇒ From Other Sources ⇒ **EXCEL FILE** option.

2. In the Friendly connection name field, type Import by Range Name.

3. Select the Products With Range Names workbook.

4. On the Select Tables and Views screen, you will see the range options shown in Figure 6-7 ⇒ Check the Range 2 table.

    When the import is finished, you will see that 500 records were imported. Even though the Products table in Exercise 6.1 came from a different workbook then the Products table in this exercise, the data in both spreadsheets is the same.

    Notice that there are no column headings for the data in the Power Pivot workbook. That is because the range of data that was selected, does not have column headings.

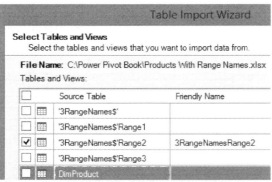

Figure 6-7 Range selected to be imported

If you know that you will import data from a spreadsheet that has a range, add column headings to the range, if needed.

5. Save the workbook as E6.3 Import by Range Name.

Using Data Feeds To Import Data

Select this option when the data that you need to import is on a web site, corporate intranet or is in a SharePoint list. A data feed is an **XML DATA STREAM** that is created from an online source. This data stream is sent to a document or application. Like the other import options that you have learned about, data feeds are also imported using the Table Import Wizard. Data imported from a data feed can be refreshed.

Exercise 6.4: Import Data From A Data Feed

This exercise will show you how to import data from a public data feed on a web site. The web site address used in this exercise, points to a **CLOUD-BASED DATABASE** that has the data that you will import. There are two options that you can use, to get the Data Feed URL, as described below.

① Select an **.ATOMSVC** document.
② Type in the web site address (the URL) of the data feed.

1. Power Pivot window ⇒ From Data Service ⇒ From OData Data Feed.

2. In the Friendly connection name field, type `Public Data Feed`.

3. In the **DATA FEED URL** field, type `http://services.odata.org/northwind/northwind.svc/`

4. Click the Test Connection button to make sure that your computer is connected to the database.

If the test fails, make sure that you typed the URL in correctly, in step 3 above, and that your computer is connected to the Internet.

You should have the options shown in Figure 6-8 ⇒ Click Next.

Figure 6-8 Data Feed connection options

Like other types of data that can be imported, you can give source tables in a data feed a different name and filter the data, before it is imported.

5. Import all of the tables. (**Hint**: Click the check box to the left of the Source Table heading.) When the import is finished, you will see the tables from the data feed in Power Pivot.

6. Save the workbook as `E6.4 Import data from a data feed`.

Exercise 6.5: Import Data From Multiple Sources Into One Data Model

This exercise will show you how to import a list of orders from a Comma Separated Values (.csv) file and a table of order detail records from a dBASE database. The data in tables from multiple sources does not have to be related. This is helpful if you need to create several reports in the same workbook that have unrelated data.

Import Data From A CSV File

1. Power Pivot window ⇒ From Other Sources ⇒ Text File option.

2. In the Friendly connection name field, type `Import Orders CSV`.

3. Check the Use first row option, then select the Import Orders.csv file.

4. Make the Connect to Flat File screen wider, then clear the check marks illustrated in Figure 6-9, for all of the address columns that start with "Ship", so that they will not be imported.

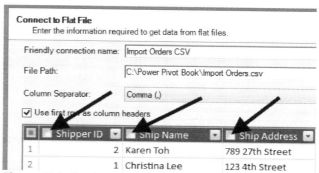

Figure 6-9 Check mark box illustrated

5. Save the workbook as `E6.5 Import from a dBASE database`. Leave the workbook open to complete the next part of the exercise.

Import A Table From A dBASE Database

In this part of the exercise, you will learn how to set up an ODBC connection for a database.

Create The ODBC Connection

1. Power Pivot window ⇒ From Other Sources ⇒ **OTHERS** data source option ⇒ Click Next.

2. Click the **BUILD** button on the Connection String screen ⇒ On the Provider tab of the Data Link Properties dialog box, select the Microsoft OLE DB Provider for ODBC Drivers option.

3. Connection tab ⇒ Select the **USE CONNECTION STRING** option ⇒ Click the **BUILD** button.

4. Machine Data Source tab ⇒ Select the dBase database option. If you do not see this option, follow the steps in the tip box below ⇒ Click OK.

5. Select Directory dialog box ⇒ Click on your folder, on the right ⇒ Click on the Order DE.dbf file on the left, (the file will not be highlighted) ⇒ Click OK ⇒ Click OK to close the Data Link Properties dialog box.

> **How To Create A New Data Source Option**
> 1. Click the New button ⇒ Select the User Data Source option ⇒ Click Next ⇒ Select the Microsoft dbase driver (*.dbf) option illustrated in Figure 6-10 ⇒ Click Next ⇒ Click Finish.
> 2. On the ODBC dBase Setup dialog box, in the Data Source Name field, type `dBase database` ⇒ Click OK.

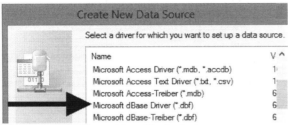

Figure 6-10 dBase driver illustrated

Import The Data

1. In the Friendly name field, type
   `MyODBCConnection`.

   The connection string should look like the one shown in Figure 6-11.

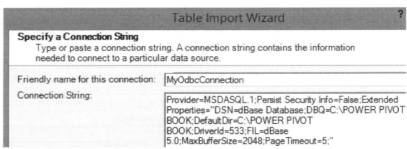

Figure 6-11 Connection string

2. Click Next twice ⇒ On the Select Tables and Views screen, check the Order DE table ⇒ Change the Friendly Name to `Order Details` ⇒ Click Finish. You should see the Order Details table from the dBASE database in the Power Pivot window, next to the Import Orders table.

Exercise 6.6: Import Data From A Text File And A Database

In this exercise you will import data from a text file and three tables from an Access database into the same workbook.

Import Data From A Text File

1. Power Pivot window ⇒ From Other Sources ⇒ Text File option.

2. In the Friendly connection name field, type `Customers` ⇒ Check the Use first row option ⇒ Click the Browse button ⇒ Select the Import Text File.txt file.

3. Clear the check mark for the following columns: E-mail Address, Home Phone, Mobile Phone, Web Page, Notes and Attachments ⇒ Click Finish.

4. Rename the tab to `Customers`.

5. Save the workbook as `E6.6 Import from a text file and a database`.

. . . .

Import Multiple Tables

In this part of the exercise you will import three tables from a database.

1. Power Pivot window ⇒ From Database ⇒ From Access.

2. In the Friendly connection name field, type Import 3 tables ⇒ Select the Import DB database ⇒ Click Next.

3. Select the Tables and Views option ⇒ Click Next ⇒ Select the Orders, Order Details and Products tables ⇒ Click Finish.

4. In Power Pivot, move the Order Details table after the Orders table, by right-clicking on the Order Details tab and selecting Move.

   On the dialog box shown in Figure 6-12, click on the Products table ⇒ Click OK.

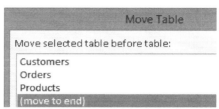

Figure 6-12 Move Table dialog box

 Rearranging The Table Order In Power Pivot
You just learned how to use the Move Table dialog box to rearrange the order of the tables. Like the tabs in an Excel workbook, you can use drop and drag to rearrange the order of the tables in the Power Pivot window.

Exercise 6.7: Import Tables From The Same Database At Different Times

In Exercise 6.6, the Customers table was imported before the Orders table. This means that there is a possibility that a link was created that will produce unexpected results.

In this exercise you will import four related tables at two different times. As you will see in Chapter 9, relationships that are in the database will not be imported, when related tables are imported at different times.

Import The Customers And Orders Tables

1. Power Pivot window ⇒ From Database ⇒ From Access.

2. In the Friendly connection name field, type Customers-Orders ⇒ Select the Import DB database ⇒ Click Next.

3. Select the Tables and Views option ⇒ Click Next ⇒ Select the Customers and Orders tables ⇒ Click Finish.

Import The Order Details And Products Tables

1. Power Pivot window ⇒ From Database ⇒ From Access.

2. In the Friendly connection name field, type Order Details-Products ⇒ Select the Import DB database ⇒ Click Next.

3. Select the Tables and Views option ⇒ Click Next ⇒ Select the Order Details and Products Tables ⇒ Click Finish.

4. Save the workbook as E6.7 Import tables at different times.

Exercise 6.8: Import Data From Databases And Excel Files

In this exercise you will import data from two Access databases and two Excel files. This workbook will be used later in the book to create a pivot table.

1. Open a new workbook ⇒ Import all of the tables in the Contoso Sales database.

2. Save the workbook as E6.8 Contoso database.

3. Import the DimProductCategory table in the Product Categories database.

4. Import the DimGeography worksheet in the Geography workbook.

5. Import the Stores worksheet in the Stores workbook.

Getting Data Out Of The Data Model

All of the exercises in this chapter have shown you how to get data into the data model. There may be times when you need to get data out of the data model. An example that comes to mind is when you need to make changes to the data.

Other examples include needing all or part of the data for another file or you cannot find the data source. If you are going to paste the data into a spreadsheet, keep in mind the million row limitation. The steps below show you how to get data out of a table in the data model.

1. Open the workbook that has the data that you want to paste into a spreadsheet ⇒ Open the Power Pivot window.

2. Select the entire table by clicking on the square to the left of the first column heading if you want to paste the entire table into the spreadsheet or select the cells or columns that you want to use in another file.

3. Home tab ⇒ Click the Copy button.

4. Display the application that you want to paste the data into ⇒ Press Ctrl+V ⇒ Save the changes to the software that you pasted the data into.

Exercise 6.9: Upgrading A Data Model

It is very possible that you will need to use workbooks that have tables that were created in a previous version of Power Pivot. You will see the message shown in Figure 6-13, when you try to view the Power Pivot window, if the workbook was last saved in a previous version of Power Pivot. If that is the case, you can refer back to this exercise. When I have had to do this, I make a copy of the workbook first and use the copy for the upgrade. That way, if something goes wrong, the original workbook is still protected.

1. Save the Data Model To Upgrade workbook as E6.9 Upgraded Data Model ⇒ On the Power Pivot tab, click the Manage button. You will see the message shown in Figure 6-13 ⇒ Click OK.

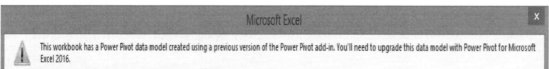

Figure 6-13 Upgrade data model message

 Clicking the **ADD TO DATA MODEL** button on the Power Pivot tab, will also display the message shown above in Figure 6-13.

2. Click OK on the dialog box shown in Figure 6-14. In a few seconds, you will see the dialog box shown in Figure 6-15.

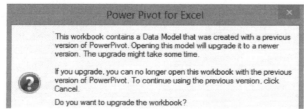

Figure 6-14 Power Pivot for Excel upgrade message

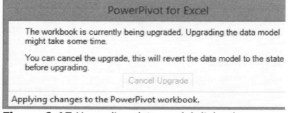

Figure 6-15 Upgrading data model dialog box

3. When you see the dialog box shown in Figure 6-16, click Yes.

   The upgrade changes will be saved, and the workbook will reopen.

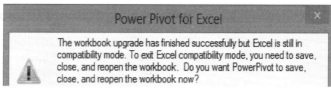

Figure 6-16 Upgrade successful message

Handling A Corrupt Data Model

The previous exercise covered upgrading a data model that was last saved in a previous version of Power Pivot. If you find that you cannot upgrade a data model, it could be corrupt. In Excel 2010 and 2013, any of the items listed below could corrupt the data model.

① Delete an imported column.
② Rename an imported column.
③ Rename a table.

I suspect that one reason that data models got corrupt is because until Excel 2016, when an object was renamed, the new name was not updated throughout the data model automatically, like it is in Excel 2016 and beyond. The fact that Power Pivot and Power Query were separate add-ins, probably did not help either, as I don't think that they "talked" to each other, like they can now that they are both built into Excel 2016. Don't hold me to this though, as I could be wrong <smile>.

What I find interesting is that in prior versions of Power Pivot, the data in a corrupt data model could sometimes be refreshed several times, giving you the impression that nothing was wrong.

I didn't have a problem with a corrupt data model while using it in Power Pivot. I had the problem in Power Query, when I tried to refresh the data in a Power Pivot data model. I saw a message that said that the properties could not be changed because the connection was modified in Power Pivot. I could not find a way to fix this problem. I wound up having to delete the table in Power Pivot that I could not refresh, then import it again and recreate the measures. Thankfully, it was only two measures that had to be recreated <smile>.

Summary

This chapter covered importing data from non database sources. You also learned how to import data from different sources into the same workbook. As you saw, the process is not scary. Upgrading a data model that was last saved in a previous version of Power Pivot was also covered. I will say that sometimes the upgrade does not always work the first time for me. I haven't been able to find out why this happens. I finally resorted to closing Excel, turning the laptop off, then restarting it. And for whatever reason it worked. Go figure! Maybe not on the first try, but on the second or third try.

Another Way To Filter Imported Data

In Chapter 5 and this chapter, you learned how to filter data before it is imported. That is great to reduce columns and rows that you know you will never use. After reviewing the imported data in Power Pivot, what do you do if you realize that there are still rows or columns of data that you do not need? More then likely, you would edit the import connection.

Chapter 3 covered the **TABLE PROPERTIES** button. I did not include this information in that chapter because I wanted you to have more experience importing and filtering data. Just like data can be filtered in Power Pivot, data displayed on the **EDIT TABLE PROPERTIES** dialog box, can also be filtered. This dialog box displays the tables in the data source. The grid in the middle of the dialog box has the same column filter options that the **PREVIEW SELECTED TABLE SCREEN** has on the Table Import Wizard.

This means that you can filter the data displayed in Power Pivot because you can save the filter options on the Edit Table Properties dialog box. Even better, filter options that you save on this dialog box, are applied when the table is refreshed. I guess the downside to that is that at some point, you no longer need to filter the data and forget that you created a filter on this dialog box. What I like about this way of creating a filter is that I do not have to modify the connection properties. You can walk through the steps below to learn how to use this feature.

Import Data From Non Database Sources

1. Save the E5.4 workbook with a different name.

2. In the new workbook, display the Orders table. Notice that the table has 2,192 records ⇒ Design tab ⇒ Table Properties button.

3. Display the filter options for the Order Date column ⇒ Select Date Filters ⇒ Between.

4. Create a filter to select records between 1/1/2010 and 12/31/2010.

5. Click the Save button on the Edit Table Properties dialog box. The data in the table will automatically be refreshed. You will see that there are only 181 records in the Orders table.

If you remove the filter created in step 4 above, the data in the table will automatically be refreshed again and all of the records will be displayed.

It's time to link tables!

LINKING TABLES, PASTING AND APPENDING DATA

 Overview

After reading this chapter and completing the exercises you will be able to:

☑ Link an Excel table to a table in the data model
☑ Copy and paste data
☑ Append data

CHAPTER 7

Linking Data In Excel To The Data Model

You have learned how to import Excel data. You have also learned that you cannot make changes to data in the data model and that if you needed to change the data, you would have to make the changes in the data source (or use Power Query) and then refresh the data or import the data again.

Importing is not the only way to get data into the data model. There are other options: Linking to tables in Excel, pasting data and appending data. These options are explained below.

① A **LINKED TABLE** is a table that is created from data on an Excel worksheet that has the table properties applied to it. It is linked to a table (in the data model) in the same workbook. After the initial link to the data in an Excel workbook is set up, the data in the data model will be updated (refreshed) with the new or modified data from the table in Excel. In environments where spreadsheets are on a server and updated by a few people on a regular basis, linking to the worksheet will save you a lot of work.

② **COPY AND PASTE** the data into the data model. This option is the same process as copying and pasting data between any other types of documents. Keep in mind that once data is pasted into the data model, there is no connection back to the data source. This means that if 2500 records are added to the data source tomorrow, you have to copy and paste the new records into the data model again. For a small amount of data, it may be acceptable to copy and paste data, but what about data sources that have tens of thousands of new records added on a regular basis? Do you really want to keep copying and pasting that many records on a regular basis?

In order to copy and paste the new records in the data source into the data model, you would have to know specifically which records are new. How will you handle data that has been deleted from the source, but is still in the data model? As you can see, the data model can quickly become outdated. The best solution is to link to the data source, if importing the data is not an option. The benefit that linking has is that the data model is automatically updated.

③ **APPENDING DATA** into the data model is similar to copying and pasting. One difference is that the data to append to a table in the data model, has to have the same data type in each column that the data in the data model has. Another difference is that the data to append must have the same number of columns that the table in the data model has, that you want to append the data to.

Linked And Pasted Tables
If you plan to publish a Power Pivot workbook to a SharePoint server, keep in mind that linked and pasted tables cannot be updated from SharePoint. To update the data you have to update it in the Power Pivot window in Excel, then republish the workbook to the SharePoint server.

Linked Table Advantages
New records (rows of data) that are added to the original table on the spreadsheet, are automatically added to the linked tables, in the data model. The linked data can be modified in Excel and the data does not have to constantly be re-imported. Data in Excel can be changed, including adding and deleting rows and columns. Because linked table changes are automatically updated in the data model, this is a way of getting around Power Pivots rule of not being able to edit data in the data model, but you did not hear this from me <smile>.

Creating Tables
If the data that you want to link to is not in a table, you can follow the steps in Exercise 7.1, in the "Prepare The Data To Be Linked" section, before the **ADD TO DATA MODEL** button is clicked. This is not a requirement because if you click the Add to Data Model button and the data in the spreadsheet is not in table format, you will be prompted to create the table before the link to the data can be created.

One benefit of creating the table first is that you can change the table name, which is the name that will be used for the table in the data model. This will keep you from having to rename the table in Power Pivot.

Add To Data Model Option

For data in an Excel spreadsheet that is in a layout that Power Pivot supports, using the Data Model option is an easy way to create a table in Power Pivot. As stated earlier in this chapter, data in a Power Pivot table cannot be changed.

Data Model Benefits That Copy And Paste Do Not Have

① New columns can be added.
② Data in Power Pivot can be updated.

Exercise 7.1: Link Data In An Excel Table To A Table In The Data Model

This exercise will show you how to link data in an Excel workbook to a table in the data model.

Prepare The Data To Be Linked

In this part of the exercise you will convert the data in the spreadsheet to a table. In your own workbooks, if the data in the spreadsheet is already in a table you can skip step 2.

1. Save the Store Data workbook as `E7.1 My Store Data`.

2. Click in a cell that has data, then press Ctrl+T.

   You will see the dialog box shown in Figure 7-1. You should see the range A1:S307 in the field.

   Check the My table has headers option, if it is not already checked ⇒ Click OK.

Figure 7-1 Create Table dialog box

Name The Table

By default, Excel creates generic table names like Table 1, Table 2, Table 3, etc. The table name is what appears in the Pivot Tables Fields list, so it is a good idea to change the table name to something meaningful.

1. On the Table Tools Design tab in Excel, type `Stores` in the Table Name field, as illustrated on the left of Figure 7-2 ⇒ Click on any cell in the table ⇒ Save the changes.

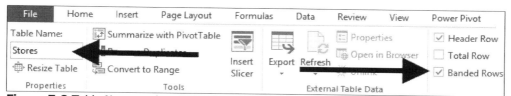

Figure 7-2 Table Name and Banded Rows options illustrated on the Excel Table Tools Design tab

Converting Excel Data To Table Format

Once data in a spreadsheet is converted to a table, you will see some differences, as explained below.

① Bands of color are automatically added to the rows in the table. You can remove the band formatting by clearing the check mark for the **BANDED ROWS** option, illustrated above, on the right side of Figure 7-2.
② Auto Filter drop-down lists are added to the first row of the table, as shown at the top of Figure 7-3. The first row is usually the header row. You can turn this feature off.
③ If you scroll down the spreadsheet, the column letters will be replaced with the data in the first row, which should be the column headings, as shown in Figure 7-3. This only happens when the Freeze Column option is not enabled.

	StoreId	SalesTerritory	StoreManag	StoreName
29	31	23	57	Contoso Greeley No.2 Store
30	32	29	63	Contoso Milliken Store
31	33	30	64	Contoso Berthoud Store

Figure 7-3 Auto Filter option enabled and column letters replaced with column headings

Link The Excel Table To The Data Model

In this part of the exercise you will create the link between the Excel table and a table in the data model.

1. Click in any cell in the Excel table ⇒ Power Pivot tab ⇒ Add to Data Model button. You will see the data (from the Excel worksheet) in the Power Pivot window.

   If you look at the tab in the lower left corner of the Power Pivot window, you will see a **LINK TABLE ICON** in front of the tab name, as illustrated in Figure 7-4.

   This is how you can visually see which tables in the Power Pivot window have linked data. Notice that the tab name is the name of the table on the Excel worksheet.

Figure 7-4 Link icon illustrated

 Possible Error Creating The Link
A few people have contacted me saying that they got an error message after clicking the Add to Data Model button. I don't know which version of excel they were using, nor could I duplicate the error. My suggestion was to close the workbook and Excel, then try it again. That worked for the people that contacted me.

Modify The Excel Data

In this part of the exercise you will modify data in the Excel table and observe how the changes are automatically updated in the table in the data model.

1. On the Stores worksheet in the E7.1 workbook, type the date 12/31/2015 in the Close Date column, for the first two rows of data.

2. View the data in Power Pivot.

   The first two rows in the table should look like the ones shown in Figure 7-5.

Status	OpenDate	CloseDate
On	4/12/2004 12...	12/31/2015 12:00:00 AM
On	2/14/2004 12...	12/31/2015 12:00:00 AM
On	2/12/2004 12...	

Figure 7-5 Data updated in the table

Add Data To An Excel Table

In Figure 7-4 shown earlier, you saw that there are 306 rows of data, in the table in the data model. In this part of the exercise you will paste rows of data from a different workbook to the end of the Excel table in the E7.1 workbook. If done correctly, the data that you paste to the end of the table in Excel will also be added to the table in the E7.1 workbook.

1. Open the New Stores workbook.

2. Select the range A2:S21 ⇒ Press Ctrl + C.

3. Switch to the E7.1 workbook ⇒ Scroll to the end of the Excel table ⇒ Right-click on the first empty row below the table and select Paste ⇒ Save the changes.

4. View the table in Power Pivot. The table should now have 325 rows of data ⇒ Close the New Stores workbook.

 Inserting And Deleting Rows Of Data
An Excel table that is linked to a table in the data model is no different then a table that is not linked, in terms of inserting and deleting rows of data. If you insert a row of data in the Excel table, it is automatically added to the table in the data model. The same applies to deleting rows of data in the Excel table, they are automatically removed from the table in the data model.

 Creating Links
When instructed to create a link to a table, follow the steps below.
1. In the Excel workbook, click in a cell of the table (or range) that has data that you want to link to.
2. Power Pivot tab ⇒ Tables group ⇒ Add to Data Model button.
3. Unless specified otherwise, check the My table has headers option, on the Create Table dialog box.

Exercise 7.2: Linking To Non Table Data In Excel

In the previous exercise you created a link to data that was in an Excel table before you started the steps to link to the data. In this exercise you will learn how to create the table in Excel during the process of linking to the data. You will also create links for data that is on three worksheets in the same workbook.

1. Save the Import Spreadsheet workbook as `E7.2 Link non table data`.

2. On the Customers tab, click the Add to Data Model button.

> **Selecting A Different Table Range In Excel**
> By default, Power Pivot will select the entire range of adjacent cells on the worksheet to link to. If you do not want to link to all of the data in the range that Excel selects, you can type in the range you want to link to or click the button at the end of the range on the Create Table dialog box shown earlier in Figure 7-1, then select the range of cells that you want to link to.

3. You will see the range A1:Q30, on the Create Table dialog box ⇒ Click OK.

4. Power Pivot window ⇒ Rename the tab to `Customers` ⇒ Save the changes.

5. Repeat steps 2 to 4 above to create links for the data on the Orders worksheet (use the range A1:T49) and the Order_Details worksheet (use the range A1:J59). Rename the tables in the Power Pivot window accordingly.

Using Multiple Data Sets On The Same Worksheet

In the previous exercise you learned how to link to data that originally was not in an Excel table. It is not uncommon to see a worksheet that looks like the one shown in Figure 7-6.

The data on this worksheet could have been placed on separate worksheets in the workbook. It is just a matter of preference. As you read earlier, Excel data must be in table format to be linked to a table in the data model. You also read that data in non adjacent cells cannot be created as one table. The good news is that each of the three data sets shown in Figure 7-6, can individually be converted to a table, then linked to tables in the data model.

Customers						Order Header						Order Details				
Customer ID	Last Name	First Name	City	State		Order ID	Customer	Order Date	Shipped Date	Payment Type		ID	Order ID	Product ID	Quantity	Unit Price
1	Bedecs	Anna	Seattle	WA		30	1	1/15/2006	1/22/2006	Check		27	30	34	100	14.00
2	Gratacos Solsona	Antonio	Boston	MA		31	4	1/20/2006	1/22/2006	Credit Card		28	47	80	30	3.50
		.					.						.			
		.					.						.			
		.					.						.			
17	Bagel	Jean Philippe	Seattle	WA		48	8	4/5/2006	4/5/2006	Check		43	45	6	10	25.00
18	Autier Miconi	Catherine	Boston	MA								44	46	4	10	22.00
19	Eggerer	Alexander	Los Angelas	CA								45	42	19	10	9.20
												46	43	80	20	3.50
												47	43	81	50	2.99

Figure 7-6 Multiple data sets on a worksheet

Exercise 7.3: Create Three Tables In The Data Model From One Worksheet

This exercise will show you how to convert the three data sets shown above in Figure 7-6, into three tables and link them to individual tables in the data model.

1. Save the Multiple Data Sets workbook as `E7.3 Multiple data sets`.

2. Create a link to the Customers data section. You should see the range A3:E22 on the Create Table dialog box.

3. Power Pivot window ⇒ Rename the table to `Customers` ⇒ Save the changes.

4. Repeat steps 2 and 3 above for the Order Header (range G3:K20) and Order Details (range M3:Q24) sections of the worksheet, to create linked tables.

Linked Table Errors

Linking Excel table data to a table in the data model provides the ability to keep the data in the data model updated easily. If you use a lot of spreadsheets, over time you may not remember which tables are linked to tables in the data model.

If you make certain changes to the linked table in Excel, then click the **UPDATE ALL** button on the Power Pivot tab, it will cause errors in the data model. For example, if the linked table in Excel is deleted, an error will occur.

Exercise 7.4: Create And Fix Linked Table Errors

Normally, you would not create an error on purpose, but it is necessary to create errors in this exercise to demonstrate how to fix an error.

Create The Errors

In this part of the exercise, you will create errors in an Excel table to learn how to fix errors in the next part of this exercise.

1. Save the E7.3 workbook as `E7.4 Linked table errors`.

2. On the Data Sets worksheet tab in Excel ⇒ Delete the Orders Details table ⇒ Save the changes.

Generate And Fix The Errors

In the previous part of the exercise, you made a change to a linked table in Excel. By default, Power Pivot does not automatically let you know that there are any problems with the data. The way that you find out that there is a problem with the data is to refresh it.

1. Power Pivot tab ⇒ Update All button.

    You will see the dialog box shown in Figure 7-7.

    This is how you know that something has changed in the linked table in Excel.

    Click the Options button.

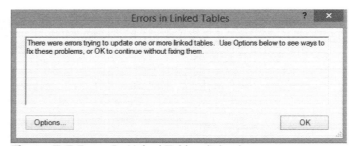

Figure 7-7 Errors In Linked Tables dialog box

 The **UPDATE ALL** and **UPDATE SELECTED** buttons, on the Table Tools Linked Table tab in the Power Pivot window, will also check for errors, like deleted or renamed columns, in linked tables.

Select Action Dialog Box

This dialog box is used to select what to do when the link between a table in the data model and the Excel table has changed.

The options shown in Figure 7-8 are used to let you know that there is a problem with the Order Details table and what the options are to fix the error.

Table 7-1 explains the options on the dialog box.

Figure 7-8 Select Action dialog box

Option	Description
Do Nothing	This option leaves the error unchanged. The error dialog box shown earlier in Figure 7-7 will continue to appear every time data in the Power Pivot table is refreshed.
Change Excel Table Name	This option is not enabled. This may be because tables in the data model can now be renamed and the name change is replicated throughout the workbook.
Remove Link To Excel Table	Selecting this option removes the link between the Excel table and the table in the data model. This means that the data in the data model will no longer be updated.
Delete Power Pivot Table	Selecting this option deletes the link and the table in the data model.

Table 7-1 Select Action dialog box options explained

2. In this exercise you want to continue to use the Order Details table. Select the **REMOVE LINK TO EXCEL TABLE** option.

Copy And Paste Excel Data Into The Data Model

Unlike the requirement of the data having to be in the same workbook for linking data in an Excel table, to a table in the data model, copying and pasting data does not have this requirement. This means that the data that you want to paste into a table in the data model can be in a different workbook or other data source, like a web page. This is usually the reason why copying and pasting is sometimes used instead of linking data. The other advantage of copying and pasting data is support of the Paste Append and Paste Replace options in Power Pivot.

Limitations Of Copying And Pasting Data
① If the source data that is pasted into the data model is updated and the changes are needed in the data model, all of the data has to be pasted into the data model again, because pasted data cannot be updated in the data model. This process is also known as **REPLACING DATA**. Individual rows of pasted data cannot be replaced. Therefore, pasting data is best suited for data that will not change or data that does not change often.
② Additional columns cannot be pasted in the table after the initial data has been pasted in the data model. If you need to paste data with additional columns, you have to create a new table in the data model to paste the data into.

Exercise 7.5: Copy And Paste Data

This exercise will show you how to copy data in an Excel spreadsheet in one workbook and paste it into a data model table in a new workbook.

Selecting Data In A Spreadsheet To Copy
You should only select the data that you want to copy and paste. Do not select empty rows, columns or the entire spreadsheet, because the empty rows and columns will be pasted into the data model, which is not what you want.

1. Open the Product Categories workbook ⇒ On the Products tab, select all of the data, not the entire spreadsheet ⇒ Press Ctrl + C. Leave the workbook open for the next exercise.

2. Open a new workbook, then open the Power Pivot window.

3. Home tab ⇒ Paste button. You will see the Paste Preview dialog box with the data that you copied from the other workbook.

4. In the Table Name field, type `Products`.

   If the Use first row as column headers option is not checked, check it now.

   Your dialog box should look like the one shown in Figure 7-9.

   Click OK. The table will be created in the data model.

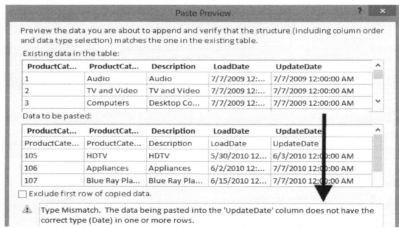

Figure 7-9 Paste Preview dialog box

5. Save the workbook as `E7.5 Copy and paste`.

Appending Data

There may be times that you need to add more data to an existing table in the data model. As long as the structure of the new data has the same structure as the data that it will be appended to, appending the new data will work. This means that the file type of the new data does not matter.

 | When appending data, it is not a requirement to copy the column headings.

Exercise 7.6: Append Data To A Table In The Data Model

In this exercise you will append data to the data model that you created in the previous exercise.

1. Save the E7.5 workbook as `E7.6 Append Data`.

2. Open the Product Categories workbook ⇒ Click on the Append_Products tab ⇒ Select the range A1:E8 ⇒ Press Ctrl + C ⇒ Leave the Product Categories workbook open for the next exercise.

3. Display the Power Pivot window in the E7.6 workbook.

4. Home tab ⇒ Paste Append.
   You will see the dialog box shown in Figure 7-10.

   You may have to make the dialog box larger (by dragging the lower right corner of the dialog box) to see the data.

   The top section of the dialog box displays the data that is already in the table in the data model.

   The next section displays the data that will be pasted (appended) into the data model table.

Figure 7-10 Paste Preview warning message illustrated

At the bottom of the dialog box is an option to exclude the first row of data from being pasted. Any errors in the data that will be pasted are also displayed.

As you can see, a warning message is displayed about the data that you want to paste. This **TYPE MISMATCH** message is letting you know that at least one cell in the Update Date column of data that will be pasted, has data that is a different type then the same column in the data model table. In this case, the mismatch data is the column heading, because Power Pivot recognizes the Update Date column as a date field.

5. Check the **EXCLUDE FIRST ROW OF COPIED DATA** option. Notice that the Type Mismatch warning at the bottom of the dialog box is gone ⇒ Click OK. The Products table in the data model now has 27 records, instead of 20.

Exercise 7.7: Appending Bad Data

As much as we strive to keep data correct and up to date, there will be data that does not meet the minimum requirements. In spreadsheets that do not have a lot of data, it is easier to fix bad data. Spreadsheets that have 100,000 rows of data for example, are a little more difficult to maintain. The previous exercise showed an example of what Power Pivot considers bad data.

As you have read, when data is appended to an existing table in the data model, Power Pivot compares the data type of each column of data that you want to append, to the existing column in the same location in the table in the data model. In this exercise you will purposely try to append bad data to a table in the data model.

1. Save the E7.6 workbook as E7.7 Appending Bad Data.

2. In the Product Categories workbook, click on the Append_Bad_Data tab ⇒ Select the range A1:E8 ⇒ Press Ctrl + C. Leave the workbook open for the next exercise.

3. In the E7.7 workbook, display the Power Pivot window ⇒ Click the Paste Append button.

This **TYPE MISMATCH** warning message on the Paste Preview dialog box is letting you know that the first column in the data model table has been designated as a whole number data type and that at least one cell in the data that you want to append to the column has a different data type. In this exercise, selecting the Exclude first row option will not fix the problem.

4. Click OK. Power Pivot will attempt to paste the data.

   You will see the message shown in Figure 7-11 when you click the **DETAILS** button.

   This message provides information on why the data could not be appended.

   While Power Pivot allows you to format data, it does not allow you to change the actual data.

   The only way to change the data is to change it in the source file, then try appending it again. It would be nice if the message would display all of the data errors at one time.

   Click OK to close the message window ⇒ Close Power Pivot.

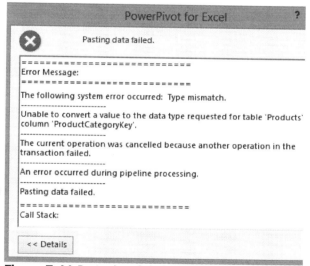

Figure 7-11 Paste data failed message

Different Types Of Bad Data

In the previous two exercises, you learned about appending bad data. These exercises showed you that the Type Mismatch validation feature is also used to check more than the actual data. The exercises that you will complete now, cover some of the more popular types of data errors that you may come across when appending or importing data.

Exercise 7.8: Appending More Bad Data

In this exercise you will attempt to append the following types of bad data: Fewer columns then the data model table has, invalid dates and cells that are missing data.

Append Fewer Columns Of Data

In this part of the exercise you will append four columns of data to a table in the data model, that has five columns of data.

1. Save the E7.6 workbook as `E7.8 Append more bad data`.

2. Product Categories workbook ⇒ On the Fewer_Columns tab, select the range A2:D14 ⇒ Right-click on the selected cells and select Copy.

3. In the E7.8 workbook, display the Power Pivot window ⇒ Home tab ⇒ Click the Paste Append button. You will see the message shown in Figure 7-12 ⇒ Click OK. You will see that the data is not appended to the data model table.

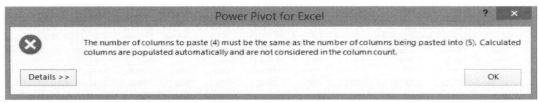

Figure 7-12 Fewer Columns error message

 Appending More Columns Of Data
You will see the same message shown above in Figure 7-12 if you try to append more columns of data then the table in the data model has.

Append Invalid Dates

In this part of the exercise you will append data that has dates that are in a different format then the dates in the same column in the data model table.

1. In the Product Categories workbook, click on the Invalid_Dates tab.

   Figure 7-13 illustrates three of the dates that are not valid.

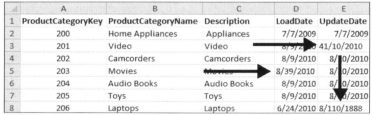

	A	B	C	D	E
1	ProductCategoryKey	ProductCategoryName	Description	LoadDate	UpdateDate
2	200	Home Appliances	Appliances	7/7/2009	7/7/2009
3	201	Video	Video	8/9/2010	41/10/2010
4	202	Camcorders	Camcorders	8/9/2010	8/10/2010
5	203	Movies	Movies	8/39/2010	8/10/2010
6	204	Audio Books	Audio Books	8/9/2010	8/10/2010
7	205	Toys	Toys	8/9/2010	8/10/2010
8	206	Laptops	Laptops	6/24/2010	8/110/1888

Figure 7-13 Invalid dates illustrated

2. Copy the range A2:E8, then Paste Append the data to the Products table in the E7.8 workbook.

   You will see that data in the Update Date column (in the Data to be pasted section) does not have the correct data type, as shown in Figure 7-14.

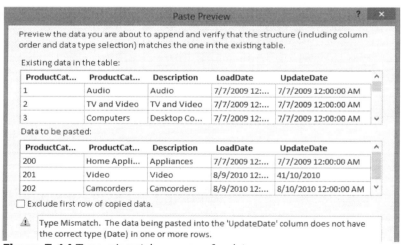

Figure 7-14 Type mismatch message for dates

3. Click OK. You will see the Paste data failed message letting you know that the data that you want to append cannot be appended ⇒ Click OK.

 Pasting Invalid Dates
The steps above walked you through attempting to append data that has invalid dates. As you saw, the data could not be appended. You can paste data with invalid dates, but the data type for the column, in the data model, will automatically be changed to Text instead of staying a date column.

Append Empty Cells

If you have created a pivot table in Excel, you know that an empty cell in a numeric column can change the function or formula that is used to calculate the values. In this part of the exercise you will append a range of data that has empty cells.

1. In the Product Categories workbook, click on the Missing_Data tab ⇒ Copy the range A2:E11 ⇒ Paste Append it to the Products table in the data model. You will see the Paste Preview dialog box. Notice that no errors are reported ⇒ Click OK.

2. If you scroll to the bottom of the Products table, you will see the appended data with the empty cells, as illustrated in Figure 7-15.

   You will also see that the data type of the Product Category Key column is still a whole number.

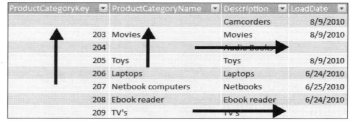

Figure 7-15 Appended data with empty cells illustrated

3. Close the Product Categories workbook.

Exercise 7.9: Importing Bad Data

In the previous exercise you attempted to paste a variety of data to see the types of error messages that Power Pivot will generate. In this exercise, you will import data to see how Power Pivot handles different types of bad data.

Import Data With Different Date Formats

In this part of the exercise you will import a date column that has two date formats in it.

1. Save the E7.6 workbook as E7.9 Import bad data.

2. Power Pivot window ⇒ Select the Excel File connection option.

3. In the Friendly connection name field, type Date Format ⇒ Check the Use first row option ⇒ Click the Browse button ⇒ Select the Product Categories workbook ⇒ Click Next.

4. Select the Date Format table ⇒ Click Finish.

Notice in the Load Date column, in the table shown in Figure 7-16, that the first three dates in August have the same format as the other dates in the column. That is because Power Pivot converted them.

ProductCategoryKey	ProductCategoryName	Description	LoadDate	UpdateDate
200	Home Appliances	Appliances	7/7/2009	7/7/2009
201	Video	Video	8/9/2010	8/10/2010
202	Camcorders	Camcorders	8/9/2010	8/10/2010
203	Movies	Movies	8/9/2010	8/10/2010
204	Audio Books	Audio Books	8/9/2010	8/10/2010
205	Toys	Toys	8/9/2010	8/10/2010
206	Laptops	Laptops	6/24/2010	8/10/2010

Figure 7-16 Date_Format tab in Power Pivot

If you look at the data on the Date_Format tab, in the Products Categories workbook, shown in Figure 7-17, you will see that the three dates in August are in a different date format.

	A	B	C	D	E
1	ProductCategoryKey	ProductCategoryName	Description	LoadDate	UpdateDate
2	200	Home Appliances	Appliances	July 7, 2009	7/7/2009
3	201	Video	Video	August 9, 2010	8/10/2010
4	202	Camcorders	Camcorders	August 9, 2010	8/10/2010
5	203	Movies	Movies	August 9, 2010	8/10/2010
6	204	Audio Books	Audio Books	8/9/10	8/10/2010

Figure 7-17 Date_Format tab in the Product Categories workbook

Import Data With Invalid Dates

In this part of the exercise you will import data that has invalid dates.

1. Select the Excel File connection option.

2. In the Friendly connection name field, type Invalid Dates ⇒ Select the Use first row option ⇒ Click the Browse button ⇒ Select the Product Categories workbook ⇒ Click Next.

3. Select the Invalid_Dates table ⇒ Click Finish. Notice in Figure 7-18 that three cells in the date columns are empty. In this example, that is because Excel could not convert the data in the cells illustrated earlier in Figure 7-13.

ProductCategoryKey	ProductCategoryName	Description	LoadDate	UpdateDate
200	Home Appliances	Appliances	7/7/2009	7/7/2009
201	Video	Video	8/9/2010	
202	Camcorders	Camcorders	8/9/2010	8/10/2010
203	Movies	Movies		8/10/2010
204	Audio Books	Audio Books	8/9/2010	8/10/2010
205	Toys	Toys	8/9/2010	8/10/2010
206	Laptops	Laptops	6/24/2010	

Figure 7-18 Empty cells in the Power Pivot table

How To Change The Connection To An Existing Data Source

You must select the same type of data source as the one that you are going to change. This means that if the current data source is a text file, you cannot change the connection to a database file now. The steps below show you how to change the connection for a data source.

1. Open the Power Pivot window in the workbook that you need to change the connection information of.

2. Home tab ⇒ Existing Connections button.

   As shown in Figure 7-19, you will see the connections for the workbook.

   In this scenario, the location of the Product Categories workbook has changed.

   Click on the connection that you want to change, then click the Edit button.

   You will see the Edit Connection dialog box.

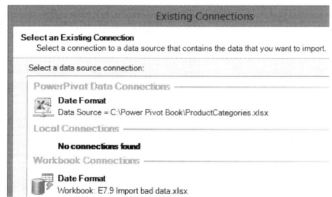

Figure 7-19 Existing Connections dialog box

3. Click the Browse button ⇒ Navigate to the location of the new file that you want to connect to ⇒ Click on the file, then click the Open button. You should see the new location and file in the Excel File Path field, as shown in Figure 7-20.

Notice the message at the bottom of the dialog box. This message lets you know that Power Pivot recognizes that the data source has changed and that the data needs to be refreshed.

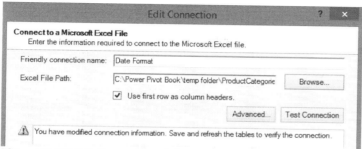

Figure 7-20 Edit Connection dialog box

4. Click the Save button.

    You should see the new location of the data source that you changed.

    Compare the Data Source path illustrated in Figure 7-21, to the Product Categories workbook shown earlier in Figure 7-19.

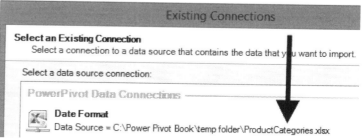

Figure 7-21 Modified connection illustrated

5. Select the connection ⇒ Click the Refresh button ⇒ Click the Close button on the Data Refresh dialog box ⇒ Click the Close button on the Existing Connections dialog box.

 Considerations For Changing The Location Of A File In An Existing Connection
Keep in mind that file paths in a data connection are relative to the computer that they are created on. If you create the connection and are the only person using the workbook, changing the location of a data source is not a problem. If someone else needs to use the workbook and the data source is on your computers hard drive, that person may have to edit the connection information so that it points to the location where they put the data source. From experience, if you have to send the data source, have the person create the same folder structure that you have on your computer. That usually reduces the errors that they may have.

How To Import Data From A New Table In An Existing Data Source

Over time, the structure of a database (or Excel workbook for that matter) may change and new tables will be added. If that is the case and you want to import data from a new table in a database that already has a connection to the data model, follow the steps below to add the new table.

1. Open the Power Pivot window in the workbook (that has an existing connection) that you want to import data from.

2. Home tab ⇒ Existing Connections button ⇒ On the Existing Connections dialog box, click on the file that has the table(s) that you want to add ⇒ Click the Open button.

3. On the Select Tables and Views screen ⇒ Select the table(s) that you want to add, then create any filters that are necessary ⇒ Click Finish. You will see the new table(s) in the Power Pivot window.

Summary

What I hope that you take away from this chapter is how important it is to create links properly. Incorrect links will prevent you from creating reports that display the data correctly. The other thing that I hope that you are starting to realize is how helpful and important it is to have an above average understanding of the data that you use. Otherwise, you may not know that the data being displayed is not correct.

USING FILTERS AND SORTING DATA

 Overview

In addition to learning how to sort and filter the data in Power Pivot, you will also learn about the following:

☑ Changing data types
☑ Formatting data
☑ Freezing columns
☑ Rearranging the column order
☑ Hiding and unhiding columns

CHAPTER 8

Overview

Now that you have learned how to import data from a variety of data sources, link to data in Excel worksheets, paste and append data, it is time to learn how to format, filter and sort the data in preparation of analyzing the data in Power Pivot. These features do not interfere with creating relationships or using the data to create reports.

Chapter 5 covered how to filter records while using the Table Import Wizard to select which records would be imported. Filtering records in Power Pivot basically works the same way. Filtering data in Power Pivot is useful when you need to analyze data in preparation to create reports. Often, the columns used to filter data are good choices for slicers for a pivot table.

Changing Data Types

Once the data is imported into the data model you may need to change the data type for some columns. The formatting options on the Home tab in Power Pivot are used to change the data type. During the data import process, the data being imported is mapped to one of the data types listed below.

① Text   ③ Whole Number   ⑤ Date

② Decimal Number   ④ Currency   ⑥ True/False

If you select a data type that is not compatible with the data in the column, you will see a warning message similar to the one shown in Figure 8-1.

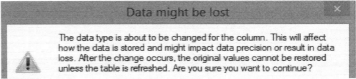

Figure 8-1 Data might be lost message

Not all of the data types are available for each column of data. The options shown in the Data Type field drop-down list, on the Home tab, are the options that are most compatible with the data in the selected column. Keep in mind that just because a data type is in the drop-down list does not mean that the data in the column, can or should be converted to any of the data types in the list.

For example, Figure 8-2 shows the Whole Number data type options for the Shipper ID field. If you selected the True/False option, you would see the warning message shown above in Figure 8-1.

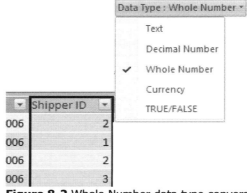

Figure 8-2 Whole Number data type conversion options

Figure 8-3 shows the Text data type options and the data in the Customer Name column. If you selected the Currency data type, you would see the warning message shown in Figure 8-4. This message lets you know why the column of data could not be converted to the currency data type.

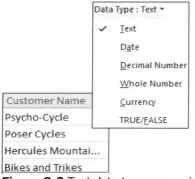

Figure 8-3 Text data type conversion options

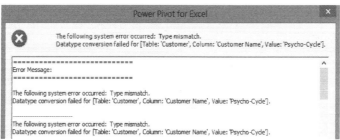

Figure 8-4 Failed change of data type message

Formatting Data

If the reason that you want to change the data type is because you want to see data in a slightly different format, it may be a better choice to change how the data is formatted. The difference between changing the data type, of a column, and changing the formatting of a column is that the data in the column is not physically changed if it is formatted. Formatting a column just changes the way that the data is displayed. This is shown in Figures 8-5 and 8-6.

Figure 8-5 shows columns of data that have the Whole Number data type with each of the available formatting options. The column heading name is the formatting option that is applied to the data in the column.

General	Decimal Number	Whole Number	Currency	Accounting	Percentage	Scientific
17	17.00	17	$17.00	17.00	1,700.00 %	1.70E+001
25	25.00	25	$25.00	25.00	2,500.00 %	2.50E+001
26	26.00	26	$26.00	26.00	2,600.00 %	2.60E+001

Figure 8-5 Whole Number formatting options

Figure 8-6 shows columns of data that have the Date data type with some of the available formatting options. The column heading name is the formatting option that is applied to the data in the column.

M D YYYY	MM DD YYYY	Weekday Month DD YY	M D	M D YY Time	Month YYYY
4/12/2004	04/12/2004	Monday, April 12, 2004	4/12	4/12/04 12:00 AM	April, 2004
2/14/2004	02/14/2004	Saturday, February 14, 2004	2/14	2/14/04 12:00 AM	February, 2004
2/12/2004	02/12/2004	Thursday, February 12, 20...	2/12	2/12/04 12:00 AM	February, 2004
3/1/2004	03/01/2004	Monday, March 01, 2004	3/1	3/1/04 12:00 AM	March, 2004

Figure 8-6 Date formatting options

No Printing From The Power Pivot Workspace
You cannot print from Power Pivot. If the table does not have more than one million rows (Excels row limit), you can copy the data from the data model and paste it into an Excel spreadsheet and print the data from Excel.

Filtering Data In Power Pivot

The next few sections cover filter options for different data types.

Numeric Filter Options And Functions

Figure 8-7 shows the filter options on the left and the numeric functions on the right, for a Whole Number field in Power Pivot.

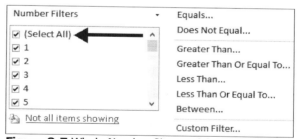
Figure 8-7 Whole Number filter and function options

Using The (Select All) Filter Option
This option is checked by default, as illustrated above in Figure 8-7. When checked, it causes all of the options below it to also be checked. If you clear this option, all of the options below it are also cleared. This is helpful when you only want to use a few of the options to filter the data because you can select them one by one.

Using Functions In Power Pivot
Use a function when the filter options, shown above on the left side of Figure 8-7, will not handle your needs. All of the functions open the Custom Filter dialog box, just like selecting the Custom Filter option, on the shortcut menu. The difference is that if a function is selected before opening the Custom Filter dialog box, the function is displayed on the dialog box.

Custom Filters

Select the **CUSTOM FILTER** option when the filter options on the shortcut menu are not sufficient enough to create the filter that you need. This option opens the dialog box shown in Figure 8-8.

The filter options that are applied, only work in Power Pivot. They are not applied to pivot tables that you create. They are also not available if the workbook is used to create a report in **POWER VIEW**.

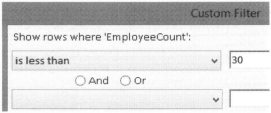

Figure 8-8 Custom Filter dialog box

Date Functions

The functions shown in Figure 8-9 are used to create criteria for date fields. The functions that reference a week, month, quarter or year, use the computers system date. The functions are explained in Table 8-1.

| Equals... |
| Before... |
| After... |
| Between... |
| Tomorrow |
| Today |
| Yesterday |
| Next Week |
| This Week |
| Last Week |
| Next Month |
| This Month |
| Last Month |
| Next Quarter |
| This Quarter |
| Last Quarter |
| Next Year |
| This Year |
| Last Year |
| Year to Date |
| Custom Filter... |

Function	Selects Records That Have . . .
Equals	The date that you entered.
Before	A date earlier than the date entered.
After	A date later than the date entered.
Between	A date in the range selected.
Tomorrow	The next days date.
Today	The current date.
Yesterday	The previous days date.
Next Week	A date in the next calendar week.
This Week	A date in the current calendar week.
Last Week	A date in the previous calendar week.
Next Month	A date in the next calendar month.
This Month	A date in the current calendar month.
Last Month	A date in the previous calendar month.
Next Quarter	A date in the next calendar quarter.
This Quarter	A date in the current calendar quarter.
Last Quarter	A date in the previous calendar quarter.
Next Year	A date in the next year.
This Year	A date in the current year.
Last Year	A date in the previous year.
Year to Date	A date from January 1 of the current year through today.
Custom Filter	A date that meets the criteria that you create on the Custom Filter dialog box.

Figure 8-9 Date functions   **Table 8-1** Date functions explained

Exercise Tip
Unless stated otherwise, after you save the workbook with a new name, open Power Pivot.

Exercise 8.1: Using Filters

In this exercise you will learn how to filter the data in the Stores table to only display stores in the United States that have less than 30 employees, that are still open.

1. Save the E7.1 workbook as `E8.1 Filter Data`.

2. Open the Region Country Name column filter list ⇒ Clear the (Select All) option.

   Scroll down the list and check the United States option, shown in Figure 8-10 ⇒ Click OK.

   Notice that the table now displays 220 rows of data instead of 325 rows.

Figure 8-10 Region Country Name filter options

3. Open the Employee Count (last column in the table) filter list ⇒ Select the Number Filters option ⇒ Select the Less Than function.

4. Type 30 in the field, as shown earlier in Figure 8-8 ⇒ Click OK. Notice that the table now displays 161 records.

5. Open the Close Date filter list ⇒ Clear the (Select All) option.

   Check the **(BLANKS)** option, illustrated in Figure 8-11. In this exercise, this option means that the store is still open.

   Click OK.

   Based on all of the filters that you created, there are 149 stores in the United States that are open and have less than 30 employees.

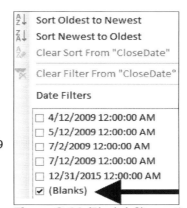

Figure 8-11 (Blanks) filter option illustrated

Exercise 8.2: Creating Custom Filters

This exercise will show you how to create custom filters to only display records with a Unit Cost between $1 and $100 and a Discount Quantity between 3 and 4 percent.

1. Save the E5.1 workbook as E8.2 Custom Filters.

2. Delete all tables except the Fact Sales table.

3. Open the Unit Cost filter drop-down list ⇒ Select the **BETWEEN** function.

4. Type 1.00 in the field across from the Greater than or equal to function.

   Type 100.00 in the field across from the Less than or equal to function.

   You should have the options shown in Figure 8-12 ⇒ Click OK. Notice that the number of records has been reduced to 1.2 million from over 2.2 million.

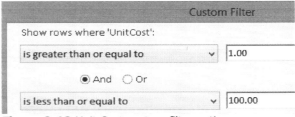

Figure 8-12 Unit Cost custom filter options

Create Another Custom Filter

In this part of the exercise you will create a custom filter to only display records that have a Discount Quantity between 3 and 4 percent.

1. Open the Discount Quantity filter drop-down list ⇒ Select the Between function.

2. Type 3 in the field across from the Greater than or equal to function ⇒ Type 4 in the field across from the Less than or equal to function ⇒ Click OK. The number of rows displayed should be 316,772.

Sorting Records

The options that are available are to sort a column are ascending or descending order. Currently, only one column in the Power Pivot window can be sorted on at a time. If you sort on Column A, then sort on Column C, the sort from Column A is removed and then the table is sorted on Column C. Sorting the data in a table does not have any effect when the data is used to create a report.

Use The Sort By Column Option

Being able to sort the data in one column by the data in another column is a very helpful feature, especially for a text column. This option will sort the data in **POWER VIEW**. A common use for this option is to sort month names in calendar order, not in alphabetical order. There is a catch though. In order to sort a column that is defined as text (in something other then ascending or descending order), you need to have a column that is designated as numeric. This new column would be sorted on to display the month names in calendar order.

If you have a table that meets this criteria, the steps below show you how to create this type of sort. To see how sorting works with a month column in the My Dates table, you can come back here after completing Exercise 14.4, or you can open a new workbook and import the My Dates tables in the My Dates workbook.

1. Power Pivot window ⇒ Click on the text column. In this case, click on the month column that you want sorted.

2. Home tab ⇒ Sort by Column button ⇒ Sort by Column option.

3. On the dialog box shown in Figure 8-13 ⇒ By Column ⇒ Select the field that has the numeric month values. (Select the Month Number column.)

The **HOW TO SORT BY A COLUMN FROM A DIFFERENT TABLE** link, displays the DAX formula that you can use to reference a field in another table in the workbook, as the By Column field.

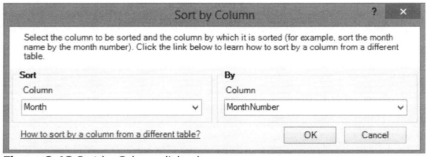

Figure 8-13 Sort by Column dialog box

Exercise 8.3: Using The Freeze Option

The Freeze option will move the selected columns to the far left of the table. These columns will always be visible without having to scroll to see them. If you have used the Freeze Panes option in Excel, you will notice that the Freeze option in Power Pivot only supports freezing columns. Freezing rows is not supported.

Usually, tables in a database have many, if not all of the ID fields (**PRIMARY** and **FOREIGN KEY FIELDS**) as the first fields in a table, as shown in Figure 8-14. That is a database standard. For end users, these fields are not the ones that will be used for analysis. In the table shown in Figure 8-14, it may be more helpful to move the Product Name, Standard Cost and List Price columns to the beginning of the table.

> **Freezing Columns**
> Once a column is frozen, you cannot move it to the right without removing the Freeze option.

Supplier IDs	ID	Product Code	Product Name	Description	Standard Cost	List Price
10	3	NWTCO-3	Northwind Traders Syrup		$7.5	$10
10	4	NWTCO-4	Northwind Traders Cajun Seasoning		$16.5	$22
10	5	NWTO-5	Northwind Traders Olive Oil		$16.0125	$21.35
2;6	6	NWTJP-6	Northwind Traders Boysenberry Spread		$18.75	$25

Figure 8-14 ID columns at the beginning of the table

The steps below show how to use the Freeze option to rearrange the column order.

1. Save the E6.6 workbook as E8.3 Freeze option.

2. Products table ⇒ Click on the Product Name column ⇒ Design tab ⇒ Freeze button ⇒ Freeze.
   The Product Name column should now be the first column in the table.

3. Select the Standard Cost and List Price columns ⇒ Design tab ⇒ Freeze button ⇒ Freeze. The Standard Cost and List Price columns should be the second and third columns in the table. The beginning of the table should look like the one shown in Figure 8-15.

Product Name	Standard Cost	List Price	Supplier IDs	ID
Northwind Traders Chai	$13.50	$18.00	4	1
Northwind Traders Syrup	$7.50	$10.00	10	3
Northwind Traders Cajun Seasoning	$16.50	$22.00	10	4
Northwind Traders Olive Oil	$16.01	$21.35	10	5

Figure 8-15 Freeze option applied to three columns

Notice the vertical line after the List Price column. This line is used to visually indicate which columns have the freeze option applied. Compare this table to the one shown earlier in Figure 8-14.

4. Scroll to the right until you see the Category column. You will still see the Product Name, Standard Cost and List Price columns on the left.

Rearranging The Column Order

This option is used to move the selected columns to another part of the table. If you have the need to change the order of the columns, follow the steps below.

1. Power Pivot window ⇒ Display the table that has the columns that you want to rearrange.

2. Click on the heading of a column that you want to move ⇒ Drag the column heading to the right or left, until it is in the location that you want ⇒ Release the mouse button.

Hiding And Unhiding Columns

Having the ability to hide columns in a table that you currently do not need for analysis can be helpful. When a column is hidden, it is disabled (grayed out) on the Grid view. The steps below show you how to hide and unhide columns, as well as view the hidden columns.

How To Hide Columns

1. Power Pivot window ⇒ Display the table that has columns that you want to hide.

2. Right-click on the column that you want to hide ⇒ Hide from Client Tools.

Hiding More Than One Column At The Same Time
To hide more than one adjacent column at a time, click on the left most column that you want to hide. Hold the Shift key down, then click on each column that you want to hide. You will see a thick black border around the selected columns, as shown in Figure 8-16, then go to step 2.

EntityId	▾	RegionCounrtyName	▾	StateProvinceName	▾	CityName	▾
635		United States		Washington		Seattle	
636		United States		Washington		Seattle	
934		United States		Washington		Kennewick	

Figure 8-16 Multiple adjacent columns selected

How To Unhide A Column

1. Power Pivot window ⇒ Display the table that has columns that you want to unhide ⇒ Home tab ⇒ Data View.

2. Home tab ⇒ View group ⇒ Show Hidden button. The hidden columns are displayed, but not enabled ⇒ If you want to fully restore a column, right-click on a disabled (grayed out) column heading and select **UNHIDE FROM CLIENT TOOLS**.

Hiding vs Deleting Columns

Below are some tips and guidelines that you may find helpful in deciding whether to hide or delete a column.

① If a column is deleted from a table, the data in the column is no longer available.

② If you are going to delete a column, make sure that it is not a column that is needed to create a relationship with another table.

③ When in doubt about deleting a column, hide it instead.

④ Hiding a column prevents it from being displayed in the Pivot Table Fields list.

⑤ Hide columns of data used to create a relationship. The reason to consider doing this is because these fields are rarely used to create a report because the end user probably will not understand the numeric values in the field.

⑥ As you have seen, many tables that you imported have a lot of fields. Having to sift through all of the fields in the Pivot Table Fields list can take a lot of time. If you know that some fields will not be used, hide them if you do not want to delete them.

Summary

The focus of this chapter was to show the formatting, filtering and sorting options that are available in Power Pivot. These features are also available for the pivot tables. Hopefully, introducing these topics here, will make using them with pivot tables easier later on, because it is one less thing you have to learn about later.

CREATING RELATIONSHIPS

 Overview

In this chapter you will learn about the following:

- ☑ Data models
- ☑ Relational databases
- ☑ Primary key fields
- ☑ Types of database relationships
- ☑ Manually creating relationships

CHAPTER 9

Overview

Chapter 1 provided an overview of what relationships are. The data model concept was briefly explained. Once the data has been cleaned, filtered and imported, relationships need to be created, especially for tables that were imported from different data sources. This chapter covers both of these topics in more detail. I guess the best way to start this chapter is with a few questions.

What Is A Relationship?

In order to be able to use the tables in a workbook together, to create a report, there has to be a connection between the tables. The actual connection is called a **LINK**. The result of a link between tables is called a **RELATIONSHIP**. The ability to create relationships to join (combine) tables and use the data from multiple tables to create one report, may be the number one reason that many people will use Power Pivot.

Relationships are created between a column of data that two tables have in common. Relationships between tables allow for a higher level of analysis, because columns of data from different tables can be used to create one report. Data in one table can be filtered by data in another table, which provides even more flexibility and control over the data that is displayed on a report.

What Is A Data Model?

A data model is a way to create a relational database, if you will, inside an Excel workbook. Each workbook can only have one data model. Imported tables are automatically added to the data model. So yes, you have already created data models. You will create relationships for some of the data models, in this chapter.

A data model contains tables (of data) and their relationships. Chapter 2 demonstrated from beginning to end how to get data from an external data source, import the data into the data model, then create a pivot table. One benefit of using a data model is that calculations are processed faster because the data in a data model is loaded into the computers memory (RAM).

Other benefits of using a data model include:

① Saves disk space because an efficient data compression algorithm is used.
② Supports complex calculations.
③ Tables can store more than 1 million rows of data.
④ Data models support KPI's and hierarchies.

When viewed, a data model contains tables with lines between them that point to the field (in the table) that they have in common. These lines represent the relationships between the tables. Figure 9-1, displays a data model that includes the Orders, Orders Detail, Customer, Order Subtotals and Employee tables and their relationships.

Data modeling is an important concept to understand because even though Power Pivot recreates the relationships saved in a database, at best, it only works on database tables that are imported at the same time. You will see examples of this later in this chapter, when you view the relationships in the E6.7 workbook. Power Pivot does not automatically create relationships from data that is imported from other file types, like spreadsheets.

What Is A Star Schema?

Now that you have created data models and have a better understanding of them, it is time to clearly define what the data model will be used for. Data models covered in this book are used for analyzing and reporting on data. The three schema types for data models are:

① **STAR** Has one level of **CHILD TABLES**.
② **SNOWFLAKE** Can have multiple levels of child tables. Some people say that this schema can cause performance issues because of the increased number of relationships. My advice is to try it and see for yourself.
③ **CONSTELLATION** Is used when there is more than one fact table.

The Star schema has what is called a **FACT TABLE** (the parent or primary table in the data model). I wonder if this is the reason why the Fact Sales table in Exercise 5.1, has the name that it does. My personal preference for Power Pivot is the Star schema because it handles large datasets. That, and it is easy to understand.

The primary table is surrounded by the other tables in the data model, forming, you guessed it, a star, as shown in Figure 9-1.

This is also known as **DIMENSIONAL MODELING** because it describes the logical way that data should be structured to obtain the best performance.

The Orders table is the fact table in this figure. It is not a requirement to arrange the tables in this layout in the Diagram view.

On your own, if you are not sure which table is the fact table, create the relationships for the tables and see which one has the most relationships.

More than likely, the table with the most relationships with other tables is the fact table.

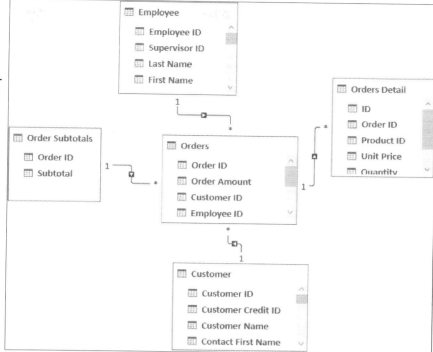

Figure 9-1 Star schema

The fact table usually has some or all of the following characteristics:

① It has measurable data, meaning that it will answer a question. For example, the Orders table has an order amount. It could be used to answer which five states have the most sales.
② Other tables are linked to it.
③ It has one or more date fields, which confirm when something happened, like when the order was placed or the date of each basketball game.
④ Fact tables usually have more of rows of data, then any other table in the data model. (Date tables are not included when determining the fact table, because they do not contain data that will be analyzed).

The other tables (known as the **DIMENSION** or **CHILD TABLE**) in the schema contain supporting data, if you will, that provide additional information about a field in the fact table. For example, in Figure 9-1 above, the Customer table contains information on who placed each order. The Order Details table contains the items for each order. Notice that each dimension table is linked to the fact table and none of the dimension tables are linked to each other.

Dimension tables can be linked to each other. An example would be adding a Products table to the schema in Figure 9-1. It would be linked to the Orders Detail table, using the Product ID field. That would allow the product name to be displayed on the report. If the schema rules were strictly followed, adding the Product table would make the star schema shown above in Figure 9-1, a Snowflake schema, because the Product table does not have a direct relationship with the fact table (the Orders table).

The arrows on the link line between tables, point in the direction of the relationship.

The number "1", on the link line, indicates that the field used to create the link, has unique values.

The asterisk * on the link line, indicates the "many" table in the relationship.

How Power Pivot Handles Data

Power Pivot uses what is known as a **COLUMNAR DATABASE**. This type of database reduces the need to figure out a normalization strategy. There are two normalization strategies, as explained below:

① **DENORMALIZATION** is the process of combining several tables (usually small tables) into one big table. While this causes the new table to have redundant data, it is done on purpose because it allows the queries to process faster against the table(s) in the data model.

② **NORMALIZATION** is the process of removing redundancy in the data model. It works the opposite of denormalization. It takes a large table and turns it into two or more smaller tables. If a value occurs more than once in a column, it is only saved once in the table. The other occurrences of the value in the column are replaced with a reference to the first occurrence.

For example, in a customers table, a zip code will often appear more than once in the zip code column. The first occurrence of the zip code is saved. The remaining occurrences of the same zip code are replaced with a pointer to the first location in the column that has the zip code.

After the tables have been imported into the data model, you have to determine if the tables are set up to run in the most efficient way. This is known as **NORMALIZING THE DATA MODEL**. This process organizes the data to make querying it more efficient. This includes tasks like verifying that the data in a table only has one value per column (for example, the first and last name should be in two columns) and that all of the columns in a table are related (meaning the customer zip code should not be in the products table). As much as possible, I fix items like these before or during the import process.

Relational Databases

The reason that tables can have relationships created between them is because there is at least one column of data in each table that has related data, thus the term "Relational Databases". Yes, this is a complicated topic and there are a lot of books on the concepts associated with relational databases and how to create them, so I won't bore you with all of the details, but please hear me out and don't skip this section. Creating relationships in Power Pivot and creating relationships in a database have a lot in common.

While databases are not the primary focus of this chapter, it is important that you understand a little more than the fundamentals. My goal is to explain, as painless as possible, how all of the components fit together <smile>. The reason that you need to understand this database concept is because it will probably be the foundation of the reports that you create and modify. If you have never created a database, or have very little experience creating them, the next few sections in this chapter will be your crash course in databases and relationships. Figures 9-2 and 9-3 illustrate the layout of two tables.

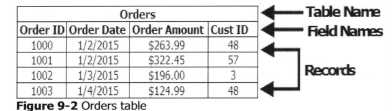

Figure 9-2 Orders table

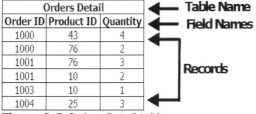

Figure 9-3 Orders Detail table

Primary Key Fields

Primary key fields and ID fields are terms that are used interchangeably. I prefer to use the term ID field because primary key fields in databases often have "ID" as part of the field name. Recently, I have seen the word "Key" at the end of a field name to signify that the field is a primary key field.

 ID is short for identification. It is jargon that the computer programming community uses to reference a field that can be used to link one table to another table.

The majority of the tables in the databases that you use in the this book have at least one ID field. Hopefully, you will find that this is also true out in the real world. The reason ID fields are used is because by design they provide a way for each record in the table to have a unique way to be identified. A **FOREIGN KEY** points back to a primary key in a related table.

I have taught several database classes and almost without fail, this topic causes a lot of confusion. For some reason, people want to create links on string (text) fields. Please don't do that for tables in databases. It can cause you problems and should be avoided. It is a bad table design choice. However, creating relationships for tables in the data model on text fields is acceptable, in particular, for data that is not imported from a database.

If you needed to create a pivot table that displays all of the orders and what items were on each order, you would need a way to link the Orders and Orders Detail tables. Think of creating relationships as having the ability to combine two or more tables "virtually" and being able to display the result of this "virtual linking" on a report. This linking is different from linking to tables in Excel that was covered in Chapter 7. The linking covered in Chapter 7 provides the ability to keep the data in a table up to date from the data in the spreadsheet that it is linked to. The relationship linking covered in this chapter refers to the process of joining two tables based on data in a column, that the tables have in common.

In Figures 9-2 and 9-3 above, the common ID field is the Order ID field. If you look at the data in the Orders Detail table, you will see that some records have the same Order ID number. That's okay. This means that some customers placed orders with more than one item. Each record in the Orders Detail table represents one item that a customer ordered. If you were to "virtually" join the data in the tables shown in Figures 9-2 and 9-3 above, the virtual table would look like the one shown in Figure 9-4.

This "virtual" join is what happens when tables are **LINKED** (have a relationship). If all of this data was stored in one table instead of two, at the very minimum, all of the fields in the Orders table would be repeated for every record that is in the Orders Detail table, which is exactly what the virtual table, in Figure 9-4, shows.

Orders				Orders Detail		
Order ID	Order Date	Order Amount	Cust ID	Order ID	Product ID	Quantity
1000	1/2/2015	$263.99	48	1000	43	4
1000	1/2/2015	$263.99	48	1000	76	2
1001	1/2/2015	$322.45	57	1001	76	3
1001	1/2/2015	$322.45	57	1001	10	2
1002	1/3/2015	$196.00	3			
1003	1/4/2015	$124.99	48	1003	10	1
				1004	25	3

Figure 9-4 Virtually joined tables

Repetition of data is why this information is stored in two tables in a database, instead of one. In this example, an additional row would be added to the Orders table for each row in the Orders Detail table. It is considered poor table design to have the same information (other than fields that are used to join tables) stored in more than one table.

Usually if you see a record in the Orders Detail table, like Order ID 1004 shown above in Figure 9-4, or any **CHILD TABLE** that is in a **PARENT-CHILD RELATIONSHIP**, there is a problem with the data in at least one of the tables because all of the records in the child table should have a matching record in the parent table. Parent tables are used to get data from a **CHILD TABLE**. In this scenario, the record for Order ID 1004, in the Orders Detail table, would not be retrieved or shown on a report.

Types Of Database Relationships

To create an orders report would require at least two tables in a database. These tables are linked by a common field, the Order ID field. This field is what connects (joins) data from both tables and allows you to use data from both tables seamlessly.

An ID field in the Orders table is how you find the matching record (known as a **ONE-TO-ONE RELATIONSHIP**) or matching records (known as a **ONE-TO-MANY RELATIONSHIP**, which is the most popular type of relationship) in another table. These are the two most common types of relationships. The **MANY-TO-MANY RELATIONSHIP** is a third type of relationship. It is not used as much as the other two relationship types. Power Pivot currently does not support this type of relationship, as shown at the bottom of Figure 9-5.

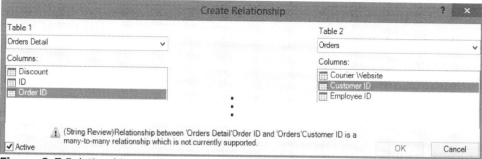

Figure 9-5 Relationship warning message

Power Pivot Relationships

A relationship between tables may appear to work in the reverse of what you may be use to. They work in a **MANY-TO-ONE RELATIONSHIP** because Table 1, is the "many" table and Table 2, is the "one" table. [See Figure 9-8] The good thing though, is that you can create relationships traditionally with, the "one" table on the left and the "many" table on the right. Fortunately, if you create a relationship between tables that Power Pivot wants in the opposite direction, you will see the message shown above in Figure 9-5.

How Relationships Work

More than likely, many of the reports that you create will require data from more than one table in a database or another data source. Reports that display the equivalent of a Product List report will probably only use one table, so there is no linking involved. For reports that require two or more tables, the tables need to be linked by creating a relationship between them.

When you need to view or modify existing relationships, you can do so by opening the Manage Relationships dialog box. Even though some of the time the relationships that you need are automatically created in Power Pivot for you, it is important to understand what is going on behind the scenes, as they say. The best way to understand the basic concept of creating relationships between tables, especially if you are not familiar with the data, is to take the time to view at least some of the data in the tables that need to have a relationship created.

Figures 9-6 and 9-7 show the records in the Employee and Employee Addresses tables. The field that these tables have in common is the Employee ID field. This would be the primary key field used to create a relationship between these two tables.

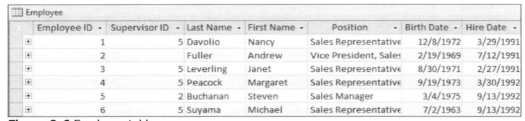

	Employee ID	Supervisor ID	Last Name	First Name	Position	Birth Date	Hire Date
+	1	5	Davolio	Nancy	Sales Representative	12/8/1972	3/29/1991
+	2		Fuller	Andrew	Vice President, Sales	2/19/1969	7/12/1991
+	3	5	Leverling	Janet	Sales Representative	8/30/1971	2/27/1991
+	4	5	Peacock	Margaret	Sales Representative	9/19/1973	3/30/1992
+	5	2	Buchanan	Steven	Sales Manager	3/4/1975	9/13/1992
+	6	5	Suyama	Michael	Sales Representative	7/2/1963	9/13/1992

Figure 9-6 Employee table

	Employee ID	Address1	Address2	City	Region	Country	Postal Code
+	1	507 - 20th Ave. E.		Port Moody	BC	Canada	V3D 4F6
+	2	908 W. Capital Way	Suite 100	Coquitlam	BC	Canada	V3H4J7
+	3	722 Moss Bay Blvd.		Vancouver	BC	Canada	V6M 8S9
+	4	4110 Old Redmond Rd.		Richmond	BC	Canada	V5S 6H7
+	5	14 Garrett Hill		London		UK	SW1 8JR
+	6	Coventry House		London		UK	EC2 7JR

Figure 9-7 Employee Addresses table

Depending on the table structure, tables can have more than one field that they can be linked on. An example of this would be the Orders Detail table. This table has an ID field that would be used to link it to the Orders table. There is a Product ID field in the Orders Detail table that would be used to retrieve the Product Name from another table (the Product table) to display on the report, instead of displaying the Product ID number. Displaying the product name is more meaningful then displaying the Product ID field, which contains a number. If you are asking why the Product Name is not stored in the Orders Detail table, there are three reasons that I can think of, as explained below.

① The ID field takes up less space then the Product Name field, thereby keeping the size of the Orders Detail table (and any other table that stores the Product Name field instead of the Product ID field) smaller.

② If a Product Name has to be changed for any reason, it only has to be changed in the Product table. Every report that the Product Name field is displayed on would automatically be updated with the revised product name, the next time the report is run. If the product name was stored in the Orders Detail table, every record in the Orders Detail table that had that product name would have to be changed, as well as, any other table that stored the product name. That would be a lot of extra work (for you) and increase the chance for inaccurate data.

③ Without a Product table, there would be no place to add new products.

Relationship Requirements

Having the ability to create relationships between tables provides a lot more flexibility. The requirements (the do's and don'ts) are explained below.

① **MANY-TO-MANY RELATIONSHIP** DAX functions can be used to imitate this type of relationship. (1)

② **COMPATIBLE DATA TYPES** The column in each table that will be used to create a relationship must have the same or compatible data type. For example, the primary key column in the main table can have a whole number data type and the lookup column in the second table can have a text data type. In this example, the lookup column could not be a date, currency or True/False data type.

③ **COMPOSITE KEYS** Are a unique value that is created by combining the values in two or more fields. To emulate this type of key, you have to combine the values in the fields before creating the relationship. There are two options for combining values: 1) Import the columns and create a calculated column using DAX or 2) Combine the values in the data source and import the new column. (1)

④ **SELF JOINS** In many types of databases, this is also known as a **RECURSIVE JOIN**. This type of join uses one column in the table to reference data in another column in the same table. A recursive join example would be using the Supervisor ID field (shown earlier in Figure 9-6) to create a report that displays a list of supervisors and the people in their department. (1)

⑤ **ONLY ONE RELATIONSHIP PER COLUMN** A primary key column cannot be used to create multiple relationships. If you need to use the same column in a table to create a relationship with another table, you would have to import another instance of the table into the data model and use the copy to create the second relationship.

⑥ **UNIQUE COLUMN OF DATA FOR EACH TABLE** A table used as the primary or fact table, to create a relationship must have one column that has a unique value that can be used to identify each row of data. This means that no two rows of data can have the same value in this column. At most, there can only be one empty cell in this column. This is because empty cells are the same as a blank cell, which is a data type. [See Chapter 5, Power Pivot Supported Data Types]

(1) Power Pivot does not support this type of relationship.

 Keep in mind that if the relationships are incorrect, the data displayed on reports that are created from the tables, in the relationship, will not display the correct data.

Inferred Relationships

This is a type of relationship that occurs when two relationships are manually created between three tables. For example, if Relationship #1 and #2 below were created manually, relationship #3 is inferred and will automatically be created.

Relationship #1 Orders and Products tables
Relationship #2 Products and Product Types tables
Relationship #3 Orders and Product Types tables

 Sometimes, I have noticed that in Power Pivot some of the relationships that are created via the **AUTO DETECTION** method are wrong. Why, I am not sure. I delete all of the relationships that are automatically created and create what I need. This keeps me from having to "guess" why the reports that I create are not displaying the data that I think they should.

View Relationships

In this section, you will view relationships that were detected from the database, during the import.

View The Relationships In The E6.6 Workbook

In Exercise 6.6 you imported a Customers table from a text file and an Order, Order Details and Product tables from an Access database. The steps below show you how to view the relationships that were detected.

1. Open the E6.6 workbook ⇒ Open Power Pivot.

2. Design tab ⇒
    Manage Relationships button.

    You should see the relationships
    shown in Figure 9-8.

Active	Table 1	▲	Cardinality	Filter Direction	Table 2
Yes	Order Details [Order ID]		Many to One (*:1)	<< To Order Details	Orders [Order ID]
Yes	Order Details [Product ID]		Many to One (*:1)	<< To Order Details	Products [ID]

Figure 9-8 Exercise 6.6 relationships

View The Relationships In The E6.7 Workbook

In Exercise 6.7 you imported a Customer, Order, Order Details and Product tables from an Access database.

1. Open the E6.7 workbook ⇒ Open Power Pivot.

2. Design tab ⇒
    Manage Relationships button.

    You should see the relationships
    shown in Figure 9-9.

Active	Table 1	▲	Cardinality	Filter Direction	Table 2
Yes	Order Details [Product ID]		Many to One (*:1)	<< To Order Details	Products [ID]
Yes	Orders [Customer ID]		Many to One (*:1)	<< To Orders	Customers [ID]

Figure 9-9 Exercise 6.7 relationships

In Exercises 6.6 and 6.7, the same data was imported. Notice that the relationships that were automatically created are different (See Figures 9-8 and 9-9 above). The difference is that in Exercise 6.6 no relationship was created between the Orders and Customers tables. The Customer table was imported from a text file and the other tables were imported from a database. Text files do not have or save relationship information like databases do.

Relationships Are Not Updated Automatically When Importing From The Same Database Twice
In Exercise 6.7, no relationship was created between the Orders and Order Details tables, even though both tables were imported from the same database. That is because the tables were imported at different times. This lets you know that Power Pivot does not check tables already in the workbook during the import process to see if there are any relationships that can automatically be created for the tables that are being imported, even if they are from the same database. Keep this in mind if you have to import from the same database more than once in the same workbook. I tried refreshing all of the tables, in attempt to import the relationships, but that did not work either. When fields from tables that do not have a relationship are added to a pivot table, you will see a message stating that a relationship may need to be created. If you find that this happens to you often and you do not want to create the relationships manually, delete all of the tables in Power Pivot and create a new connection to the database that includes all of the tables that you need.

Another Way To View Relationships

If you want to see which field in each table the relationship was created with, switch to the Diagram view. Hold the mouse pointer over the connecting line between the tables.

The fields used to create the relationship will be displayed with a box around them, as shown in Figure 9-10.

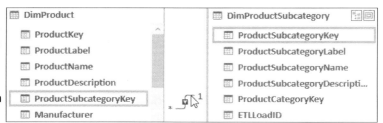
Figure 9-10 Fields used to create a relationship

Right-clicking on the arrow allows you to edit the relationship. Right-clicking on the line allows you to mark the relationship as inactive, edit or delete the relationship.

Exercise 9.1: Create Your First Relationship

This exercise will show you how to create a relationship between data that was imported from a table and data that was imported from a view. The relationships shown in Figure 9-11 were automatically detected when the data was imported.

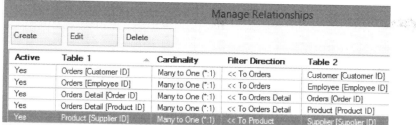

Figure 9-11 Auto detection created relationships

1. Save the E5.4 workbook as E9.1 Create a relationship.

2. Power Pivot window ⇒ Design tab ⇒ Create Relationship button.

Another Way To Open The Create Relationship Dialog Box
Double-clicking on a relationship on the Manage Relationship dialog box opens the relationship on the Create Relationship dialog box.

3. Open the Table 1 drop-down list ⇒ Select the Orders table ⇒ Select the Order ID field, in the Columns list below.

4. Open the Table 2 drop-down list ⇒ Select the Order Subtotals table.

   The Order ID field should have automatically been selected, as shown in Figure 9-12.

   Click OK.

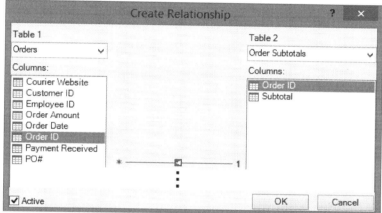

Figure 9-12 Create Relationship dialog box

Exercise 9.2: Create Relationships Between Data From Different Data Sources

In Exercise 6.8 you created a data model that contains tables from two databases and two Excel workbooks. During the import process, five relationships were detected. In this exercise, you will create the rest of the relationships that are needed for an exercise in Chapter 10.

1. Save the E6.8 workbook as E9.2 Create three relationships.

2. Create the relationships in Table 9-1. When finished, you should have all of the relationships shown in Figure 9-13.

Table 1	Column	Table 2	Column
FactSales	StoreKey	Stores	StoreKey
DimProductSubcategory	ProductCategoryKey	DimProductCategory	ProductCategoryKey
Stores	GeographyKey	DimGeography	GeographyKey

Table 9-1 Relationships to create for Exercise 9.2

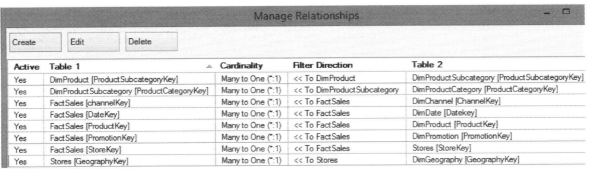

Figure 9-13 E9.2 workbook relationships

Exercise 9.3: Creating Relationships For Linked Tables

In Exercise 7.3 you created three linked tables from data on a single worksheet. Even though the linked tables have a common field, Power Pivot does not create relationships for linked tables. As you will see in this exercise, creating relationships for tables that are linked, is no different then creating relationships from data that was imported.

1. Save the E7.3 workbook as E9.3 Relationships for linked tables.

2. Create the relationships in Table 9-2.

Table 1	Column	Table 2	Column
Order Header	Customer ID	Customers	Customer ID
Order Header	Order ID	Order Details	Order ID

Table 9-2 Relationships to create for Exercise 9.3

Understanding The Power Of Relationships

As discussed at the end of Chapter 2, there is nothing stopping you from creating a pivot table that uses fields from tables that do not have relationships. The tables that you created relationships for in Exercise 9.3 is a good example.

If you opened the E7.3 workbook (which has the same tables as the E9.3 workbook), you could create the pivot table shown in Figure 9-14, using data from all three tables, even though there are no relationships for the tables.

At first glance, the pivot table may look okay, until you realize that the values in the Sum of Quantity column are all the same. The other thing that you should notice is the message illustrated at the top of the Pivot Table Fields list on the right side of Figure 9-14. This message means that Power Pivot cannot use data from different tables correctly, if there is no relationship between the tables. If you created the same pivot table in the E9.3 workbook, the values in the Sum of Quantity column would be calculated and displayed correctly, as shown in Figure 9-15.

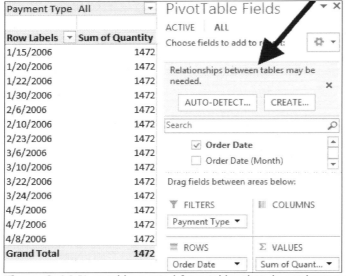

Payment Type	All

Row Labels	Sum of Quantity
1/15/2006	100
1/20/2006	20
1/22/2006	15
1/30/2006	30
2/6/2006	20
3/24/2006	280
4/5/2006	20
4/7/2006	10
4/8/2006	30
(blank)	320
Grand Total	1472

Figure 9-15 Pivot table created with tables that have a relationship

Figure 9-14 Pivot table created from tables that do not have a relationship

Summary

This chapter covered data models, the star schema and relationships. Data models and relationships are the most important topics to understand in this chapter. On your own, if you have trouble creating relationships between tables, it is usually for one of the following reasons:

① At least one table is missing a primary or foreign key.
② Another table needs to be imported.

The **STAR SCHEMA** was discussed as being the easiest schema to understand, in terms of the data model. As you saw, there are two types of tables, as discussed below.

① The **PRIMARY TABLE** is also known as the "fact", "parent" or "transaction table". Usually, primary tables have a lot of rows, when compared to child tables. Primary tables also tend to have less columns then child tables. Primary tables have the data that needs to be analyzed. This table type has a key field for each table that it needs to get additional data from, to create the report. These key fields are the ones used to link to the child tables.

② The **CHILD TABLE** is also known as the "dimension" or "lookup table". This table type is used to look up an item that is being reported on. For example, when displaying orders, it is helpful to display customer information for the order. The customer information has to be looked up, as it is not stored in the Order table. Child tables usually have one row for each unique value in the parent table. Usually, only one field is used to make each row of data unique.

One exception that comes to mind is an order or sales detail table. This table contains one row for each item on each order. This means that if one order contains five items, the detail table has five rows for the order. Each of the five rows, in the detail table, have the same Order ID number. The table also often has another field that has a unique value for each row in the detail table. This field is not the field that is linked on.

CREATING PIVOT TABLES

 Overview

In addition to learning how to create pivot tables, you will learn about the following:

☑ Pivot Table Tools contextual tabs options
☑ Pivot Table Options dialog box
☑ Field Settings dialog box
☑ Basic pivot table and pivot chart layout options
☑ Top N pivot tables

CHAPTER 10

Overview

This chapter covers how to create pivot tables, as well as, how to use the Pivot Table Fields list. While the focus of this chapter is on creating pivot tables, there will be some mention of pivot charts. The reason is to keep from presenting the same information again in Chapter 11, which covers pivot charts.

The Pivot Table Tools contextual tabs options that are part of Excel are also covered because the options on these tabs can be used to enhance the pivot tables that are created using tables in the data model.

Getting Started With Pivot Tables And Pivot Charts

I have taught beginner and intermediate college level Excel classes and noticed that little to no time in the curriculum, was devoted to learning about pivot tables and pivot charts, even though they are very popular tools that are used in the workplace. Because I wrote this book primarily for people that do not have a lot of experience creating pivot tables and pivot charts, I feel that the more information that I can provide, the better you will be able to create pivot tables and pivot charts with ease.

The purpose of pivot tables is to analyze numeric data, primarily in a summarized format. By summarized format, I mean that there are usually not a lot of detail records in a pivot table. It is very common to see reports that have detail records and summary data in paper based reports. If this is the type of report that you are use to, think of it this way. The data displayed in Power Pivot is the detail report and the pivot table (in the Excel window) that you create, is the summary report that is based on the detail report in the Power Pivot window. Pivot tables are also used to answer "What-If" scenario questions.

Pivot tables and pivot charts that use tables in the data model are great business intelligence tools because they allow large amounts of data to be summarized and analyzed easily. There are eight layouts for pivot tables and pivot charts that you can select from. Many of these layout configurations are similar. If you understand how the three basic layouts (One pivot table, one pivot chart and flattened pivot table) work, you should not have a problem using the other layouts. These three layouts are discussed later in this chapter.

How Pivot Tables Are Created

Pivot tables are used to summarize rows of (detail) data. Pivot tables are often used for comparison analysis. Pivot tables retrieve data that meets specific criteria. Examples of reports that can be created with pivot tables are:

① Sales by sales rep, by year.
② Sales by region.
③ Summarizing the number of orders, by year and by zip code, that each sales rep has.
④ Summarizing how many customers by region, purchased certain products, by month or by year.

Pivot tables often give new report designers difficulty. I suspect that this is because this type of report requires one to think in dimensions. If you have seen, used or created a **CROSS TAB REPORT**, or worked with data stored in a **CUBE**, you will see that overall, the thought process of creating a pivot table is the same as creating a cross tab report or using data stored in a cube. Like spreadsheets, pivot tables have rows and columns. Each cell in a spreadsheet contains one piece of data. In a pivot table, the cell contains one piece of summary data (count, sum, average etc.) that is the equivalent of the sub totals for each group of data in a spreadsheet.

Behind the scenes, pivot tables take the detail records that you are use to seeing in a spreadsheet, and summarizes the data and places the result in a cell. Hopefully, the following scenario will make the concept of creating pivot tables easier to understand.

Going From Spreadsheets To Pivot Tables

This scenario will use the first pivot table example mentioned above; Sales by sales rep, by year. The goal of this pivot table from a spreadsheet perspective, is to show sales for a year, for each sales rep.

The spreadsheet shown in Figure 10-1 is a basic spreadsheet list report that sorts the sales by sales rep and by year. It contains all of the data one would need to determine sales for each sales rep, by year. Because there aren't any totals for the groups (in this case, the groups are the sales rep and year), it would take a while to manually do the math, especially if there were hundreds of sales reps.

Sales By Rep By Year

Last Name	First Name	Order Date	Order Amount	Customer Name
Davolio	Nancy	02/19/2010	$789.51	Belgium Bike Co.
Davolio	Nancy	02/19/2010	$58.00	Spokes for Folks
Davolio	Nancy	02/26/2010	$68.90	Mountain Madmen Bicycles
Davolio	Nancy	02/27/2010	$1,529.70	Cycle City Rome
Davolio	Nancy	02/27/2010	$1,079.70	Mountain Madmen Bicycles
Davolio	Nancy	02/27/2010	$2,698.53	Pedals Inc.
Davolio	Nancy	12/02/2010	$41.90	City Cyclists

Last Name	First Name	Order Date	Order Amount	Customer Name
Suyama	Michael	02/06/2012	$5,879.70	Biking's It Industries
Suyama	Michael	02/08/2012	$863.74	Alley Cat Cycles
Suyama	Michael	02/09/2012	$5,219.55	Spokes
Suyama	Michael	02/10/2012	$659.70	Psycho-Cycle
Suyama	Michael	02/11/2012	$32.21	Whistler Rentals

Figure 10-1 Basic sorted list in Excel of sales by sales rep, by year

Yes, I know what you are thinking, group the data by sales rep and year, then create the totals.

Figure 10-2 shows that report.

Can you tell how many customers Nancy Davollo sold to in total? Or can you tell me who had the lowest number of sales in 2010?

Like the report shown in Figure 10-1, the report in Figure 10-2 has all of the raw data that you need to answer these questions.

Sales By Rep By Year

Last Name	First Name	Order Date	Order Amount	Customer Name
Nancy Davolio				
2010				
Davolio	Nancy	02/19/2010	$58.00	Spokes for Folks
Davolio	Nancy	02/19/2010	$789.51	Belgium Bike Co.
Davolio	Nancy	02/26/2010	$68.90	Mountain Madmen Bicycles
Davolio	Nancy	02/27/2010	$1,529.70	Cycle City Rome
Davolio	Nancy	02/27/2010	$2,698.53	Pedals Inc.
Davolio	Nancy	02/27/2010	$1,079.70	Mountain Madmen Bicycles
Davolio	Nancy	12/02/2010	$41.90	City Cyclists
Davolio	Nancy	05/02/2012	$1,082.50	Warsaw Sports, Inc.
			$138,028.42	
			$660,756.95	
Janet Leverling				
2010				
Leverling	Janet	02/21/2010	$5,219.55	Tienda de Bicicletas El Pard
Leverling	Janet	02/21/2010	$8,819.55	Bikes, Bikes, and More Bike
Leverling	Janet	02/25/2010	$2,246.25	Folk och fä HB
Leverling	Janet	02/26/2010	$61.35	Bike Shop from Mars
Leverling	Janet	02/26/2010	$267.76	Hooked on Helmets

Figure 10-2 Data grouped by sales rep and by year

The problem is that the data is spread out in the spreadsheet which makes it difficult for comparison analysis. As you will see after completing the exercises in this chapter, this same data in a pivot table will be in an easy to read format. With a pivot table, you can quickly answer questions like the ones listed above.

How To Create The Report Shown Above In Figure 10-1 As A Pivot Table

Yes, I hear you grumbling and saying, "Great, I now see the advantages of creating a pivot table, but how do I get the data shown earlier in Figure 10-1 into pivot table format?" Okay, here goes:

① Usually, the field down the left side of a pivot table (that creates the rows) is the data element that there are more occurrences of. In this example, there are more sales reps then years. You can put the sales reps across the top of the pivot table and still get the same results, but you would probably find it a little awkward to read.

② The field that goes across the top (that creates the columns) represents the data element that there are less occurrences of. In this example, that would be the years.

③ The cells in the middle of the pivot table are the sum of order amounts that the sales rep had for each year. This is the equivalent to grouping and sorting data. This is how multiple rows of data in a spreadsheet are summarized in a pivot table. In this example, all of the order total amounts for one sales rep, for one year, are placed in one cell.

④ The totals at the bottom of the pivot table display the total amount of sales for each year, for all sales reps and a grand total of sales for the entire pivot table, in the cell in the lower right corner of the pivot table. These totals are automatically calculated in a pivot table. If you do not need these totals, you can remove them.

⑤ I have saved the best for last; the placement of the fields on the Pivot Table Fields list. The fields for the rows and columns were answered above. That leaves the field for the cells in the middle of the pivot table. Recall the original report criteria: Sales by sales rep, by year. You have already determined that the sales rep field, is what will be used to create the rows. You have also determined that the Order Year will be used to create the columns. The only field left is the sales (the order amount). This is the field that goes in the Values area of the Pivot Table Fields list. In this example, the cells represent a sum of order amounts.

The pivot table would look like the one shown in Figure 10-3.

Now you should be able to figure out which sales rep had the highest sales amount each year.

	2010	2011	2012	Total
Davolio	$71,862.70	$450,865.83	$138,028.42	$660,756.95
Dodsworth	$29,049.94	$513,545.52	$140,253.75	$682,849.21
King	$21,093.75	$512,406.60	$215,255.59	$748,755.94
Leverling	$44,121.64	$447,235.19	$157,745.16	$649,101.99
Peacock	$38,458.39	$446,150.56	$147,190.82	$631,799.77
Suyama	$54,804.22	$496,881.48	$158,715.78	$710,401.48
Total	$259,390.64	$2,867,085.18	$957,189.52	$4,083,665.34

Figure 10-3 Sales per year, per sales rep pivot table

What Is The Difference Between A Pivot Table And A Pivot Table Report?

A **PIVOT TABLE**, like the one shown above in Figure 10-3, provides static summary information, meaning that there are no options for the person using the pivot table to provide "What-If" scenarios. Basically, all you can do with a pivot table is look at the data that is presented in it.

A **PIVOT TABLE REPORT** is an interactive pivot table that includes any or all of the following: filters, slicers or timelines. When used, these tools cause the pivot table to display data based on the options that are selected. This is how you provide What-If analysis functionality. For example, you could add filters or slicers for the Product name and Ship to state fields to the pivot table shown above in Figure 10-3. That would let you select the specific products to display tools for, instead of displaying totals for all products. When referenced in this book, to keep things easy, I do not make a distinction between pivot tables and pivot table reports, except here, to explain what the difference is.

The Pivot Table Fields List

When you select the type of pivot table that you want to create, you will see the Create PivotTable dialog box. This is how you select where on the worksheet the pivot table will be placed.

Once the location is selected, which you can move if necessary, you will see the Pivot Table Fields list.

The top section shown in Figure 10-4, displays all of the tables and fields that are in the data model. This section is used to select and add the fields to the pivot table.

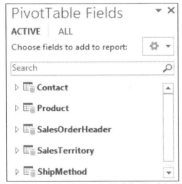

Figure 10-4 Pivot Table Fields list

Drop Zones

The options at the bottom of the Pivot Table Fields list are called **DROP ZONES**. Each of the zones shown in Figure 10-5, are also called **AREAS**, which is how I refer to them most of the time in this book. They are used to select where the fields are placed on the pivot table. These areas are explained in Table 10-1. Figure 10-6 illustrates where the drop zone areas are displayed on a pivot table.

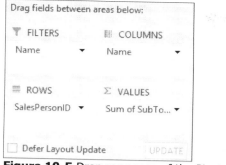

Figure 10-5 Drop zone area of the Pivot Table Fields list

Figure 10-6 Drop zone areas illustrated on a pivot table

Area	Fields Added To This Area Are . . .
Filters	Used to filter the data displayed in the pivot table. The filters are added to the worksheet, above the pivot table.
Columns	The headings that are placed across the top of the pivot table. The values are displayed as **COLUMN LABELS** on the pivot table. This list of values should be shorter then the list of values in the Rows area. (1)
Rows	Placed down the left side of the pivot table. The values are displayed as **ROW LABELS** on the pivot table. They are usually not calculated fields. Often, they are text fields. Fields placed in this area usually are the longer list of values that need to be displayed. (1)
Values	Numeric values the majority of the time. A Sum calculation is automatically created for fields that are added to this area. You can also create a field to place in this area by clicking the Measures button on the Power Pivot tab.

Table 10-1 Pivot Table Fields list area options explained

(1)   Fields added to this area can be nested.

General Guidelines For Adding Fields To A Drop Zone Area
① Text fields are usually added to the Rows area.
② Numeric fields are usually added to the Values area.
③ Date and Time fields are usually added to the Columns area.

Pivot Table Fields List Check Box Functionality
The check box next to each field in the top section of the Pivot Table Fields list is used to automatically add fields to an area based on the field type, as explained below.
① Numeric fields are added to the Values area with a Sum calculation.
② Text and date fields are added to the Rows area.

Pivot Table Tools Contextual Tabs

The tabs shown in Figures 10-7 and 10-13 are part of Excel, but they are available when a pivot table is selected, even if the pivot table was created using data in the data model. The options on these tabs are used to customize the appearance of pivot tables.

Analyze Tab

The dialog boxes that the **OPTIONS AND FIELD SETTINGS BUTTONS** shown in Figure 10-7 open, are helpful when modifying a pivot table. These options are explained below.

Figure 10-7 Analyze tab

Figure 10-7 Analyze tab (Continued)

Pivot Table Options Dialog Box

Clicking the **OPTIONS BUTTON**, in the Pivot Table group, shown above in Figure 10-7, opens the dialog box shown in Figure 10-8. The options on the first two tabs are used to change the layout, format, totals and filter options for the pivot table. As shown in Figure 10-9, grand totals are added by default to the pivot table. They can be removed. The way that filters change how the total amounts are calculated can also be changed.

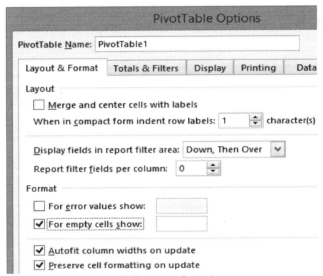

Figure 10-8 Layout & Format tab options

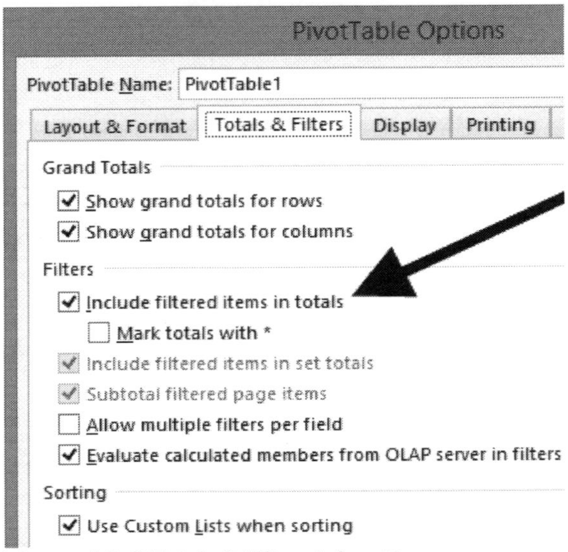

Figure 10-9 Totals & Filters tab options

Including Filtered Rows Of Data In Totals

Be default, when a pivot table uses a filter, like the Top 10 filter shown later in Figure 10-54, the totals displayed are only for the rows of data that are displayed. This is what you expect to happen.

If checked, the **INCLUDE FILTERED ITEMS IN TOTALS** option, illustrated above in Figure 10-9, will include rows of data that are filtered (not shown in the pivot table), in the total calculation field. For example, if the pivot table has a top 10 filter, the total fields only include values for the 10 rows of data displayed on the pivot table, not all of the rows that would be displayed if the filter was not applied.

If checked, the **MARK TOTALS WITH** * option, shown above in Figure 10-9, will display an asterisk next to the row and column heading to indicate that the total includes filtered rows of data. This option controls whether or not the asterisk is displayed, as illustrated in Figure 10-10.

If you need the totals to include data in the filtered rows, select the **INCLUDE FILTERED ITEMS IN TOTALS** option in one of the following places:

   ① On the Pivot Table Options dialog box, shown above in Figure 10-9.
   ② On the Pivot Table Tools Design tab, on the Subtotals button, shown later in Figure 10-14.

If this option is applied to the pivot table shown later in Figure 10-56, the grand totals would look like ones shown in Figure 10-10. Notice that even though the totals for each store are the same, the grand total amounts are different on these two figures.

Sum of SalesAmount	Column Labels			
Row Labels	2007	2008	2009	Grand Total *
Contoso Asia Online Store	$156,883,859.58	$188,427,344.54	$212,850,715.76	$558,161,919.88
Contoso Asia Reseller	$114,185,396.49	$122,563,956.44	$125,585,967.89	$362,335,320.82
Contoso Catalog Store	$273,924,905.90	$211,973,099.70	$210,006,950.16	$695,904,955.76
Contoso Europe Online Store	$167,679,516.43	$170,444,136.21	$175,239,722.44	$513,363,375.09
Contoso Europe Reseller	$122,337,430.46	$111,492,926.96	$104,077,933.71	$337,908,291.13
Contoso North America Online Store	$189,940,381.44	$208,983,212.70	$215,622,220.78	$614,545,814.92
Contoso North America Reseller	$139,379,974.11	$135,938,379.30	$128,986,735.50	$404,305,088.91
Contoso Sydney No.2 Store	$8,306,886.65	$8,920,073.26	$9,487,219.85	$26,714,179.76
Contoso Sydney No.1 Store	$7,694,245.94	$9,125,764.60	$9,830,374.39	$26,650,384.93
Contoso Taipei Store	$7,728,609.19	$9,090,492.56	$9,621,821.55	$26,440,923.31
Grand Total *	$3,144,393,292.13	$2,642,413,217.03	$2,554,417,855.67	$8,341,224,364.83

Figure 10-10 Filtered rows included in grand totals

Field Settings Dialog Box

Clicking the **FIELD SETTINGS BUTTON,** in the Active Field group, shown earlier in Figure 10-7, opens the dialog box shown in Figure 10-11. The options on this dialog box are used to customize the field in the pivot table that was selected before this dialog box was opened. If you know that the pivot table will be printed, you may have the need to change the default options shown in Figure 10-12.

As shown later in Figure 10-38, there is another Field Settings dialog box. The tab shown is used to change the field name that is displayed on the pivot table and to select a different Sum function. The difference between the dialog boxes is that the one shown in Figure 10-38 is only for fields in the Values area.

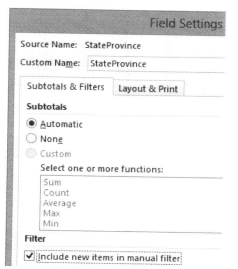

Figure 10-11 Subtotals & Filters tab options

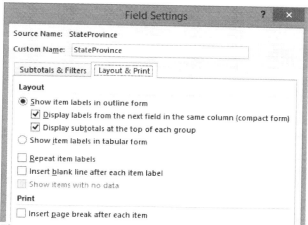

Figure 10-12 Layout & Print tab options

Design Tab

The options shown in Figure 10-13 are used to change the appearance of the pivot table. The options are explained in Table 10-2.

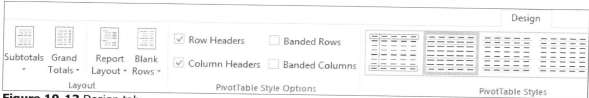

Figure 10-13 Design tab

Option	The Options . . .
Subtotals	Shown in Figure 10-14 are used to show or hide sub totals on the pivot table. (2)
Grand Totals	Shown in Figure 10-15 are used to show or hide grand totals on the pivot table. (2)
Report Layout	Shown in Figure 10-16 are used to select a different layout for the pivot table. The **SHOW IN TABULAR FORM** option changes the layout shown in Figure 10-17 to the one shown in Figure 10-18. This option moves each field in the Rows area to its own column. After the move, the fields are still in the Rows area.
Blank Rows	Shown in Figure 10-19 are used to add blank rows to or remove blank rows from the pivot table. This is done to make the pivot table easier to read.
Pivot Table Style Options	In this section are used to format specific parts of the pivot table. For example, selecting the **BANDED ROWS** option will change the background color of every other row in the pivot table, as shown in Figure 10-20. Enabling this option may make it easier to read the data in a pivot table that has a lot of rows.
Pivot Table Styles	In this section are used to format the entire pivot table. If you hold the mouse pointer over the style options, you can see how it will look on your pivot table. You can also create your own style, by selecting the **NEW PIVOT TABLE STYLE** option on the drop-down list. The dialog box shown in Figure 10-21 displays the options to create your own style.

Table 10-2 Design tab options explained

(2)   If shown, you can also select where the total will be displayed.

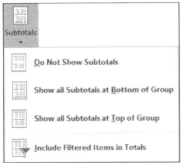

Figure 10-14 Subtotals options

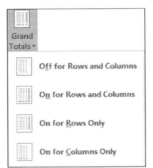

Figure 10-15 Grand Totals options

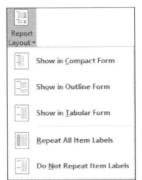

Figure 10-16 Report Layout options

Sum of SalesAmount	Column Labels			
Row Labels	2007	2008	2009	Grand Total
⊟Armenia	$7,940,032.42	$8,662,141.74	$9,482,761.09	$26,084,935.24
⊟Contoso Yerevan Store	$7,940,032.42	$8,662,141.74	$9,482,761.09	$26,084,935.24
⊟Audio	$52,884.99	$180,801.20	$250,527.25	$484,213.44
Bluetooth Headphones	$9,148.38	$40,768.11	$106,332.32	$156,248.81
MP4&MP3	$30,147.82	$68,799.40	$79,658.04	$178,605.26
Recording Pen	$13,588.79	$71,233.69	$64,536.90	$149,359.38
⊟Cameras and camcorders	$2,785,514.40	$2,727,453.28	$2,512,621.30	$8,025,588.97
Camcorders	$1,634,654.50	$1,581,742.35	$1,230,821.10	$4,447,217.95
Cameras & Camcorders Accessories	$24,799.73	$45,675.10	$109,827.31	$180,302.13

Figure 10-17 Pivot table without the Show in Tabular Form option applied

Sum of SalesAmount					CalendarYear			
RegionCountryName	StoreName	ProductCategory	ProductSubcategoryName		2007	2008	2009	Grand Total
⊟Armenia	⊟Contoso Yereva	⊟Audio	Bluetooth Headphones		$9,148.38	$40,768.11	$106,332.32	$156,248.81
			MP4&MP3		$30,147.82	$68,799.40	$79,658.04	$178,605.26
			Recording Pen		$13,588.79	$71,233.69	$64,536.90	$149,359.38
		Audio Total			$52,884.99	$180,801.20	$250,527.25	$484,213.44
		⊟Cameras and cam	Camcorders		$1,634,654.50	$1,581,742.35	$1,230,821.10	$4,447,217.95
			Cameras & Camcorders Accessories		$24,799.73	$45,675.10	$109,827.31	$180,302.13
			Digital Cameras		$392,388.91	$369,581.62	$346,682.82	$1,108,653.35
			Digital SLR Cameras		$733,671.26	$730,454.21	$825,290.08	$2,289,415.55

Figure 10-18 Pivot table with the Show in Tabular Form option applied

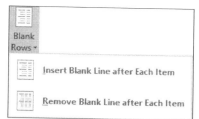

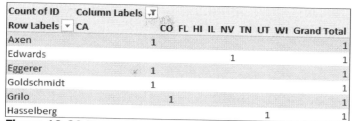

Figure 10-19 Blank Rows options

Figure 10-20 Pivot table with the Banded Rows option applied

Styles that you create will be displayed at the top of the Pivot Table Styles list in the Custom section.

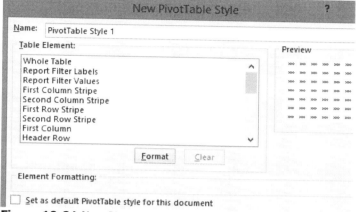

Figure 10-21 New Pivot Table Style dialog box

Basic Pivot Table And Pivot Chart Layout Options

The next three sections explain the basic pivot table and pivot chart layouts. For a review of the other layout options, see Chapter 3, Table 3-4.

One Pivot Table

Select this option when you need to create a pivot table without a pivot chart. The **PIVOT TABLE TOOLS** tabs discussed earlier in this chapter are available. This means that you can use the options on the Analyze and Design tabs, that you may already be familiar with, to enhance the pivot tables that you create. (3)

One Pivot Chart

Select this option when you need to create one pivot chart without a pivot table. Some of the drop zone areas are different then the ones for a pivot table. (3)

(3) Selecting this option does not mean that no more pivot tables or charts can be added to the worksheet. These options are just to get started.

Flattened Pivot Table

The Flattened Pivot Table option is only available for tables in a data model. The data values are not arranged as row and column headers. Instead, new columns are added to a pivot table and a Total row is added after each group.

Figure 10-22 shows a regular pivot table.

Figure 10-23 shows the same pivot table with the Flattened Pivot Table layout applied.

This option is often used when the pivot table needs to be printed.

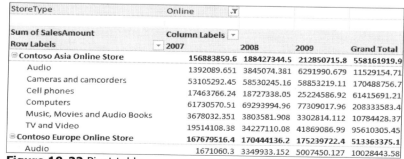

Figure 10-22 Pivot table

As shown in Figure 10-23, notice that some of the column headings are easier to understand in the Flattened pivot table and that each row displays the filter group name. To me, a flattened pivot table looks similar to a spreadsheet because of the repetition of data in columns.

You can see the features that a flattened pivot table has that a standard pivot table does not have. It would be great if there was a way to turn an existing pivot table into a flattened pivot table, if needed. The closet that I was able to get is to select the **SHOW ITEM LABELS IN TABULAR FORM** and **REPEAT ITEM LABELS** options on the Layout & Print tab, on the Field Settings dialog box, shown earlier in Figure 10-12.

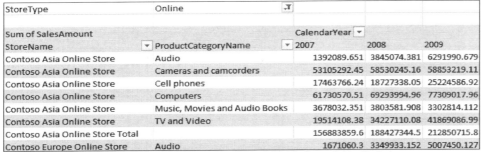

StoreType	Online			
Sum of SalesAmount		CalendarYear		
StoreName	ProductCategoryName	2007	2008	2009
Contoso Asia Online Store	Audio	1392089.651	3845074.381	6291990.679
Contoso Asia Online Store	Cameras and camcorders	53105292.45	58530245.16	58853219.11
Contoso Asia Online Store	Cell phones	17463766.24	18727338.05	25224586.92
Contoso Asia Online Store	Computers	61730570.51	69293994.96	77309017.96
Contoso Asia Online Store	Music, Movies and Audio Books	3678032.351	3803581.908	3302814.112
Contoso Asia Online Store	TV and Video	19514108.38	34227110.08	41869086.99
Contoso Asia Online Store Total		156883859.6	188427344.5	212850715.8
Contoso Europe Online Store	Audio	1671060.3	3349933.152	5007450.127

Figure 10-23 Pivot table with the Flattened Pivot Table layout applied

> **Pivot Table Creation Tips**
> ① There are two ways to create a pivot table: **Option 1** Power Pivot window ⇒ Home tab ⇒ Pivot Table button ⇒ Pivot Table. You will see the dialog box shown in Figure 10-24. **Option 2** Insert tab ⇒ Pivot Table button ⇒ Select the Use this workbook's Data Model option.
> ② Unless the exercise states otherwise, select the Existing Worksheet option. Do this after step 1, for the exercises in this chapter.
> ③ Fields can be added to a drop zone by dragging them there, from the Pivot Table Fields list.

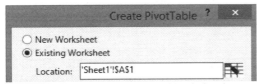

Figure 10-24 Create Pivot Table dialog box

Exercise 10.1: Use The Check Boxes To Create A Pivot Table

This exercise will show you how to create a basic pivot table by using the check boxes in the Pivot Table Fields list. The pivot table will display customers and their order subtotal amount.

1. Save the Customers workbook as E10.1 Use check boxes to create a pivot table.

2. Pivot Table Fields list ⇒ Orders table ⇒ Add the Ship Name field to the Rows area.

3. Order Subtotals table ⇒ Add the Subtotal field to the Values area. The drop zone area should look like the one shown in Figure 10-25. The pivot table should look like the one shown in Figure 10-26.

Figure 10-25 Drop zone area

	A	B
1	**Row Labels** ▼	**Sum of Subtotal**
2	Amritansh Raghav	$15,432.50
3	Anna Bedecs	$2,410.75
4	Christina Lee	$4,949.00
5	Elizabeth Andersen	$4,683.00
6		
7		
13	Run Liu	$3,625.25
14	Soo Jung Lee	$2,905.50
15	Sven Mortensen	$3,786.50
16	Thomas Axen	$2,550.00
17	**Grand Total**	**$68,137.00**

Figure 10-26 Order subtotal pivot table

Basic Sorting In A Pivot Table

By default, data is displayed in the order it is retrieved from the tables. This may or may not be what you need. The pivot table shown above in Figure 10-26 can be sorted on either column. Currently, the pivot table is sorted by the first letter of the first name in the first column.

Row Labels drop-down list ⇒ More Sort Options (illustrated in Figure 10-27), opens the Sort dialog box (shown in Figure 10-28). The options shown in Figure 10-28 are used to change or customize the sort order of the data displayed in the pivot table.

The **ASCENDING** and **DESCENDING** options can be used by any field displayed in the pivot table. Once one of these options is selected, you can select the field to sort the data by.

The options that you select are displayed in the **SUMMARY** section on the dialog box. This is helpful if you are not sure or want confirmation that you selected the options needed to display the data the way you need it.

The **MORE OPTIONS** button is covered later in this chapter. [See How To Change The Sort Order Of The Month Names]

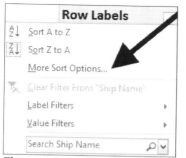

Figure 10-27 Row Labels filter options

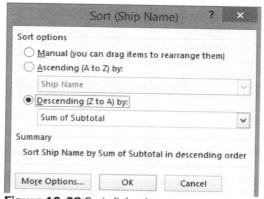

Figure 10-28 Sort dialog box

The pivot table shown earlier in Figure 10-26, may be more useful if the data is displayed in descending order by the Sum of Subtotal values.

Selecting the sort options shown above in Figure 10-28, changes the pivot table shown earlier in Figure 10-26, to the one shown in Figure 10-29.

Row Labels	Sum of Subtotal
Amritansh Raghav	$15,432.50
Ming-Yang Xie	$13,800.00
Francisco Pérez-Olaeta	$8,007.50
Christina Lee	$4,949.00
Elizabeth Andersen	$4,683.00
Sven Mortensen	$3,786.50
Run Liu	$3,625.25
Soo Jung Lee	$2,905.50
Thomas Axen	$2,550.00
Anna Bedecs	$2,410.75
Karen Toh	$1,505.00
Roland Wacker	$1,412.50
John Edwards	$1,190.00
Peter Krschne	$1,019.50
John Rodman	$860.00
Grand Total	**$68,137.00**

Figure 10-29 Pivot table sorted by the Sum of Subtotal values

Another Way To Sort The Values In A Pivot Table
Right-click on a cell in the column that you want to sort on ⇒ Sort ⇒ More Sort Options, as shown in Figure 10-30, displays the dialog box shown in Figure 10-31.

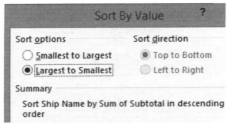

Figure 10-31 Sort By Value dialog box

Figure 10-30 Path to the Sort By Value dialog box

Exercise 10.2: Create A Customers By State Pivot Table

This exercise will show you how to create a pivot table that displays a count of customers per state. You will also add a filter that will be used to select the order dates to filter the pivot table by.

Select The Pivot Table Layout

1. Save the Customers and Orders workbook as E10.2 Customers by state pivot table.

2. Click the button at the end of the Location field ⇒ Click in cell B3. You should see this cell in the dialog box shown in Figure 10-32, if you used the Pivot Table option in the Power Pivot window.

   If you used the Pivot Table button in Excel, you will see the Create Pivot Table dialog box.

Figure 10-32 Range Selection dialog box

Select The Fields For The Pivot Table

In this part of the exercise you will select the fields for the Columns, Rows and Filters areas.

1. Display the fields in the Customers table, in the Pivot Table Fields list.

   Right-click on the Customer Full Name field (it's at the bottom of the list) and select Add to Row Labels, on the shortcut menu shown in Figure 10-33. The options on this shortcut menu are explained in Table 10-3.

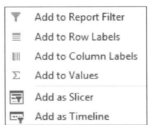

Figure 10-33 Pivot Table Fields list shortcut menu for fields

2. Customers table ⇒ Add the State Province field to the Columns area.

3. Orders table ⇒ Add the Order Date field to the Filters area.

Pivot Table Fields List Shortcut Menu For Measures

Figure 10-34 shows the additional options on the shortcut menu when a measure field is selected.

Having these options here, keeps you from having to use the Manage Measures dialog box to edit or delete a measure. [See Chapter 3, Measure Options]

The measure options are explained in Table 10-3.

Figure 10-34 Pivot Table Fields list shortcut menu for measures

Option	Description
Add to Report Filter	Adds the field to the Filters area. (4)
Add to Row Labels	Adds the field to the Rows area. (4)
Add to Column Labels	Adds the field to the Columns area. (4)
Add to Values	Adds the field to the Values area.
Add as Slicer	[See Chapter 12, Slicers] (4)
Add as Timeline	[See Chapter 15, Timelines] (4)
Edit Measure	Opens the Measure dialog box to modify the formula. (5)
Delete Measure	Deletes the selected measure. (5)

Table 10-3 Pivot Table Fields list shortcut menu options explained

(4)   This option is not available for a measure.
(5)   This option is only available for a measure.

Add A Field To The Values Area

In Chapter 3, implicit measures were covered. The reason that I am showing you how to use them is because this book does not cover creating calculations or writing DAX formulas. What may not be obvious is that an **IMPLICIT MEASURE** is created for each field that is added to the Values area.

These formulas cannot be modified. Like KPI's, they are placed in the **CALCULATION AREA** in Power Pivot. You can change the name of the measure and how the data is formatted, but that's about it. When you learn how to create measures, you should create them and add them to the Values area instead of using implicit measures.

If you viewed the calculation area for the Customers table now, you would not see the implicit measures shown in Figure 10-35. After you complete this exercise, view the calculation area and you will see the implicit measures below the Customer ID column. If you don't see them, click the **SHOW IMPLICIT MEASURES** button on the Advanced tab.

Figure 10-35 Implicit measures for the Customer ID column

In this part of the exercise, you will add the fields that will be summarized to the Values area. The goal is to get a count of customers by state. This means that you need to select a customer field that has a unique value for each customer.

1.   Customers table ⇒ Add the Customer ID field to the Values area.

If you look at the pivot table shown in Figure 10-36, the values in each state column are not a count, they are the actual Customer ID number. In cell B3, you will see the Values field (Sum of Customer ID) and how it is summarized. To get a count, the Customer ID field in the Values area needs to be changed to Count. Remember that the default aggregation is Sum. If you find that the majority of totals that you create is something other then Sum, you can change the default aggregation to the one that you use most.

	A	B	C	D E F G H I J K L M N O P Q	R
1		Order Date	All		
2					
3		Sum of Customer ID	Column Labels		
4		Row Labels	CA	CO FL HI ID IL MA MN NV NY OR TN UT WA WI	Grand Total
5		Alexander Eggerer	19		19
6		Amritansh Raghav		28	28
7		Andre Ludick		13	13
8		Anna Bedecs		1	1
9		Antonio Gratacos Solsona		2	2
10		Bernard Tham		21	21

Figure 10-36 Pivot table with incorrect values

2.   In the Pivot Table Fields list, click on the Sum of Customer ID field in the Values area. You will see the shortcut menu shown in Figure 10-38 ⇒ Select the **VALUE FIELD SETTINGS** option. The options on the drop-down list are explained in Table 10-4.

3.   On the Value Field Settings dialog box, select the Count option. Your pivot table should look like the one shown in Figure 10-37. Compare the values in this pivot table to the values shown above in Figure 10-36.

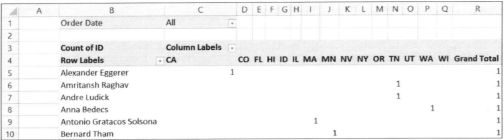

Figure 10-37 Customers by state pivot table

Pivot Table Fields Drop-Down List Options

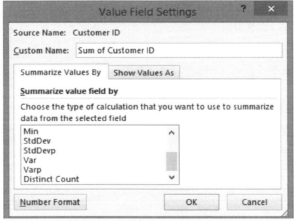

Figure 10-38 Pivot Table Fields drop-down list for the Values area

Option	Description
Move Up	Moves the selected field up one in the area that it is in.
Move Down	Moves the selected field down one in the area that it is in.
Move to Beginning	Moves the selected field to the top of the area that it is in.
Move to End	Moves the selected field to the bottom of the area that it is in.
Move to Report Filter	Moves the selected field to the Filters area.
Move to Row Labels	Moves the selected field to the Rows area.
Move to Column Labels	Moves the selected field to the Columns area.
Move to Values	Moves the selected field to the Values area.
Remove Field	Deletes the field from the area.
Value Field Settings	Opens the dialog box shown in Figure 10-39. This option is only available for the Values area.
Field Settings	Opens the dialog box shown earlier in Figure 10-11. This option is available for all areas except the Values area.

Table 10-4 Pivot Table Fields drop-down list Values area options explained

Value Field Settings Dialog Box

The options on the Summarize Values By tab, shown in Figure 10-39, are used to select how the field is calculated. The options on this dialog box are used to customize the fields in the Values area on the Pivot Table Fields list.

The **DISTINCT COUNT** calculation option, shown in Figure 10-39, creates a count of unique values in the column.

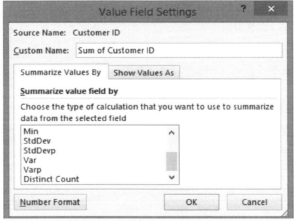

Figure 10-39 Value Field Settings dialog box

 Number Format Button
Clicking the Number Format button, on the Value Field Settings dialog box, shown above in Figure 10-39, opens the Format Cells dialog box. This is the same as selecting the **FORMAT CELLS** option, when you right-click on a cell in the pivot table. Selecting the **NUMBER FORMAT** option on the right-click shortcut menu of a numeric cell, also opens the Format Cells dialog box.

Exercise 10.3: Create A Yearly Sales By Country Pivot Table

This exercise will show you how to create a pivot table that displays the yearly sales for each country.

1. Save the E9.2 workbook as `E10.3 Yearly sales by country pivot table`.

. . . .

2. DimChannel table ⇒ Add the Channel Name field to the Filters area.

3. DimDate table ⇒ Add the Calendar Year field to the Columns area.

4. FactSales table ⇒ Add the Sales Amount field to the Values area. The pivot table should look like the one shown in Figure 10-40.

ChannelName	All ▾			
	Column Labels ▾			
	2007	2008	2009	Grand Total
Sum of SalesAmount	$3,144,393,292.13	$2,642,413,217.03	$2,554,417,855.67	$8,341,224,364.83

Figure 10-40 Yearly sales by country pivot table

5. Add the fields in Table 10-5 to the Rows area. After each field is added, the structure of the pivot table will change, as indicated by the figures in the last column in the table. I included a screen shot after each field was added, so that it would be easier for you to know what each field adds to the pivot table. Figure 10-41 shows the bottom of the Pivot Table Fields list after all of the fields have been added to the Rows area.

Table	Field	See . . .
DimGeography	Region Country Name	Figure 10-42
Stores	Store Name	Figure 10-43
DimProductCategory	Product Category Name	Figure 10-44
DimProductSubcategory	Product Subcategory Name	Figure 10-45

Table 10-5 Fields to add to the Rows area

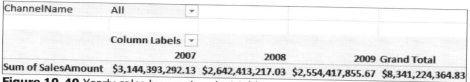

Figure 10-41 Drop zone area of the Pivot Table Fields list

	A	B	C	D	E
3	Sum of SalesAmount	Column Labels ▾			
4	Row Labels ▾	2007	2008	2009	Grand Total
5	Armenia	$7,940,032.42	$8,662,141.74	$9,482,761.09	$26,084,935.24
6	Australia	$23,168,631.98	$26,881,924.55	$29,116,033.12	$79,166,589.65
7	Bhutan	$7,837,852.03	$8,628,060.29	$13,570,713.85	$30,036,626.16
8	Canada	$77,067,627.45	$53,160,435.69	$45,714,689.59	$175,942,752.73
9	China	$308,391,585.32	$358,389,358.09	$397,075,325.59	$1,063,856,269.00

Figure 10-42 Region Country Name field added to the Rows area

	A	B	C	D	E
3	Sum of SalesAmount	Column Labels ▾			
4	Row Labels ▾	2007	2008	2009	Grand Total
5	⊟ Armenia	$7,940,032.42	$8,662,141.74	$9,482,761.09	$26,084,935.24
6	Contoso Yerevan Store	$7,940,032.42	$8,662,141.74	$9,482,761.09	$26,084,935.24
7	⊟ Australia	$23,168,631.98	$26,881,924.55	$29,116,033.12	$79,166,589.65
8	Contoso Canberra Store	$7,167,499.39	$8,836,086.69	$9,798,438.88	$25,802,024.96
9	Contoso Sydney No.2 Store	$8,306,886.65	$8,920,073.26	$9,487,219.85	$26,714,179.76
10	Contoso Sydney No.1 Store	$7,694,245.94	$9,125,764.60	$9,830,374.39	$26,650,384.93
11	⊟ Bhutan	$7,837,852.03	$8,628,060.29	$13,570,713.85	$30,036,626.16
12	Contoso Thimphu No.1 Store	$364,257.49		$4,575,478.11	$4,939,735.60
13	Contoso Thimphu No.2 Store	$7,473,594.54	$8,628,060.29	$8,995,235.73	$25,096,890.56

Figure 10-43 Store Name field added to the Rows area

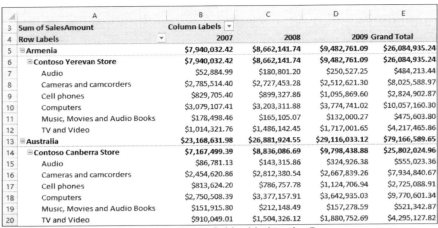

	A	B	C	D	E
3	Sum of SalesAmount	Column Labels ▼			
4	Row Labels ▼	2007	2008	2009	Grand Total
5	⊟ Armenia	$7,940,032.42	$8,662,141.74	$9,482,761.09	$26,084,935.24
6	⊟ Contoso Yerevan Store	$7,940,032.42	$8,662,141.74	$9,482,761.09	$26,084,935.24
7	Audio	$52,884.99	$180,801.20	$250,527.25	$484,213.44
8	Cameras and camcorders	$2,785,514.40	$2,727,453.28	$2,512,621.30	$8,025,588.97
9	Cell phones	$829,705.40	$899,327.86	$1,095,869.60	$2,824,902.87
10	Computers	$3,079,107.41	$3,203,311.88	$3,774,741.02	$10,057,160.30
11	Music, Movies and Audio Books	$178,498.46	$165,105.07	$132,000.27	$475,603.80
12	TV and Video	$1,014,321.76	$1,486,142.45	$1,717,001.65	$4,217,465.86
13	⊟ Australia	$23,168,631.98	$26,881,924.55	$29,116,033.12	$79,166,589.65
14	⊟ Contoso Canberra Store	$7,167,499.39	$8,836,086.69	$9,798,438.88	$25,802,024.96
15	Audio	$86,781.13	$143,315.86	$324,926.38	$555,023.36
16	Cameras and camcorders	$2,454,620.86	$2,812,380.54	$2,667,839.26	$7,934,840.67
17	Cell phones	$813,624.20	$786,757.78	$1,124,706.94	$2,725,088.91
18	Computers	$2,750,508.39	$3,377,157.91	$3,642,935.03	$9,770,601.34
19	Music, Movies and Audio Books	$151,915.80	$212,148.49	$157,278.59	$521,342.87
20	TV and Video	$910,049.01	$1,504,326.12	$1,880,752.69	$4,295,127.82

Figure 10-44 Product Category Name field added to the Rows area

	A	B	C	D	E
3	Sum of SalesAmount	Column Labels ▼			
4	Row Labels ▼	2007	2008	2009	Grand Total
5	⊟ Armenia	$7,940,032.42	$8,662,141.74	$9,482,761.09	$26,084,935.24
6	⊟ Contoso Yerevan Store	$7,940,032.42	$8,662,141.74	$9,482,761.09	$26,084,935.24
7	⊟ Audio	$52,884.99	$180,801.20	$250,527.25	$484,213.44
8	Bluetooth Headphones	$9,148.38	$40,768.11	$106,332.32	$156,248.81
9	MP4&MP3	$30,147.82	$68,799.40	$79,658.04	$178,605.26
10	Recording Pen	$13,588.79	$71,233.69	$64,536.90	$149,359.38
11	⊟ Cameras and camcorders	$2,785,514.40	$2,727,453.28	$2,512,621.30	$8,025,588.97
12	Camcorders	$1,634,654.50	$1,581,742.35	$1,230,821.10	$4,447,217.95

Figure 10-45 Product Subcategory Name field added to the Rows area

Exercise 10.4: Create A Customer Orders By Year Pivot Table

This exercise will show you how to create a pivot table that displays customer orders by year. Three filters will also be added to the pivot table.

1. Save the Pivot Tables and Charts workbook as `E10.4 Customer orders by year`.

Renaming A Field
Changing the **ACTIVE FIELD** on the PivotTable Tools Analyze tab, will rename a field.

2. Add the fields in Table 10-6 to create the pivot table.

   When finished, the pivot table should look like the one shown in Figure 10-46.

Table	Field	Add To Area	Rename The Field To
SalesOrderHeader	Total Due	Values	
SalesTerritory	Name	Filters	Select A Territory
Product	Name	Filters	Select A Product
ShipMethod	Name	Filters	Shipping Method
SalesOrderHeader	Order Year	Columns	
Contact	Last Name	Rows	
Contact	First Name	Rows	

Table 10-6 Fields to create the pivot table

The three filter fields allow you to select specific values to display on the pivot table.

	A	B	C	D	E	F
1	SelectATerritory	All				
2	SelectAProduct	All				
3	ShippingMethod	All				
4						
5	Sum of TotalDue	Column Labels				
6	Row Labels		2001	2002	2003	2004 Grand Total
7	⊟Abel				$79,447.60	$73,054.25 $152,501.84
8	Catherine				$79,447.60	$73,054.25 $152,501.84
9	⊟Abercrombie		$111,519.11	$306,635.70	$200,671.01	$70,881.23 $689,707.05
10	Kim		$111,519.11	$306,635.70	$200,671.01	$70,881.23 $689,707.05
11	⊟Acevedo		$49,873.56	$40,573.31	$9,793.17	$1,251.60 $101,491.64
12	Humberto		$49,873.56	$40,573.31	$9,793.17	$1,251.60 $101,491.64
13	⊟Achong		$5,370.28	$88,472.30	$81,925.44	$175,768.02
14	Gustavo		$5,370.28	$88,472.30	$81,925.44	$175,768.02

Figure 10-46 Customer orders by year pivot table

Custom Lists

Custom lists are used to sort data. By default, Power Pivot sorts in alphabetical order because it does not know about the custom list functionality in Excel. Often, sorting in alphabetical order is just what you need. Other times, sorting alphabetically produces unexpected results, as you will see in Exercise 10.5. Excel provides custom lists and you can create your own custom list. If you are not familiar with custom lists, follow the steps below to view the lists that come with Excel.

1. File tab ⇒ Options ⇒ Advanced.

   You will see the options shown in Figure 10-47.

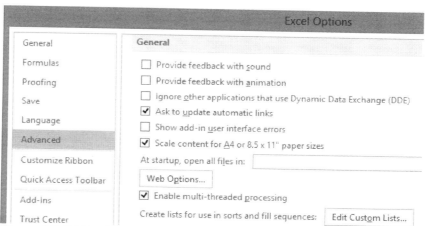

Figure 10-47 Excel Options dialog box

2. Scroll down to the bottom of the window ⇒ Click the **EDIT CUSTOM LISTS** button, shown above in Figure 10-47.

   You will see the dialog box shown in Figure 10-48.

   Click on a custom list to view all of its entries.

   As shown, a custom list exists that will sort the months in calendar month order.

   You will learn how to apply this custom list in Exercise 10.5.

Figure 10-48 Custom Lists dialog box

Exercise 10.5: Create A Customer Orders By Month And Year Pivot Table

The pivot table that you will create in this exercise is similar to the one that you created in Exercise 10.4. The difference is that the month names will be displayed in the left column, instead of the customers name. The Pivot Tables and Charts workbook has a formula that formats the Order Date field to display the full month name.

1. Save the E10.4 workbook as E10.5 Customer orders by month and year.

2. Delete both of the fields in the Rows area.

3. Add the field in Table 10-7 to modify the pivot table. The pivot table should look like the one shown in Figure 10-49. As you can see, the month names are not in the order that you are probably expecting.

I created this field because the data model did not have a dates table. On your own, it is more efficient to put date related fields in the date table.

Table	Field	Add To Area
SalesOrderHeader	OrderMonthFullName	Rows

Table 10-7 Field to add to the pivot table

	A	B	C	D	E	F
5	Sum of TotalDue	Column Labels				
6	Row Labels	2001	2002	2003	2004	Grand Total
7	April		$1,905,833.91	$3,041,865.44	$4,722,890.74	$9,670,590.09
8	August	$2,605,514.98	$5,433,609.34	$6,775,857.07		$14,814,981.40
9	December	$3,097,637.34	$3,545,522.74	$6,582,833.04		$13,225,993.12
10	February		$3,130,823.04	$3,705,635.50	$5,207,182.51	$12,043,641.05
11	January		$1,605,782.19	$2,233,575.11	$3,691,013.22	$7,530,370.53
12	July	$1,172,359.43	$3,781,879.07	$4,681,520.64	$56,178.92	$9,691,938.06
13	June		$2,546,121.96	$3,257,517.70	$6,728,034.99	$12,531,674.65
14	March		$2,643,081.08	$2,611,621.26	$5,272,786.81	$10,527,489.15
15	May		$3,758,329.29	$4,449,886.23	$6,518,825.23	$14,727,040.75
16	November	$3,690,018.67	$4,427,598.00	$5,961,182.68		$14,078,799.34
17	October	$1,688,963.27	$2,854,206.75	$4,243,366.59		$8,786,536.62
18	September	$2,073,058.54	$4,242,717.72	$6,762,753.81		$13,078,530.07
19	Grand Total	$14,327,552.23	$39,875,505.10	$54,307,615.09	$32,196,912.42	$140,707,584.82

Figure 10-49 Customer orders by month and year pivot table

How To Change The Sort Order Of The Month Names

As you can see above in Figure 10-49, the month names are displayed in alphabetical order. The data would be easier to read and understand if the month names were displayed in calendar month order. The steps below show you how to change the sort order of the month names.

1. In the pivot table, open the Row Labels filter drop-down list ⇒ Select **MORE SORT OPTIONS**.

2. Select the **ASCENDING (A TO Z) BY** option ⇒ Select the OrderMonthFullName field in the drop-down list, if necessary.

   You should have the options selected that are shown in Figure 10-50.

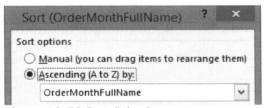

Sort (OrderMonthFullName)

Sort options
- ○ Manual (you can drag items to rearrange them)
- ● Ascending (A to Z) by:
  - OrderMonthFullName

Figure 10-50 Sort dialog box

3. Click the **MORE OPTIONS** button at the bottom of the Sort dialog box ⇒ Clear the check mark for the **SORT AUTOMATICALLY** option, at the top of the More Sort Options dialog box.

4. Open the **FIRST KEY SORT ORDER** field drop-down list and select the option with the month full names, as illustrated in Figure 10-51.

    Click OK twice to close both dialog boxes.

    The pivot table should look like the one shown in Figure 10-52, with the months displayed in calendar order.

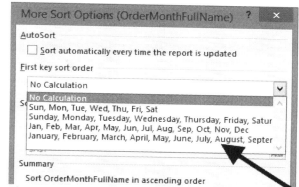

Figure 10-51 Sort order option illustrated

	A	B	C	D	E	F
5	Sum of TotalDue	Column Labels				
6	Row Labels	2001	2002	2003	2004	Grand Total
7	January		$1,605,782.19	$2,233,575.11	$3,691,013.22	$7,530,370.53
8	February		$3,130,823.04	$3,705,635.50	$5,207,182.51	$12,043,641.05
9	March		$2,643,081.08	$2,611,621.26	$5,272,786.81	$10,527,489.15
10	April		$1,905,833.91	$3,041,865.44	$4,722,890.74	$9,670,590.09
11	May		$3,758,329.29	$4,449,886.23	$6,518,825.23	$14,727,040.75
12	June		$2,546,121.96	$3,257,517.70	$6,728,034.99	$12,531,674.65
13	July	$1,172,359.43	$3,781,879.07	$4,681,520.64	$56,178.92	$9,691,938.06
14	August	$2,605,514.98	$5,433,609.34	$6,775,857.07		$14,814,981.40
15	September	$2,073,058.54	$4,242,717.72	$6,762,753.81		$13,078,530.07
16	October	$1,688,963.27	$2,854,206.75	$4,243,366.59		$8,786,536.62
17	November	$3,690,018.67	$4,427,598.00	$5,961,182.68		$14,078,799.34
18	December	$3,097,637.34	$3,545,522.74	$6,582,833.04		$13,225,993.12
19	Grand Total	$14,327,552.23	$39,875,505.10	$54,307,615.09	$32,196,912.42	$140,707,584.82

Figure 10-52 Months sorted in calendar order

Top N Reports

Top and Bottom N reports, commonly known as Top N reports, are used to display the first N or bottom N records in a group. N is a number that you select. Often, the number selected is 10. In previous exercises in this chapter, you created reports that grouped data. By default, the groups are sorted on the value in the group field. For example, in Exercise 10.4, the orders were grouped by year.

There is another way to sort groups. Just like you can filter detail records, groups can be filtered. One way to explain Top N reports is that this sort method is sorting the groups on the value of a group summary field, instead of the values in the group by field. Top N reports do not display all of the groups. They display the number of groups equal to the value of N. Top N reports rank the groups based on the summary field values. For example, if N=7, only the seven groups, with the largest value in the group summary field, would be displayed on the pivot table.

Exercise 10.6: Create A Top 10 Pivot Table

This exercise will show you how to create a Top 10 pivot table that will display the top 10 stores, based their yearly sales amounts.

1. Save the E10.3 workbook as `E10.6 Top 10 pivot table`.

2. Remove all of the fields in the Rows area, except for the Store Name field. You should see a list of stores, their sales amounts for three years and the grand total in the pivot table.

Select The Top 10 Options

1. Open the Row Labels drop-down list in cell A4.

2. Select the Value Filters option ⇒ Select **TOP 10**, as illustrated in Figure 10-53.

    You will see the dialog box shown in Figure 10-54.

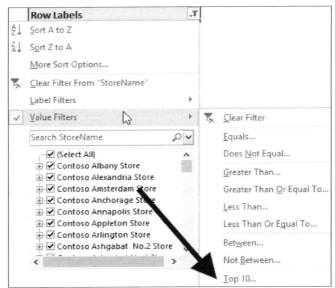

Figure 10-53 Value Filters Top 10 option selected

Top 10 Filter Dialog Box

The options on the Top 10 Filter dialog box are used to select a specific number of rows (the N value) to display in the pivot table. The options are explained in Table 10-8.

Figure 10-54 Top 10 Filter dialog box

Option	Description
Show	Is used to select and display the top (the highest or largest) values or the bottom (the lowest or smallest) values in the field.
Spinner button	Is used to select how many of the N value (the number of items, the percent or sum) to display in the pivot table. Click the Up or Down arrow button at the end of the field to select the number that you want. (6)
Third field	The options in this drop-down list are used to select how you want to filter the data to get the rows of data to display. The **ITEMS** option is used with the spinner button. It only allows a specific number of rows to be displayed in the pivot table. The **PERCENT** option retrieves enough rows to equal the percent that you select. The **SUM** option is used for What-If analysis. It is used to find out how many of something is needed to get to a certain amount. (6)
Fourth field	Displays a list of the fields in the Values area, as shown in Figure 10-55. Select the value that will be used to rank the rows of data that will be retrieved. (6)

Table 10-8 Top 10 Filter dialog box options explained

(6) I could not find an official name for this field.

Figure 10-55 Fourth field (from Values area) options

3. For this exercise, accept the default options shown earlier in Figure 10-54 ⇒ Click OK. The pivot table should look like the one shown in Figure 10-56. This Top 10 pivot table is based on three years of sales data. Notice that there are only 10 rows of data displayed.

	A	B	C	D	E
3	**Sum of SalesAmount**	**Column Labels**			
4	**Row Labels**	**2007**	**2008**	**2009**	**Grand Total**
5	Contoso Asia Online Store	$156,883,859.58	$188,427,344.54	$212,850,715.76	$558,161,919.88
6	Contoso Asia Reseller	$114,185,396.49	$122,563,956.44	$125,585,967.89	$362,335,320.82
7	Contoso Catalog Store	$273,924,905.90	$211,973,099.70	$210,006,950.16	$695,904,955.76
8	Contoso Europe Online Store	$167,679,516.43	$170,444,136.21	$175,239,722.44	$513,363,375.09
9	Contoso Europe Reseller	$122,337,430.46	$111,492,926.96	$104,077,933.71	$337,908,291.13
10	Contoso North America Online Store	$189,940,381.44	$208,983,212.70	$215,622,220.78	$614,545,814.92
11	Contoso North America Reseller	$139,379,974.11	$135,938,379.30	$128,986,735.50	$404,305,088.91
12	Contoso Sydney No.2 Store	$8,306,886.65	$8,920,073.26	$9,487,219.85	$26,714,179.76
13	Contoso Sydney No.1 Store	$7,694,245.94	$9,125,764.60	$9,830,374.39	$26,650,384.93
14	Contoso Taipei Store	$7,728,609.19	$9,090,492.56	$9,621,821.55	$26,440,923.31
15	**Grand Total**	**$1,188,061,206.20**	**$1,176,959,386.27**	**$1,201,309,662.04**	**$3,566,330,254.51**

Figure 10-56 Top 10 stores by sales amount

If you wanted to see the Top 10 stores, in terms of sales for a specific year, open the Column Labels drop-down list shown in Figure 10-57 and select the year that you want to see the Top 10 store sales for. If you select the year 2008, the pivot table would look like the one shown in Figure 10-58. In this scenario, it would be a good idea to remove the grand total column. The values are the same as the yearly values because only one year of data is displayed.

Figure 10-57 Column Labels filter options

Sum of SalesAmount	**Column Labels**	
Row Labels	**2008**	**Grand Total**
Contoso Asia Online Store	$188,427,344.54	$188,427,344.54
Contoso Asia Reseller	$122,563,956.44	$122,563,956.44
Contoso Catalog Store	$211,973,099.70	$211,973,099.70
Contoso Europe Online Store	$170,444,136.21	$170,444,136.21
Contoso Europe Reseller	$111,492,926.96	$111,492,926.96
Contoso Kolkata Store	$9,137,428.48	$9,137,428.48
Contoso North America Online Store	$208,983,212.70	$208,983,212.70
Contoso North America Reseller	$135,938,379.30	$135,938,379.30
Contoso Sydney No.1 Store	$9,125,764.60	$9,125,764.60
Contoso Tehran No.1 Store	$9,247,336.39	$9,247,336.39
Grand Total	**$1,177,333,585.31**	**$1,177,333,585.31**

Figure 10-58 Top 10 stores in 2008 pivot table

If you wanted to see the stores in the lowest 5% of sales, select the options shown in Figure 10-59, for the Row Labels. The options would display the pivot table shown in Figure 10-60.

Figure 10-59 Options to select the Bottom 5% of stores based on the sales amount

Sum of SalesAmount	**Column Labels**			
Row Labels	**2007**	**2008**	**2009**	**Grand Total**
Contoso Amsterdam Store	$7,526,105.22	$4,001,770.02	$3,336,812.99	$14,864,688.22
Contoso Bangkok No.1 Store	$786,515.33	$1,508,081.39	$8,118,519.53	$10,413,116.25
Contoso Beijing Store	$761,172.35	$4,187,640.57	$8,172,957.09	$13,121,770.00
Contoso Bellevue Store	$6,513,203.79	$4,814,163.12	$3,648,716.91	$14,976,083.83
Contoso Berlin Store	$218,948.21	$717,511.99	$2,603,316.82	$3,539,777.03
Contoso Berne Store	$7,424,788.95	$3,645,505.88	$3,478,647.52	$14,548,942.34
Contoso Carlisle Store	$7,231,510.75	$3,838,415.42	$3,684,384.63	$14,754,310.80

Figure 10-60 Bottom 5% of store sales pivot table

Summary

I suspect that this is your favorite chapter because you were able to see how all of the topics in the previous chapters come together. Learning how to create Top/Bottom N pivot tables and displaying month names in calendar order may have made going through all of the previous chapters worth it. Hopefully, this chapter did not disappoint.

I think you are starting to see why I think it is important to really understand the data in the tables. Exercise 10.5 modified an existing pivot table, which displayed the totals in a completely different way. This was done by deleting two fields and replacing it with one field. Once you get the hang of where each drop zone places the data, you will be able to take your pivot tables to another level.

The good thing is that if you are not sure how each field added to a drop zone will alter the pivot table, you can add the field and if it doesn't produce the result that you are looking for, you can move it to another drop zone or delete it.

Creating pivot charts is next.

CREATING PIVOT CHARTS

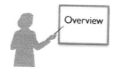

In addition to learning how to create pivot charts, you will also learn about the following:

- ☑ Pivot Chart Tools contextual tab options
- ☑ Pivot Chart Fields list options
- ☑ Pivot chart components
- ☑ Top N pivot charts
- ☑ Changing the pivot chart type

CHAPTER 11

What Is A Pivot Chart?

A pivot chart is a graphical representation of the data. This visual representation can make it easier to understand summarized data. Because of the various chart types, it is often easier to see trends and patterns in the data, in some chart types better then others, as well as, make comparisons in one chart type over another.

What Is A Pivot Chart Report?

A pivot chart report is like a pivot table report, because it has filters and slicers. Pivot charts can be interactive and display data the same way that standard charts do, because they can display data series, data markers and axis categories.

Pivot Chart Tools Contextual Tabs

Like pivot tables, there are tools in Excel specifically for pivot charts. Figures 11-2 and 11-3 show the pivot chart tools tabs. If you have created charts in Excel, you may have already used some of these options.

Analyze Tab

Figure 11-1 Analyze tab

Design Tab

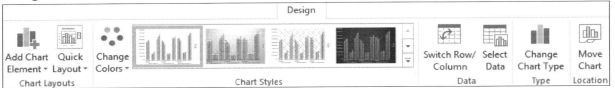

Figure 11-2 Design tab

Format Tab

Figure 11-3 Format tab

Pivot Chart Options That You May Find Helpful

Below are options that you may find helpful to enhance your pivot charts.

The **ADD CHART ELEMENT** option on the Design tab, displays the chart options shown in Figure 11-4. They are used to modify parts of the chart. The Data Labels options are used to display the actual value that the slice of a pie chart, a bar or line represents. Figure 11-5 shows the **OUTSIDE END** option applied to a chart.

The **DATA TABLE** options on the Add Chart Element button, shown in Figure 11-6, are used to add a table below the chart. The values displayed in the data table are the values displayed in the chart.

The **QUICK LAYOUT** options on the Design tab, shown in Figure 11-7, are used to rearrange chart objects, like the position and style of the legend and the grid style.

Figure 11-8 illustrates a pivot chart with a data table and legend keys below the chart. If the chart displays a lot of data, the **DATA TABLE WITH LEGEND KEYS** option can be used instead of placing the actual values on the chart, which may make the chart easy to read.

The **WALL** options are only available for 3D charts. Figure 11-9 shows a 3D bar chart without any background formatting. Right-clicking on a 3D chart displays the shortcut menu shown in Figure 11-10. Some options on the shortcut menu are explained later in Table 11-1. Selecting the **FORMAT WALLS** option, on the shortcut menu shown in Figure 11-10, displays the Format Walls fill pattern options, shown in Figure 11-11.

The **WALL** and **FLOOR** options shown in Figure 11-12 are used to add a solid color or **FILL PATTERN** color to the background of certain areas of a 3D chart. Figure 11-13 shows the chart with the chart walls fill pattern applied.

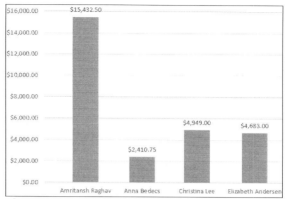

Figure 11-5 Outside End data labels option applied to a chart

Figure 11-4 Add Chart Element and Data Labels options

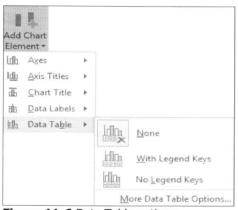

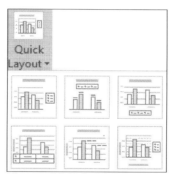

Figure 11-7 Quick Layout options

Figure 11-6 Data Table options

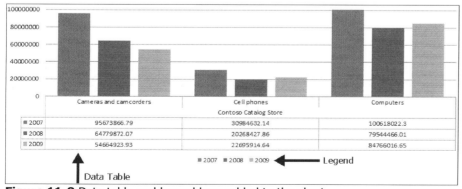

Figure 11-8 Data table and legend keys added to the chart

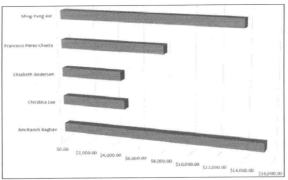

Figure 11-9 3D Bar chart

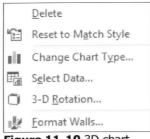

Figure 11-10 3D chart shortcut menu

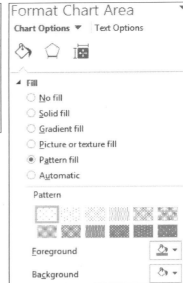

Figure 11-11 Pivot chart fill pattern options

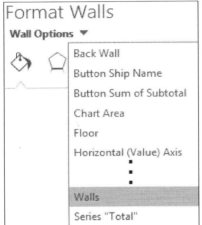

Figure 11-12 Format Walls options

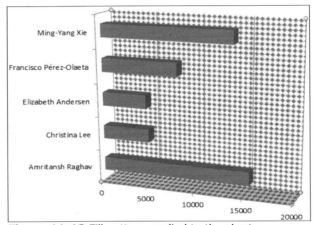

Figure 11-13 Fill pattern applied to the chart

Differences On The Fields List For Pivot Charts

Figure 11-14 shows the Pivot Chart Fields list.

The Rows and Columns areas on the Pivot Table Fields list, are not available for pivot charts.

Instead, pivot charts have the areas explained below. You can refer back to Chapter 10, Table 10-1 for an explanation of the areas that pivot tables and pivot charts have in common. Measures cannot be added to these areas.

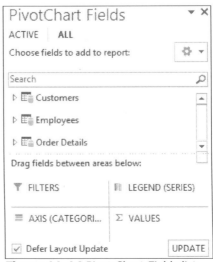

Figure 11-14 Pivot Chart Fields list

① **AXIS (CATEGORIES)** The fields placed in this area are displayed across the bottom of the chart. If a text field is checked at the top of the Pivot Chart Fields list, by default it is placed in this area. This area replaces the Rows area that pivot tables have.

② **LEGEND (SERIES)** The fields placed in this area are displayed vertically on the left side of the chart. If a text field is added to this area, each item becomes a new series in the chart. This area replaces the Columns area that pivot tables have. Like the Columns area, the Legend area can be used to filter the data.

Pivot Chart Components

Pivot charts have features that pivot tables do not have. These features are explained below.

① **DATA SERIES** are related points of data that are plotted on a chart. More than one data series can be plotted on a chart, except for pie charts. Each color on a chart represents a different series of data. For example, the chart shown in Figure 11-15 has three series of data. The easiest way to tell how many series of data a chart has is to count the number of items in the legend. The legend contains one entry for each series of data.

② A **LEGEND** displays the color of each data series on the chart.

③ **DATA MARKERS** are symbols that represent a single value on the chart. Data markers that are related, create a data series. Figure 11-46 shows a line chart that has markers.

④ A **DATA LABEL** provides more information about the data points on the chart. Usually, this is the value of the data point because it can be difficult to tell what the exact value of a data point is. The data label is the value above each column in the chart shown earlier in Figure 11-5.

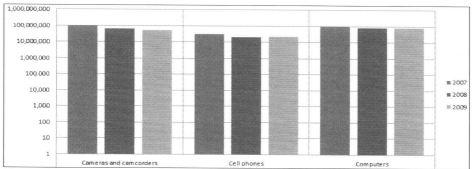

Figure 11-15 Data series

Pivot Chart Creation Tips
① There are two ways to create a pivot chart: **Option 1** Power Pivot window ⇒ Home tab ⇒ Pivot Table button ⇒ Pivot Chart. **Option 2** Insert tab ⇒ Pivot Chart button ⇒ Select the Use this workbook's Data Model option.
② Unless the exercise states otherwise, select the Existing Worksheet option. Do this after step 1, for the exercises in this chapter.
③ Fields can be added to a drop zone by dragging them there, from the Pivot Chart Fields list.

Exercise 11.1: Create A Customer Order Subtotal Pivot Chart

This exercise will show you how to create a pivot chart that displays customer order subtotal information.

1. Save the Customers workbook as `E11.1 Customer order subtotal pivot chart`.

2. Orders table ⇒ Add the Ship Name field to the Axis area.

3. Order Subtotals table ⇒
    Add the Subtotal field to the Values area.

    The bottom of the Pivot Chart Fields list should look like the one shown in Figure 11-16.

Figure 11-16 Pivot Chart Fields list drop zone area

The pivot chart should look like the one shown in Figure 11-17. This chart layout works because there are not a lot of customers. If there were thousands of customers, this pivot chart would need filters and/or slicers to reduce the number of customers displayed on the chart, to make it legible.

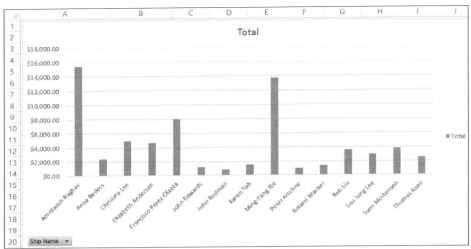

Figure 11-17 Pivot chart

Selecting fewer names in the Ship Name filter, in the pivot chart shown above in Figure 11-17, would cause the chart to look like the one shown in Figure 11-18.

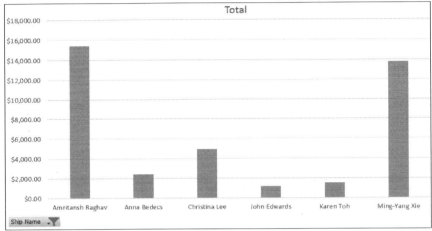

Figure 11-18 Fewer ship names selected

If the Employee ID field (in the Orders table) was added to the Filters area, sales reps could be selected to only display orders for specific sales reps.

Selecting the Employee ID filter options shown in the upper left corner of Figure 11-19 would display the chart shown in the figure.

If the Employee ID field was moved to the Legend area, the pivot chart would look like the one shown in Figure 11-20.

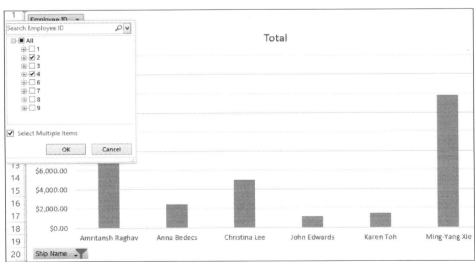

Figure 11-19 (Report) Filter added to the pivot chart

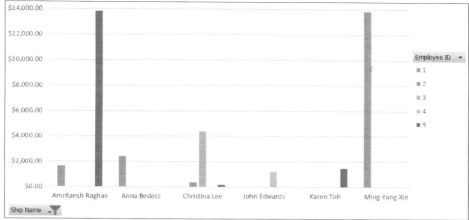

Figure 11-20 Employee ID field added to the Legend

Chart Button Options

To the right of the pivot chart, you should see the buttons shown in Figure 11-21. They provide shortcuts for options on the Pivot Chart Tools tabs.

Clicking the **PLUS SIGN** button displays the options shown in Figure 11-22. The options are used to add or remove elements on the chart. Selecting a chart element displays options that you can customize for the chart, as shown on the right side of Figure 11-22.

Figure 11-21 Chart shortcut buttons

Clicking the **PAINT BRUSH** button displays the chart style and color options shown in Figure 11-23.

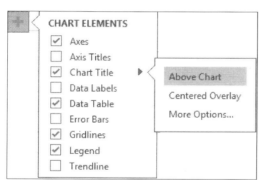

Figure 11-22 Chart Elements options

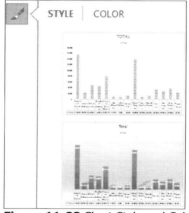

Figure 11-23 Chart Style and Color options

Pivot Chart Shortcut Menus

Right-clicking on a blank space (outside of the plot area) on the pivot chart displays some of the formatting options shown at the top of Figure 11-24 and the shortcut menu below the formatting options.

Some of the options on the shortcut menu are explained in Table 11-1.

Right-clicking in the plot area of the chart displays the shortcut menu shown in Figure 11-25.

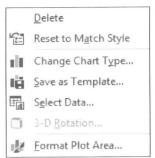

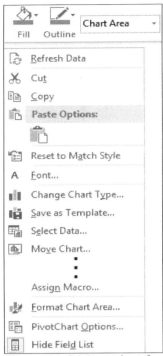

Figure 11-25 Plot area shortcut menu

Figure 11-24 Pivot chart formatting options and shortcut menu

Option	Description
Refresh Data	Refreshes the data used in the pivot chart.
Reset to Match Style	Select this option to remove the custom formatting that you applied to the pivot chart and restore the original style.
Change Chart Type	[See Change Chart Type Dialog Box]
Select Data	Opens the dialog box shown in Figure 11-26. The options are used to add, change or rename a data series.
Move Chart	Opens the dialog box shown in Figure 11-28. The options are used to move the pivot chart to an existing or new sheet in the workbook.
Assign Macro	Opens the dialog box shown in Figure 11-29. You can create a new macro to add to the worksheet or select an existing macro to apply to the worksheet.
Format Chart Area	Displays the panel shown earlier in Figure 11-11.
Pivot Chart Options	Opens the Options dialog box, which has the same functionality as the **PIVOT TABLE OPTIONS** dialog box, that was covered in Chapter 10.
Hide Field List	Hides the Pivot Chart Fields list.

Table 11-1 Pivot chart shortcut menu options explained

Clicking the **SWITCH ROW/COLUMN** button changes the pivot chart shown earlier in Figure 11-17 to the one shown in Figure 11-27.

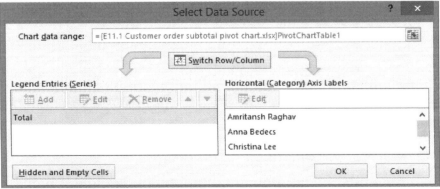

Figure 11-26 Select Data Source dialog box

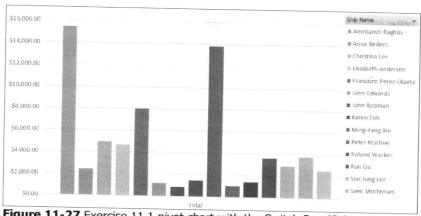

Figure 11-27 Exercise 11.1 pivot chart with the Switch Row/Column option applied

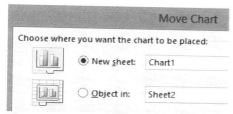

Figure 11-28 Move Chart dialog box

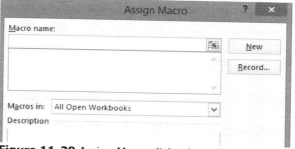

Figure 11-29 Assign Macro dialog box

Exercise 11.2: Create A Customers By State Pivot Chart

This exercise will show you how to create a pivot chart that displays a count of customers per state. You will also add a filter that will be used to select the order dates to filter the pivot chart by.

Select The Fields For The Pivot Chart

In this part of the exercise you will select the fields for the Legend, Axis and Filter areas.

1. Save the Customers and Orders workbook as `E11.2 Customers by state pivot chart`.

2. Click in cell B3 ⇒ Add a pivot chart to the worksheet. Doing this will cause the upper left most column of the chart to start in this cell. Selecting a cell using the Pivot Chart button in Excel did not start the chart in cell B3 for me, but you can drag the place holder to where you want the chart to be located.

3. Customers table ⇒
    Right-click on the Customer Full Name field ⇒
    Select Add to Axis Fields, as shown in Figure 11-30.

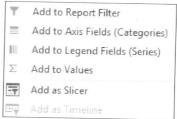

Figure 11-30 Pivot Chart Fields list shortcut menu

4. Customers table ⇒ Add the State Province field to the Legend area.

Add A Field To The Values Area

In this part of the exercise you will add the fields that will be summarized, to the Values area. The goal is to get a count of customers for each state. That means that you need to select a field that has a unique value for each customer.

1. Customers table ⇒ Add the Customer ID field to the Values area.

2. Click on the Sum of Customer ID field in the Values area.

   You will see the drop-down list shown in Figure 11-31. Select the Value Field Settings option.

   Change the **SUMMARIZE VALUES FIELD BY** option to Count.

   The majority of options on this drop-down list were explained in Chapter 10, Table 10-4.

   The remaining options are explained in Table 11-2.

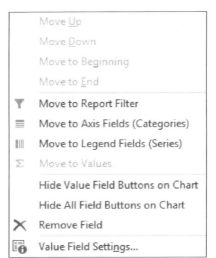

Figure 11-31 Values field drop-down list

Values Field Drop-Down List Options

Option	Description
Move to Axis Fields (Categories)	Moves the selected field to the Axis area.
Move to Legend Fields (Series)	Moves the selected field to the Legend area.
Hide Value Field Buttons on Chart	Hides the buttons on the chart from fields in the Values area.
Hide All Field Buttons on Chart	Hides all of the buttons on the chart.

Table 11-2 Values field drop-down list options explained

3. Orders table ⇒ Add the Order Date field to the Filters area.

4. Click the State Province button on the chart ⇒ Change the Filter options to only select records in CA, FL, HI and IL. Your pivot chart should look like the one shown in Figure 11-32.

As you can see, the pivot chart does not look like what you expected.

The values on the vertical axis need to be changed to only display whole numbers, because the pivot chart is suppose to display a count of customers by state.

If the Customers table had more records, the chart would be of more value.

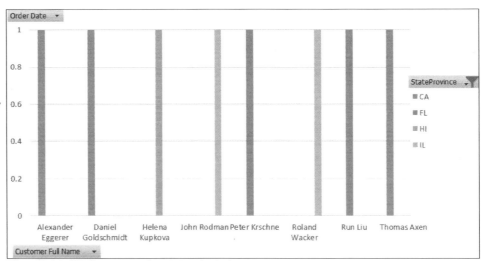

Figure 11-32 Customers by state pivot chart

Exercise 11.3: Create A Customer Orders By Year Pivot Chart

This exercise will show you how to create a pivot chart that displays customer orders by year. You will also learn how to move fields to a different area of the chart. Do not add a chart place holder to the Excel window until step 2 is completed.

1. Save the Pivot Tables and Charts workbook as `E11.3 Customer orders by year pivot chart`.

2. In Power Pivot, rename the Name field in each table, listed in Table 11-3.

Table	Rename The Name Field To
Product	SelectAProduct
ShipMethod	ShippingMethod
SalesTerritory	SelectATerritory

Table 11-3 Fields to be renamed

3. Add the fields in Table 11-4 to create the pivot chart.

Table	Field	Add To Area
SalesOrderHeader	Total Due	Values
SalesTerritory	SelectATerritory	Filters
Product	SelectAProduct	Filters
ShipMethod	ShippingMethod	Filters
SalesOrderHeader	Order Year	Legend
Contact	Last Name	Axis

Table 11-4 Fields to create the pivot chart

4. Select the filter options in Table 11-5 for the pivot chart.

   Your pivot chart should look like the one shown in Figure 11-34.

Filter	Option
Order Year	2002 and 2004
SelectATerritory	NorthEast
SelectAProduct	See Figure 11-33
ShippingMethod	Cargo Transport 5

Table 11-5 Filter options for the pivot chart

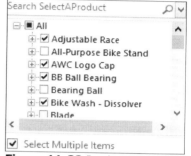

Figure 11-33 Product filter options to select

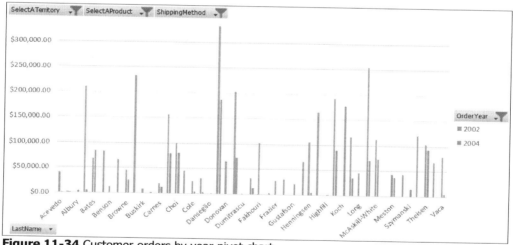

Figure 11-34 Customer orders by year pivot chart

Exercise 11.4: Create A Yearly Sales By Country Pivot Chart

Exercise 10.3 covered creating a pivot table that displayed a lot of data [See Chapter 10, Figure 10-44]. Sometimes, displaying that amount of data in a pivot chart does not look good. It can also be difficult in some chart types to see the trends or patterns in a large amount of data. When you have that much data, it is sometimes a good idea to create a few pivot charts on the same worksheet.

In this exercise you will create a pivot chart that has fewer Axis fields, then there are Rows in the pivot table that was created from the same data.

1. Save the E10.3 workbook as E11.4 Yearly sales by country pivot chart.

2. Add the pivot chart to a new worksheet ⇒ Add the fields in Table 11-6 to create the pivot chart.

Table	Field	Add To Area	Rename The Field To
FactSales	Sales Amount	Values	
Stores	Store Type	Filters	
Stores	Store Name	Axis	
DimDate	Calendar Year	Legend	
DimProductCategory	ProductCategoryName	Axis	Product Category

Table 11-6 Fields to create the pivot chart

3. On the chart, select the filter options in Table 11-7.

Filter	Option
Store Type	Online
Product Category	See Figure 11-35

Table 11-7 Filter options for the pivot chart

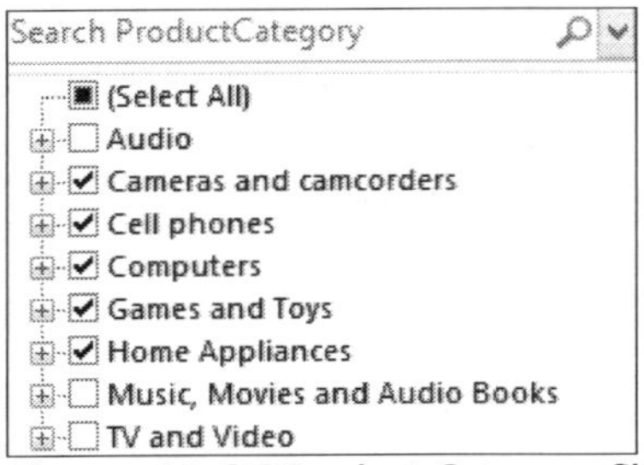

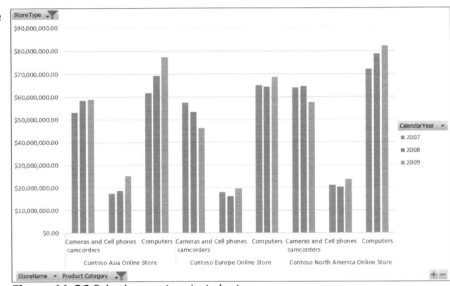

Figure 11-35 Product Category filter options to select

Your pivot chart should look like the one shown in Figure 11-36.

This chart is legible. If you selected all of the store types, the chart will look like the one shown in Figure 11-37.

As you can see, the chart in Figure 11-37 is not legible.

Figure 11-36 Sales by country pivot chart

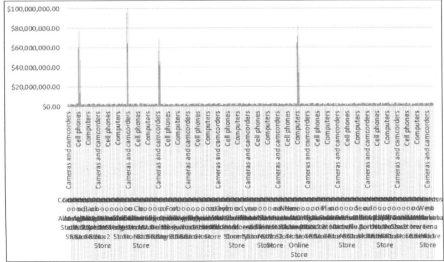

Figure 11-37 Sales by country pivot chart with all of the store type filter options selected

Exercise 11.5: Create A Top 10 Pivot Chart

This exercise will show you how to create a Top N pivot chart that shows the top 10 stores and their yearly sales amounts.

1. Save the E9.2 workbook as E11.5 Top 10 pivot chart.

2. Add the fields in Table 11-8 to the Pivot Chart Fields list, to create the pivot chart.

Table	Field	Add To Area
FactSales	Sales Amount	Values
DimChannel	Channel Name	Filters
DimDate	Calendar Year	Legend
Stores	Store Name	Axis

Table 11-8 Fields to create the pivot chart

3. Open the Store Name filter on the pivot chart and select the stores shown in Figure 11-38. The pivot chart should look like the one shown in Figure 11-39.

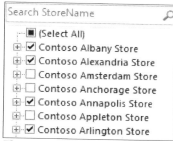

Figure 11-38 Store Name filter options

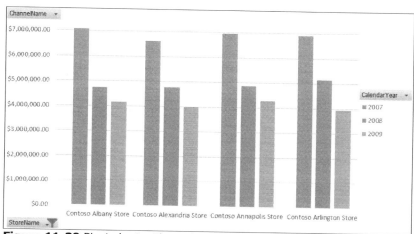

Figure 11-39 Pivot chart without the Top 10 filter

Apply The Top 10 Filter To The Pivot Chart

In this part of the exercise you will add the Top 10 filter functionality to the pivot chart.

1. Open the Store Name filter shortcut menu and select all of the stores.

2. Select the Value Filters option on the Store Name filter shortcut menu ⇒ Select the **TOP 10** option, shown at the bottom of Figure 11-40.

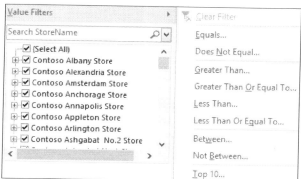

Figure 11-40 Value Filters Top 10 option

3. Accept the default Top 10 filter options ⇒ Click OK.

   The pivot chart should look like the one shown in Figure 11-41.

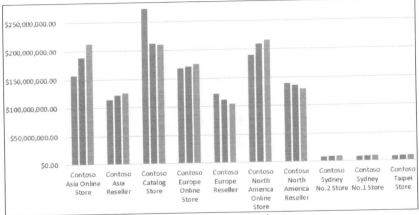

Figure 11-41 Top 10 filter applied to the pivot chart

4. Open the Channel Name filter and clear all of the options except Store.

   The Top 10 pivot chart should look like the one shown in Figure 11-42. This pivot chart displays the top 10 stores for all three years.

   Figure 11-43 shows the top 10 stores by sales, just for 2008.

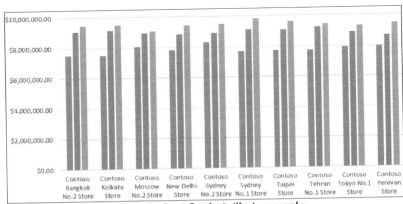

Figure 11-42 Top 10 pivot chart for (retail) stores only

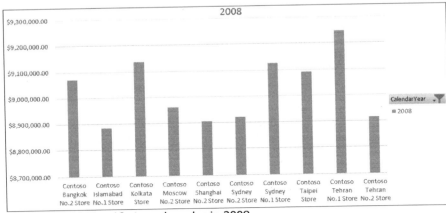

Figure 11-43 Top 10 stores by sales in 2008

Change Chart Type Dialog Box

The default chart type for pivot charts is a Clustered Column chart. The good thing is that you can use many of chart types that Excel has. Once you have created a pivot chart, you can change the chart type, by right-clicking on the chart and selecting **CHANGE CHART TYPE**. This option will open the dialog box shown in Figure 11-44. The dialog box is used to select a different chart type. The chart types that are available for pivot charts are explained in Table 11-9.

 The chart types that cannot be used to create a pivot chart that uses data in the data model are **XY (SCATTER)**, **BUBBLE** (in the XY Scatter section), **STOCK, TREEMAP, SUNBURST, HISTOGRAM, PARETO** (in the Histogram section), **BOX, WHISKER** and **WATERFALL**. If you select one of these chart types, you will see the message illustrated in Figure 11-44.

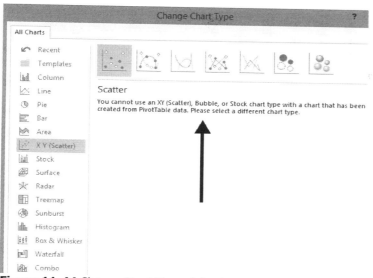

Figure 11-44 Change Chart Type dialog box

 Enlarging The Chart Preview
After selecting a chart type on the Change Chart Type dialog box, holding the mouse pointer over it, enlarges it, as shown in Figure 11-45.

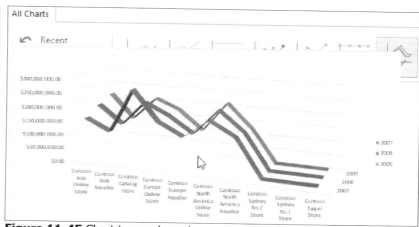

Figure 11-45 Chart type enlarged

Chart Types

Chart Type	Description
Column	Column charts, as shown earlier in Figure 11-39, show differences between items and relationships between grouped data. This is probably the most used chart type. Stacked column charts show each item as a percent of the total.
Line	Line charts, as shown in Figure 11-46, show trends and changes over a period of time. A good use of **3D LINE CHARTS** is when the data lines cross each other often. This makes a line chart easier to read.
Pie	Pie charts show data for one point in time. Figure 11-47 shows store sales for a year. Each slice of the pie represents the percent of sales for a different store in the year that is selected. (1)
Doughnut	This chart type is in the Pie chart section. It is similar to pie charts. The difference is that there is a hole in the center, as shown in Figure 11-48. (1)
Bar	Bar charts have the same functionality as a column chart. The only difference is the direction that the bars face, as shown in Figure 11-49.
Area	Area charts show how the data has changed over a period of time. Figure 11-50 shows how the revenue of five stores has changed from year to year. Area charts are almost identical to **STACKED LINE CHARTS**. The difference is that area charts are filled in below the trendline. Area charts are probably best suited for a few groups of data.

Table 11-9 Chart types explained

Chart Type	Description
Surface	This is the 3D version of area charts. Figure 11-51 shows a surface chart. This chart type uses three series of data. The surface of the chart has a curve and shows trends in relation to time.
Radar	Radar charts compare series of data relative to a center point and shows how far the data value is from the standard (the center point value), as shown in Figure 11-52. The values that are often used to create a radar chart, are group subtotals. The data from the X axis is usually plotted in a circle and the Y values are plotted from the center of the circle out.
Combo	This chart type combines two or more chart types. It displays changes and the magnitude of the change over time. This change is usually illustrated by two chart types: A line chart and a column chart.

Table 11-9 Chart types explained (Continued)

(1) This chart type only uses one value because it shows how the whole (100%) is divided.

My 3D Chart Distortion Observations
My observations are not specific to 3D charts created from data in the data model. They also apply to 3D charts created in Excel. In my opinion, sometimes 3D charts, like the one shown in Figure 11-49, distort the height of the columns and values. By that I mean, two bars appear to represent values that are close in range, but when you look at the numbers that the bars represent, you can see that the values are not as close as the bars make them appear. I have also noticed this distortion on 3D pie charts. On bar and column charts, displaying the value that each bar represents will help clarify the value.

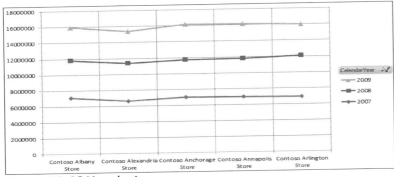
Figure 11-46 Line chart

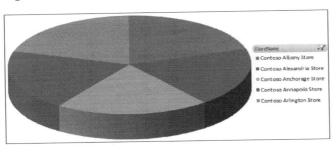
Figure 11-47 Pie chart

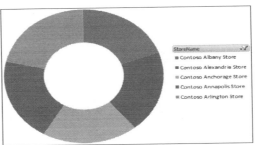
Figure 11-48 Doughnut chart

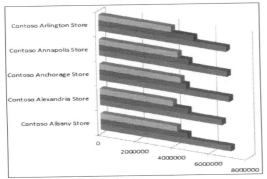
Figure 11-49 Bar chart

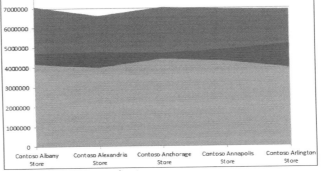
Figure 11-50 Area chart

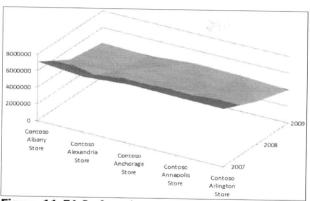

Figure 11-51 Surface chart

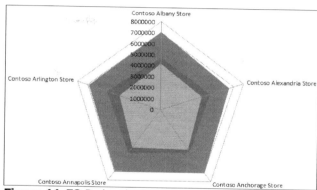

Figure 11-52 Radar chart

Combo Chart Type

The Combo chart type options, shown at the bottom of Figure 11-53, can be customized.

The **SECONDARY AXIS** option, is used to add another scale (of data) to plot a different set of data against.

A different **CHART TYPE** can be selected from the options in the drop-down list, shown in Figure 11-54, for each series.

Changing the chart type to Clustered Column-Line, for the Top 10 chart, created in Exercise 11.5, (See Figure 11-41) displays the chart shown in Figure 11-55.

This chart type is also known as a **TRENDLINE** or **VARIANCE** chart.

The major difference between line charts, column charts and combination charts is that a combination chart can use both columns and lines in the same chart and the other two chart types cannot.

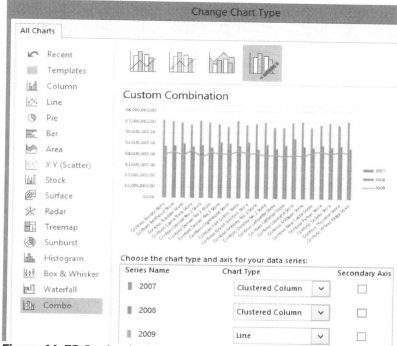

Figure 11-53 Combo chart type options

Figure 11-54 Chart type options for a series

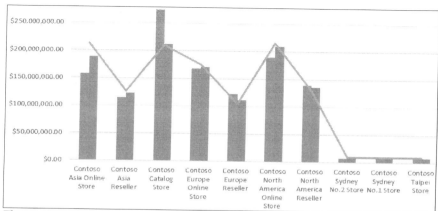

Figure 11-55 Clustered Column-Line chart

How Do I Select An Appropriate Chart Type?

So far, all of the charts that were created in this chapter used the Clustered column chart, which is the default chart type. The previous few sections covered all of the chart types that are available. If you are new to creating charts, hopefully, the rest of this section will help you select an appropriate chart type. There are four main categories that are used to help select a chart type, as explained below.

① **COMPARISON** As its name suggests, chart types in this category are used to compare more than two data points. This may be the most popular chart type category. Examples include orders by state and quantity of products sold by month. Chart types used in this category include bar, column and line.

② **COMPOSITION** Select this category when a subset of data needs to be compared to a larger set of related data. Order amount by state as a percent of the total order amount, is an example of a chart for this category. Chart types used in this category include, bar, column, donut and pie.

③ **DISTRIBUTION** This may be the second most popular chart type category. This chart type is used to display how the data is distributed, as well as, categories of data that are outside of the expected range. An example is the source of orders (phone, web site, store) by month, for last year. Chart types used in this category include column, line and scatter.

④ **RELATIONSHIP** Select this category when the relationship (or not) between categories needs to be displayed. For example, you need to display the relationship between the source of orders and a discount coupon. Meaning, you want to display how much phone and web site orders increase after existing customers receive a discount coupon. Chart types used in this category include bubble and scatter.

Exercise 11.6: Create A Total Cost By Product Category Pivot Chart

This exercise will show you how to create a pivot chart that displays the total cost by product category.

1. Save the E9.2 workbook as E11.6 Total cost by product category.

2. Add the fields in Table 11-10 to create the pivot chart.

Table	Field	Add To Area
FactSales	Total Cost	Values
DimProductCategory	Product Category Name	Axis

Table 11-10 Fields to create the pivot chart

3. Change the chart title to Total Cost By Product Category.

Change The Chart Type And Chart Style

1. Change the chart type to Pie.

2. In the Chart Styles list, on the Design tab, select the style that has a black background, that is illustrated in Figure 11-56.

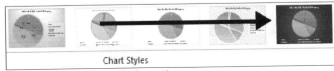

Figure 11-56 Chart Style options

Add Data Labels To The Pivot Chart

1. Design tab ⇒ Add Chart Element button ⇒ Data Labels ⇒ More Data Label Options.

2. Click on the Label Options icon illustrated in Figure 11-57 ⇒ Check the Category Name and Percentage options.

   Clear the **VALUE** option.

   Change the Separator option to **(NEW LINE)**.

   In the Label Position section, check the Outside End option.

   You should have the options selected, that are shown in Figure 11-57.

Figure 11-57 Format Data Labels panel

3. Hide the Value Field button on the chart.

   The pivot chart should look like the one shown in Figure 11-58.

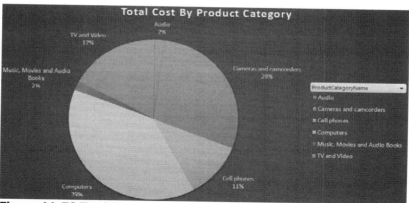

Figure 11-58 Total Cost By Product Category pivot chart

Exercise 11.7: Create A Pivot Chart And Pivot Table On The Same Worksheet

So far, all of the pivot tables and pivot charts that you have created in this book were one or the other, but not both on the same worksheet. This exercise will show you how to create both on the same worksheet and have the ability to select different filter options for the pivot table and pivot chart.

As explained below, the pivot table and pivot chart creation options have different functionality, based on where they are selected.

① All of the pivot table and pivot chart options in Power Pivot allow you to add different fields to pivot tables and pivot charts, that are created on the same worksheet.
② The Insert tab ⇒ Pivot Chart button and Pivot Table option, adds the same fields to the pivot table and pivot chart at the same time. If you want to use the Insert tab options, to be able to add different fields to the pivot table and chart on the same worksheet, you have to use the Pivot Table button and the Pivot Chart button to have the ability to add different fields to the pivot table and pivot chart.

1. Save the E9.2 workbook as E11.7 Pivot chart and table.

2. In the Power Pivot window, select the Chart and Table (Horizontal) option on the Pivot Table button drop-down list.

Create The Pivot Table

1. Click on the Pivot Table place holder ⇒ Add the fields in Table 11-11 to create the pivot table.

Table	Field	Add To Area
FactSales	Sales Amount	Values
DimChannel	Channel Name	Filters
DimGeography	State Province Name	Filters
DimDate	Calendar Year	Columns
Stores	Store Name	Rows

Table 11-11 Fields to create the pivot table

2. Open the Channel Name filter drop-down list ⇒ Select the Store option.

3. Open the State Province Name filter drop-down list and select the states: Colorado, Ohio and Texas.

4. Open the Column Labels filter and select the years: 2007 and 2009.

Create The Pivot Chart

1. Click on the Pivot Chart place holder ⇒ Add the fields in Table 11-12 to create the pivot chart.

Table	Field	Add To Area
FactSales	Sales Amount	Values
DimChannel	Channel Name	Filters
DimGeography	State Province Name	Filters
DimDate	Calendar Year	Legend
Stores	Store Name	Axis

Table 11-12 Fields to create the pivot chart

2. Open the Channel Name filter drop-down list ⇒ Select the Store option.

3. Open the State Province Name filter drop-down list ⇒ Select Colorado.

4. Open the Calendar Year filter ⇒ Select the years 2008 and 2009.

5. Change the chart type to Line. The pivot chart and pivot table should look like the ones shown in Figure 11-59.

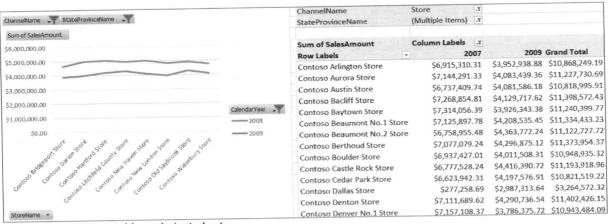

Figure 11-59 Pivot table and pivot chart

Summary

This chapter showed you how to create pivot charts using a variety of chart types. Hopefully, if you are new to creating pivot charts, you found the section on how to select an appropriate chart type helpful. Now its time to "slice" some data.

. . . .

In this chapter you will learn how to use slicers to enhance pivot tables and pivot charts. You will also learn how to create a dashboard report.

CHAPTER 12

What Are Slicers?

A slicer is an interactive tool that is used to reduce the amount of data displayed in pivot tables and pivot charts. Slicers are placed on a worksheet in Excel, with the pivot table or pivot chart. Slicers are also used to do what is known as **AD-HOC ANALYSIS** and create some types of What If scenarios. This is possible because slicers allow the data to be filtered, grouped and sorted. Slicers are useful when creating dashboards. Clicking on a button on the slicer, filters the data that is displayed in the pivot table or pivot chart.

For example, if you click on the third button on the slicer, shown in Figure 12-1, the pivot table would display the data shown in the figure.

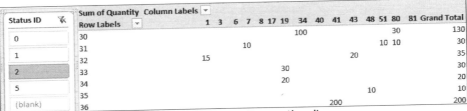

Figure 12-1 Pivot table data filtered by an option on the slicer

Excel Slicers vs Report Filters

Slicers are similar to report filters in terms of functionality. The two biggest differences between slicers and filters is: 1) Slicers display the filter values visually and 2) Each slicer can be used to filter pivot tables and charts at the same time, meaning separate slicers for each pivot table or pivot chart on the worksheet is not needed. In some respects, I think that slicers are easier to use then report filters.

In Excel, the Report filter drop-down list, shown in Figure 12-2, is used to select all values or specific values that will filter the data. As you have seen, report filters do not display all of the values that have been selected.

The Report Filter feature can be used with data on a spreadsheet, as well as, data in a table or pivot table.

Figure 12-2 Report Filter drop-down list

Slicers can only be used with pivot tables or pivot charts. If you only need to select one item from the Report Filter to filter a pivot table on, you can probably continue to use the Report Filter for pivot tables. If you need to select more than one item from the report filter to filter on, it is probably better to create a slicer because slicers make it easier to know which items are selected, because all of the items are visible in a slicer, whether or not they are selected. The biggest down side to slicers are that they take up more space on the worksheet, then a filter.

Slicer Tools Options Contextual Tab

The options on the tab shown in Figure 12-3 are part of Excel, but can be used with slicers created in Power Pivot. The options are used to change the size and orientation of the entire slicer or its buttons. The alignment of slicers can also be set. This tab is available once a slicer has been added to the worksheet. The options are explained in Table 12-1.

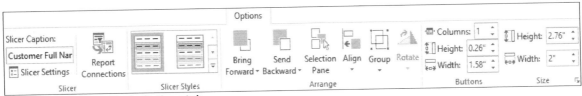

Figure 12-3 Slicer Tools Options tab

Option	Description
Slicer Caption	This field contains the name displayed above the slicer. By default, the field name that the slicer is created from is displayed. If you want to change the name, type over the name in this field.
Slicer Settings	[See Slicer Settings]
Report Connections	[See Report Connections]

Table 12-1 Slicer Tools Options tab options explained

Option	Description
Slicer Styles	[See Slicer Styles]
Bring Forward	Is used to move the selected object forward one level or to the front of all objects.
Send Backward	Is used to move the selected object back one level or all the way back.
Selection Pane	Displays the Selection panel, shown in Figure 12-8. The feature is helpful if you have trouble selecting an object on the worksheet.
Align	Is used to line up the selected objects.
Group	Treats two or more objects as one, so that they can be used as one object. This is helpful when you need to apply the same formatting to several objects. If the objects are grouped, you only have to apply the formatting options once and they will be applied to all objects in the group.
Rotate	Is used to flip or rotate the selected object.
Columns (Buttons)	Is used to change the number of columns in the slicer.
Height (Buttons)	Is used to change the height of the slicer buttons. (1)
Width (Buttons)	Is used to change the width of the slicer buttons. (1)
Height (Size)	Is used to change the height of the slicer.
Width (Size)	Is used to change the width of the slicer.

Table 12-1 Slicer Tools Options tab options explained (Continued)

(1) This can also be done manually, by resizing the frame of the slicer.

Slicer Settings

Clicking the **SLICER SETTINGS** button on the Options tab, opens the dialog box shown in Figure 12-4.

The options are used to change the display settings of the selected slicer.

The one option that you may want to change is the **CAPTION** option because it is displayed on the slicer.

As you can see, the default caption is the field name and not all field names are descriptive enough.

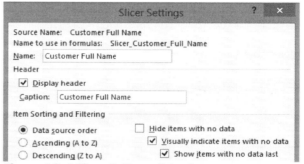

Figure 12-4 Slicer Settings dialog box

Report Connections

Clicking the **REPORT CONNECTIONS** button on the Options tab opens the dialog box shown later in Figure 12-17. The list contains all of the pivot tables in the workbook. The options are used to manage the pivot tables and charts that the slicer is connected to. You can select pivot tables and charts to connect the slicer to or remove the connection of pivot tables and charts from the slicers.

Slicer Styles

The options in this section of the Options tab, are used to change the color scheme of the slicer. If the styles in the drop-down list do not meet your needs, select **NEW SLICER STYLE** option at the bottom of the drop-down list.

The options on the dialog box shown in Figure 12-5 are used to create a new style.

The style that you create, will be displayed in the **CUSTOM** section of the slicer styles, illustrated at the top of Figure 12-6.

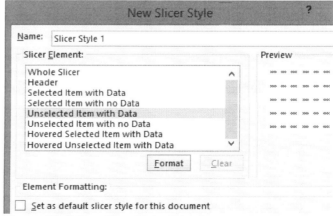

Figure 12-5 New Slicer Style dialog box

. . . .

The **FORMAT** button, on the New Slicer Style dialog box, opens the dialog box shown in Figure 12-7. The options are used to customize the selected **SLICER ELEMENT** in the middle of the New Slicer Style dialog box.

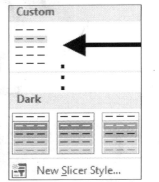

Figure 12-6 Custom slicer style illustrated

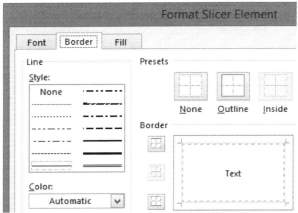

Figure 12-7 Format Slicer Element dialog box

Selection Panel

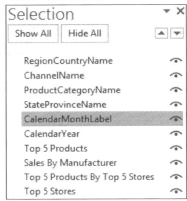

Figure 12-8 Selection panel

Insert Slicer Button And Dialog Box

The button illustrated in Figure 12-9 is on the PivotTable Tools Analyze tab for pivot tables. The options are explained below.

① **INSERT SLICER** opens the dialog box shown in Figure 12-10.
② **INSERT TIMELINE** [See Chapter 15, Insert Timeline Button And Dialog Box]
③ **FILTER CONNECTIONS** opens the dialog box shown later in Figure 12-17. The slicers can be attached (connected) to as many pivot tables and charts as necessary.

This dialog box is used to add slicers to the pivot table, just like you can use the Add as Slicer option on the shortcut menu on the Pivot Table Fields list.

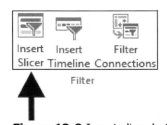

Figure 12-9 Insert slicer button illustrated

Figure 12-10 Insert Slicers dialog box

Exercise 12.1: Add Slicers To The Customers By State Pivot Table

In Exercise 10.2 you created a pivot table that displayed customers by state. In this exercise you will modify that pivot table by adding slicers for the customers state and city fields.

1.   Save the E10.2 workbook as `E12.1 Customers by state slicers`.

2.   In the Customers table, right-click on the State Province field ⇒ Select **ADD AS SLICER** ⇒ Right-click on the City field ⇒ Select Add as Slicer.

3.   Click on the State Province slicer ⇒ Slicer Tools Options Tab ⇒ Change the **SLICER CAPTION** to `State` ⇒ Change the Columns to 5.

4.   Click on the City slicer ⇒ Change the Columns to 3.

5.   Insert 8 blank rows at the top of the worksheet ⇒

   Move the slicers to the blank rows above the pivot table ⇒

   Resize the slicers as needed.

   The pivot table and slicers should look like the ones shown in Figure 12-11.

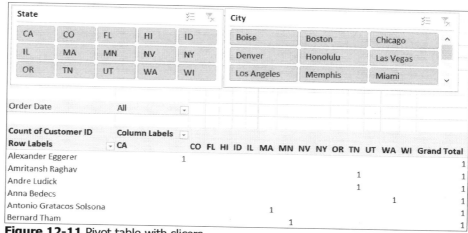

Figure 12-11 Pivot table with slicers

Using Slicers

As you read earlier, slicers are similar to the Report Filters. From a user perspective, slicers are probably easier to use and understand because all of the items are visible.

In addition to filtering data in a pivot table, a slicer can filter the options displayed in another slicer that is attached to the same pivot table. For example, the items available in the second slicer are controlled by the item selected in the first slicer. This is the same concept as the drill-down functionality that is available in some types of reports.

You can also resize the slicers, move the slicers to a different place on the worksheet. Not all slicers have to be connected to all pivot tables and charts on the worksheet or in the workbook. Slicers do not filter objects that they are not connected to. Below is an example of how one slicer filters the values in another slicer and how the slicers filter the data displayed on the pivot table.

If you click on a state in the State slicer shown in Figure 12-12, only records that have the value that you selected will be displayed in the pivot table. The pivot table displays all customers in CA.

The City slicer, shown in Figure 12-13, will only have the cities enabled for the state that is selected, in the State slicer.

After you select an option in the first slicer, the corresponding items in the second slicer will automatically be rearranged and the available options will be moved to the beginning (starting in the upper left corner) of the slicer options.

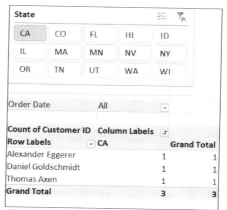

Figure 12-12 Pivot table based on the State slicer options

The options in the second slicer that are not enabled, means that they are not part of the group selected in the first slicer. For example, in the options shown in Figure 12-13, Boston is not enabled because it is not a city in California.

If you select an option in the City field, the pivot table will change to only display rows of data that match both filter options, as shown in Figure 12-13.

In this scenario, you do not have to select a state first and then select a city.

You can select a city without a state being selected first, if you know the city that you want to display data for.

Figure 12-13 Pivot table based on the State and City slicer options

Behind the scenes, multiple slicers that are connected to the same pivot table use the **AND OPERATOR**. This means that rows of data that are displayed have to meet the criteria of all of the slicers to be displayed on the pivot table or chart. Slicers that are not connected to the pivot table are not enabled.

Slicer Options

In the upper right corner of the slicer are two buttons. They are explained below.

 Clicking the **MULTI-SELECT** button allows you to select more than one value in the slicer, as shown on the left side of Figure 12-14. This is the same as selecting multiple items in a filter. If there are other slicers on the worksheet, the corresponding values in the other slicers, will be enabled, as shown on the right side of the figure. The enabled values in the second slicer are related to one of the values in the first slicer. All records that match a selected value in the first slicer are initially displayed in the pivot table.

 The **CLEAR FILTER** button displays a red X if the slicer is being used. This lets you visually know that the data displayed in the pivot table has been filtered by that slicer. If you want to remove a filter, click on the red X.

To use the Multi-Select option, click on one option on the slicer that you want to filter on ⇒ Click the Multi-Select button ⇒ Click the other options on the slicer that you want to filter on.

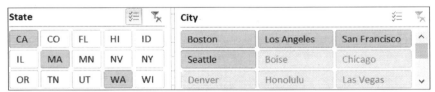

Figure 12-14 Multiple values in a slicer selected

Exercise 12.2: Create Slicers For A Pivot Table And Pivot Chart

In the previous exercise you created two slicers for a pivot table. As you have read, slicers can control more than one pivot table or pivot chart. In this exercise you will create year and month slicers that will be used to control a pivot table and pivot chart.

Modify The Pivot Chart

In this part of the exercise you will modify the pivot chart.

1. Save the E11.7 workbook as `E12.2 Mini Dashboard`.

2. Change the chart type to Clustered Column.

3. Change the Channel Name and State Province Name filters to use all options.

4. Change the Store Name filter to only display the following Contoso Stores: Albany, Alexandria, Anchorage, Annapolis and Arlington.

. . . .

5. Change the Calendar Year filter to include the year 2007.

6. Format the numbers on the vertical axis of the pivot chart to display with currency formatting, without a decimal point, by selecting the options shown at the bottom of Figure 12-15.

   The arrows indicate the changes that you should see.

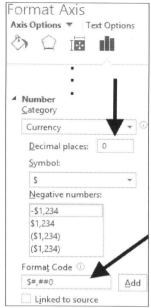

Figure 12-15 Format Axis options (pivot chart)

7. Display the Chart Elements options (click the + icon for the chart) ⇒ Select the **GRIDLINES OPTION** ⇒ Select both Primary Major Options, shown in Figure 12-16.

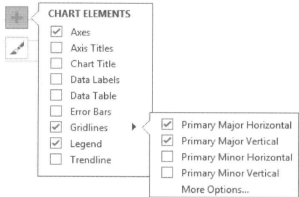

Figure 12-16 Gridline chart element options

8. Make the pivot chart smaller, then drag the chart down.

Create The Slicers

1. Select the chart.

2. Display the Dim Date table ⇒ Create slicers for the Calendar Year and Calendar Month Label fields ⇒ Place them above the pivot chart.

3. Change the Calendar Year slicer caption to `Year` ⇒ Change the Columns to 3.

4. Change the Calendar Month Label caption to `Month` ⇒ Change the Columns to 4.

5. Resize the slicers so that they fit above the chart.

Attach The Slicers To The Pivot Table

If you used the slicers now, they would only work with the pivot chart. The **FILTER CONNECTIONS** dialog box is used to attach slicers to a pivot table or chart.

1. Click on the pivot table.

2. Analyze tab ⇒ Click the Filter Connections button.

   Check both of the slicer options shown in Figure 12-17.

   The dashboard should look similar to the one shown in Figure 12-18.

Figure 12-17 Slicer options to attach to the pivot table

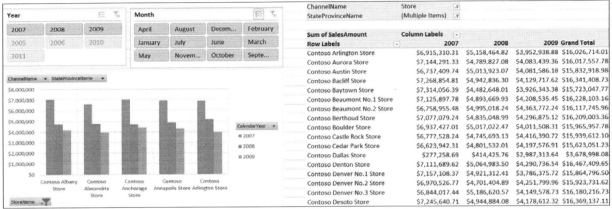

Figure 12-18 Dashboard

Not surprising, but the months in the slicer are not in calendar month order. There are currently no built-in options that can be used to sort the items in a slicer, like you can in a filter for a pivot table. Hopefully, this is something that will be worked on for a future software update. In the next chapter, I will show you how to create a solution to fix this problem. And no, you do not have to write any code <smile>.

As you can see, the pivot table and pivot chart have two other filters in common: The Channel Name and the State Province Name. You can leave them as individual filters or you can create slicers for them.

Using Filters And Slicers

The pivot table and pivot chart that you just modified in Exercise 12.2, both have a Calendar Year filter. What you will notice is that if you use the Calendar Year filter on the pivot chart, the same filter option will be applied to the pivot table automatically. This is because they are connected to the same field. Both filters do not need to be displayed. You could hide one of them. The Calendar Year slicer will also change to what you selected in the Calendar Year filter.

How To Show And Hide Filter Buttons On Pivot Charts

When a report has slicers, some of the Report Filter buttons may not be needed. An example of this is the Calendar Year legend filter button, shown above in Figure 12-18.

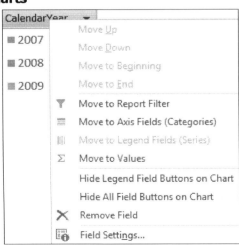

I suspect that out of habit many people will leave this button visible because slicers do not appear to have the functionality to allow more than one option to be selected at the same time.

You can hide any filter button on a pivot table or pivot chart, whether or not there is a slicer for it.

To hide the Legend filter button, right-click on the Legend button and select **HIDE LEGEND FIELD BUTTONS ON CHART**, as shown in Figure 12-19.

Figure 12-19 Legend button shortcut menu options

The legend is still displayed, even though the button is hidden, as illustrated in Figure 12-20.

Compare this chart to the one shown earlier in Figure 12-18, which displays the legend button.

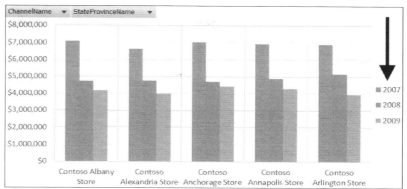
Figure 12-20 Legend filter button hidden

 Another Way To Show And Hide Filter Buttons
When a chart is selected, the **FIELD BUTTONS** options (on the Analyze tab), shown in Figure 12-21, are available to show and hide buttons.

Clearing the check mark for an option will hide the corresponding button on the pivot chart.

Selecting an option that is not checked, will display the corresponding button on the pivot chart.

Figure 12-21 Field Buttons options

Exercise 12.3: Add A Pivot Chart And Attach Slicers To An Existing Layout

In Exercise 12.1 you added slicers to a pivot table. In this exercise you will modify that layout by adding a pivot chart and then attach an existing slicer to the pivot chart.

Create The Pivot Chart

1. Save the E12.1 workbook as `E12.3 Attach slicers`.

2. Add a pivot chart to the right of the pivot table.

3. Add the fields from the Customers table in Table 12-2, to create the pivot chart.

Field	Add To Area
Customer ID	Values
State Province	Legend
Customer Full Name	Axis

Table 12-2 Fields to create the pivot chart

4. Change the chart type to 3-D Clustered column.

5. Hide all of the field buttons on the chart.

Attach The Slicers

When you add a pivot table or pivot chart to an existing report, it is not a requirement to attach it to the existing slicers. You can attach the new pivot table or chart to some slicers and not others. You can also create slicers just for the new pivot table or chart. In this part of the exercise, you will learn how to attach an existing slicer to the chart.

1. Click on the pivot chart ⇒ Pivot Chart Tools Analyze tab ⇒ Filter Connections button.

2. On the dialog box shown in Figure 12-22, you will see all of the slicers that are currently in the workbook.

   For this exercise, select the State slicer ⇒ Click OK ⇒ Save the changes.

   Now, when you use the State slicer, the data in the pivot chart will also be filtered.

Select filters to connect to this PivotChart		
Caption	Name	Sheet
City	City	Sheet1
✓ State	StateProvince	Sheet1

Filter Connections (PivotChartTable1)

Figure 12-22 Filter Connections dialog box

Test The Slicers

1. Click on the CA button in the State slicer.

2. Click on the San Francisco button in the City slicer. Notice that the pivot table changed, but the chart values did not change, which is what is expected in this exercise ⇒ Clear the City slicer.

3. On the State slicer, click the Multi-Select button ⇒ Select the following states: CO and MA. The report should look like the one shown in Figure 12-23.

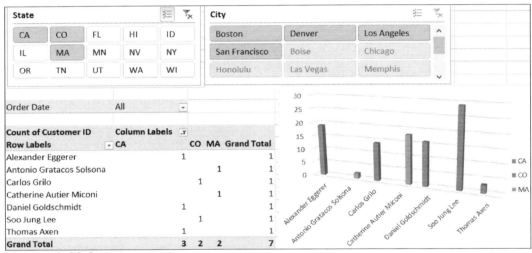

Figure 12-23 Customer report

Dashboards

You have probably heard this term before, in reference to displaying data, and wondered what is required to be considered a dashboard. In all honesty, a dashboard can consist of whatever the report designer can dream up. Typically though, to be considered a dashboard, the layout should meet the following criteria:

① Have two or more charts. Usually, dashboards do not display tables. Probably because tables can require varying amounts of space, depending on the filter or slicer options that are selected. Pivot charts do not have this issue as much because they resize automatically in its frame, to accommodate the amount of data that needs to be displayed.

② The dashboard should display the data at the level that the user needs it. For example, a CEO wants to see data in terms of whether the sales are on target (probably using key performance indicators). A Product Manager wants to see the sales on a product by product basis. The same data is required for both views, just displayed at a different level.

③ Set up the layout to fit everything in a way that doesn't require having to scroll to see all of the data.

I called the report in Exercise 12.2 a mini dashboard because it has the smallest number of objects that some people consider a requirement to be called a dashboard. Most of the time, dashboards have at least four pivot charts and three or more slicers, some of which are placed horizontally and some placed vertically.

Another reason that pivot tables generally are not displayed on a dashboard is because they do not display the data visually, like charts do. By design, charts display the same amount of data as a pivot table that has the same filters and slicers, in less space on the worksheet.

Keep in mind that a primary goal of dashboards is to display a variety of data for specific topics. Dashboards show comparisons of historical or forecast data. They also show trends in the data.

What Each Chart In Exercise 12.4 Needs
In this exercise you will be creating four pivot charts. Some of the requirements for all four charts are the same. Instead of typing the same set of instructions four times, the functionality that every chart needs is listed below. Complete the tasks below for each chart after you have completed all of the steps for the chart and added the fields to the drop zones in the Pivot Chart Fields list.
① Analyze tab ⇒ Change the Chart Name to the chart title.
② Format the values on the vertical axis to Currency, with no decimal places.
③ Resize the chart as needed.
④ Hide all of the Field buttons on charts 2, 3 and 4.
⑤ Hide the Values Field button.

Create A Chart Title
By default, pivot charts do not have a chart title. Chart 1, Chart 2 etc., that you will see at the top of charts is the chart name. The steps below show you how to create a chart title.
1. PivotChart Tools Design tab ⇒ Chart Layouts group ⇒ Add Chart Element button ⇒ Chart Title option ⇒ Above Chart option, as shown in Figure 12-24.
2. Type the title for the chart in the formula bar, then press Enter.

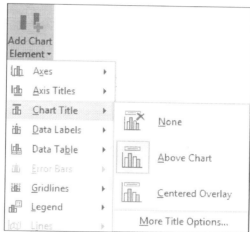

Figure 12-24 Chart Title button options

Exercise 12.4: Create A Dashboard Layout

In this exercise you will create a dashboard report that has four pivot charts and four slicers. The pivot charts will display the top five stores, top five products and the top five stores, sales by manufacturer and top five products. All of the charts will only display data for stores in the United States. The slicers will allow the charts to be filtered by year, month, state, product category and channel.

1. Save the E9.2 workbook as E12.4 Dashboard with 4 charts.

2. In the Power Pivot window, add the **FOUR CHARTS** PivotTable layout to the existing worksheet. Start the chart in Column D, on Row 9.

3. Rename the sheet to Dashboard.

Create Pivot Chart #1: Top 5 Stores

This pivot chart will display the top 5 stores based on sales.

1. Click on Chart 1 ⇒ Add the fields in Table 12-3, to create the pivot chart.

Table	Field	Add To Area
FactSales	Sales Amount	Values
DimDate	Calendar Year	Legend
DimChannel	Channel Name	Filters
Stores	Store Name	Axis

Table 12-3 Fields to create pivot chart #1

2. Open the Store Name filter list ⇒ Value Filters ⇒ Top 10 ⇒ Top 10 Filter dialog box ⇒ Change the second field to 5 ⇒ Click OK.

3. Create the chart title `Top 5 Stores`.

4. Create the slicers in Table 12-4, based on this pivot chart.

Table	Field	Rename The Field To
DimDate	Calendar Year	Year
DimDate	Calendar Month Label	Month
DimGeography	StateProvinceName	State (2)
DimGeography	RegionCountryName	Country (2)
DimProductCategory	ProductCategoryName	Product Category (2)
DimChannel	Channel Name	

Table 12-4 Fields to create the slicers for the pivot charts

How To Rename A Slicer
To rename a slicer, change the Slicer Caption on the Options tab or select the **SLICER SETTINGS** option, shown below at the bottom of Figure 12-25. On the Slicer Settings dialog box, change the Caption field.

(2) Right-click on an empty space on the slicer ⇒ Select **SORT A TO Z**, illustrated in Figure 12-25.

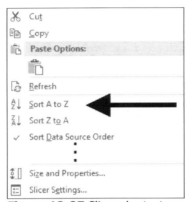

Figure 12-25 Slicer shortcut menu

5. On the Country slicer, select United States ⇒ Make this slicer smaller ⇒ Move it below the charts, so that it is not visible on the screen.

6. For now, move all of the other slicers to the top of the spreadsheet.

The chart should look like the one shown in Figure 12-26.

Figure 12-26 Top 5 Stores chart

Create Pivot Chart #2: Top 5 Products And Top 5 Stores

This pivot chart will display the sales amounts for the top 5 products and the top 5 stores that sold these products.

1. Click on Chart 2 ⇒
Add the fields in Table 12-5, to create the pivot chart.

When prompted that the maximum number of data series per chart is 255, click OK.

Table	Field	Add To Area
FactSales	Sales Amount	Values
DimProduct	Product Name	Legend
Stores	Store Name	Axis

Table 12-5 Fields to create pivot chart #2

2. Open the Product Name filter list ⇒ Value Filters ⇒ Top 10 ⇒ Top 10 Filter dialog box ⇒ Change the second field to 5.

3. Open the Store Name filter list ⇒ Value Filters ⇒ Top 10 ⇒ Top 10 Filter dialog box ⇒ Change the second field to 5.

4. Create the chart title, `Top 5 Products By Top 5 Stores`.

5. Right-click on a Store Name below the bars on the chart, at the bottom of the chart, and select **FORMAT AXIS** ⇒ On the Format Axis panel, click the **SIZE & PROPERTIES** button, illustrated at the top of Figure 12-27 ⇒ Open the Text direction drop-down list and select the **ROTATE ALL TEXT 270°** option, illustrated at the bottom of Figure 12-27 ⇒ If you do not see all five products in the legend section of the chart, make the chart larger. The chart should look like the one shown in Figure 12-28.

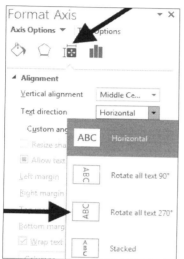

Figure 12-27 Format Axis panel (pivot chart)

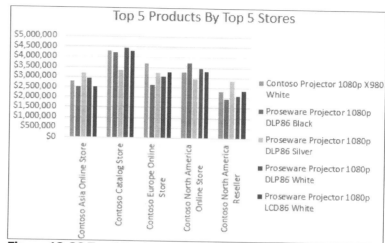

Figure 12-28 Top 5 Products By Top 5 Stores chart

Create Pivot Chart #3: Sales By Manufacturer

This pivot chart will display the sales for each manufacturer, by year.

1. Click on Chart 3 ⇒
   Add the fields in Table 12-6, to create the pivot chart.

Table	Field	Add To Area
DimDate	Calendar Year	Legend
DimProduct	Manufacturer	Axis
FactSales	Sales Amount	Values

Table 12-6 Fields to create pivot chart #3

2. Create the chart title `Sales By Manufacturer`.

3. Rotate the text on the horizontal axis to 270°.

4. Change the chart type to Stacked Line with Markers.

    The chart should look like the one shown in Figure 12-29.

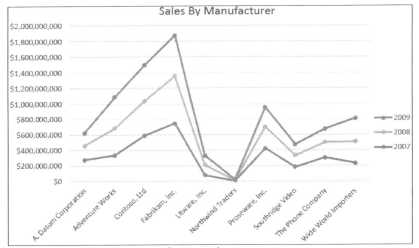

Figure 12-29 Sales By Manufacturer chart

Create Pivot Chart #4: Top 5 Products

This pivot chart will display the top 5 products for each of the calendar years that are selected.

1. Click on Chart 4 ⇒ Add the fields in Table 12-7, to create the pivot chart.

Table	Field	Add To Area
DimDate	Calendar Year	Legend
DimProduct	Product Name	Axis
FactSales	Sales Amount	Values

Table 12-7 Fields to create pivot chart #4

2. Create a Top 5 value filter for the Product Name field.

3. Create the chart title Top 5 Products.

    The chart should look like the one shown in Figure 12-30.

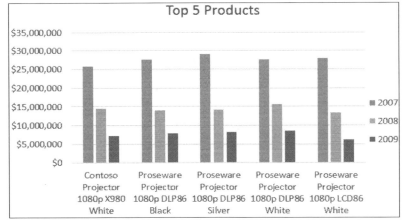

Figure 12-30 Top 5 Products chart

Change The Chart Type

1. Change the chart type to **BAR OF PIE**, as shown in Figure 12-31.

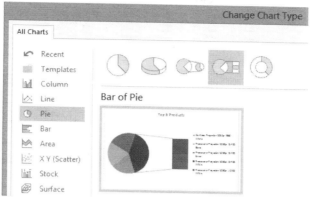

Figure 12-31 Pie chart types

2. On the Design tab, in the Chart Styles list, select the **STYLE 3** option, illustrated in Figure 12-32.

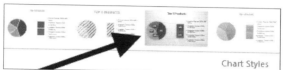

Figure 12-32 Chart Styles options

3. Design tab ⇒ Add Chart Element button ⇒ Data Labels ⇒ More Data Label Options ⇒ In the Label Options section, check the Value option ⇒ Clear the Percentage option ⇒ Change the **SEPARATOR** option to (New Line) ⇒ In the Label Position section, check the Outside End option.

   The options illustrated in Figure 12-33 are the ones you should have changed.

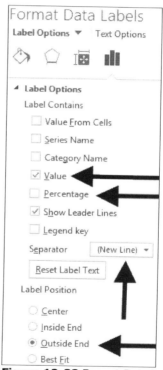

Figure 12-33 Format Data Labels options

4. Add Chart Element button ⇒ Legend ⇒ Bottom ⇒ If the Legend is touching the chart, make the chart larger or move the legend down.

5. If you want to change the colors on the chart, click the Change Colors button, shown in Figure 12-34 and select the color scheme that you want. The chart should look like the one in Figure 12-35. On the Format tab, I changed the **SHAPE FILL** and **TEXT FILL** options, so that the chart would look better printed in this book.

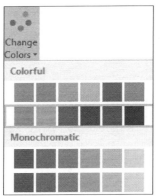

Figure 12-34 Change Colors options

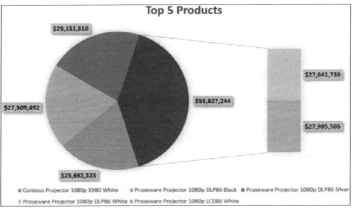
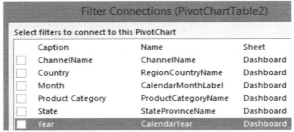

Figure 12-35 Top 5 Products chart

Attach The Slicers To The Charts

1. Click on Chart 2 ⇒ Analyze tab ⇒ Click the Filter Connections button.

    On the dialog box shown in Figure 12-36, check all of the slicers.

	Caption	Name	Sheet
	ChannelName	ChannelName	Dashboard
	Country	RegionCountryName	Dashboard
	Month	CalendarMonthLabel	Dashboard
	Product Category	ProductCategoryName	Dashboard
	State	StateProvinceName	Dashboard
	Year	CalendarYear	Dashboard

Figure 12-36 Filter connections

2. For charts 3 and 4, attach some of the filters.

Configure The Slicers

1. Move the Year slicer to the upper left corner of the sheet ⇒ Resize it, so that three years are displayed.

2. Move the Month slicer next to the Year slicer ⇒ On the Options tab, change the Columns to 4 ⇒ Resize the slicer, so that all of the months are visible.

3. Move the State slicer below the Year slicer, then make it larger.

4. Move the Channel Name slicer next to the Month slicer ⇒ Change the Columns option to 2.

5. Move the Product Category slicer next to the Channel Name slicer ⇒ Change the Columns option to 3. Figure 12-37 shows the entire dashboard report.

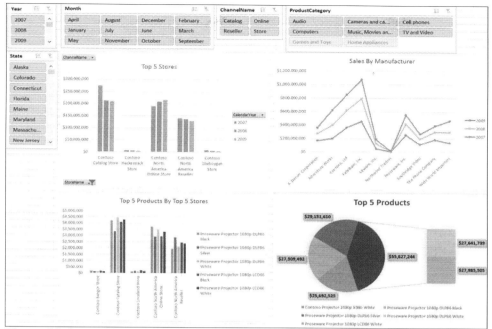

Figure 12-37 Dashboard report

Format Slicer Panel

Once a slicer has been added to the sheet, the panel shown in Figure 12-38 is accessed by right-clicking on the slicer and selecting **SIZE AND PROPERTIES**. The options are used to customize the slicer.

If you are designing the dashboard for other people to use, you may want to keep users from moving or resizing the slicers. If that is the case, check the **DISABLE RESIZING AND MOVING** option.

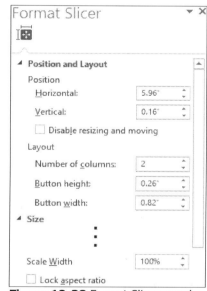

Figure 12-38 Format Slicer panel

What Can I Do If The Slicers Run Slow?

Yes, I know that the reason slicers are added to a report is to allow the data to be filtered. By now, you have seen that if a report has more than one slicer, the first slicer filters the values that are displayed in the second slicer, and so on. Behind the scenes, each time an option on any slicer is clicked on, all of the slicers, pivot tables and pivot charts are recalculated. If the data tables have millions of rows of data and/or there are a lot of formulas (that are recalculated each time the pivot table or pivot chart changes) the report can start to run slow.

It is possible that the filters are causing at least part of the problem. Below are some options that can be used to increase the performance of reports that have slicers, that are running slow.

① Reduce the number of slicers.

② Change when the formulas are calculated. Power Pivot ⇒ Design tab ⇒ Calculation Options ⇒ Manual Calculation Mode. If using this option, you have to remember to **RECALCULATE THE FORMULAS**, each time the data is refreshed. As you will learn in Chapter 14, options like refreshing data can be automated.

③ Remove columns that are not being used. You can do this in one of the following ways:

☑ By not importing them to begin with.

☑ Use the **DEFAULT FIELD SET** options to hide columns that are not being used.

☑ Disable the option that stops a slicer from being impacted (filtered) by another slicer. The option to disable this process is the **VISUALLY INDICATE ITEMS WITH NO DATA**, shown earlier in Figure 12-4. The factors that I use to help determine which slicers I should remove this option for, are listed below.

   ☑ The primary slicer in a group of related slicers. For example, if you have slicers for country, state and city, this option could be removed from the country slicer because being able to select the state and/or city that you want to display data for, can still be achieved.

   ☑ Slicers that only have a few options. For example, in Figure 12-37 shown earlier, the option could be disabled for the Channel Name slicer because it only has four options.

   ☑ Slicers whose options usually have data. In Figure 12-37 shown earlier, the year and month slicers would be candidates because they are based on the Order Date column (in the Orders table). More then likely, there are orders in the table, for each year and month in each year.

Summary

This probably goes without saying, but this chapter covered creating slicers and learning about the options available to customize them. In some respects, all of the previous chapters helped make creating dashboards a lot easier. I am sure some people want to jump right in and create dashboards right away, without taking the time to have a solid foundation of the work that is required to make creating dashboards easy. Being from the old school, as they say, I have learned that preparation is almost always a key factor to success!

In this chapter you will learn about the following options that can be used to enhance pivot tables and charts.

- ☑ Formatting cells
- ☑ Named Sets
- ☑ OLAP Tools
- ☑ Summary (group) options

CHAPTER 13

Overview

Chapters 10 and 11 covered how to create pivot tables and pivot charts. The topics covered in those chapters may handle all of your pivot table and pivot chart design needs. What I have found is that the way numbers are presented is as important as the number themselves. If you need more functionality, hopefully, the topics covered in this chapter and the next one will serve as the foundation to show how other features can enhance pivot tables and charts. Pivot tables and charts created with data in the data model can be customized, similar to how pivot tables and charts that are created from data on an Excel worksheet can be customized. Remember that any formatting that you add to the data in Power Pivot is not brought over to the pivot tables and pivot charts that you create.

Formatting Cells

To format cells, right-click on the cells in the pivot table. You will see a shortcut menu with all or some of the options shown in Figure 13-1, when the cell is not from the Values area.

When you right-click on a cell from the Values area, you will see the shortcut menu shown in Figure 13-2.

Instead of the Field Settings option shown in Figure 13-1, the **VALUE FIELD SETTINGS** option is available for cells in the Values area.

Selecting this option opens the Value Field Settings dialog box that you have used earlier in this book.

The options on Figures 13-1 and 13-2 that you may not be familiar with are explained in Table 13-1.

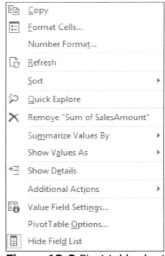

Figure 13-2 Pivot table shortcut menu for cells in the Values area

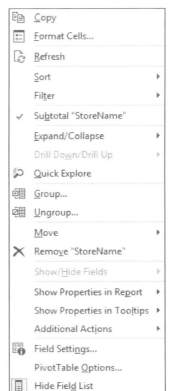

Figure 13-1 Pivot table shortcut menu for cells in the Rows and Columns areas

Pivot Table Shortcut Menu Options

Option	Description
Format Cells	Opens the dialog box shown later in Figure 13-8. The options are used to format the selected cells.
Filter	Displays the filter options shown in Figure 13-3. The options are a subset of the filter options that are available on the Row or Column Labels filter options.
Expand/Collapse	Displays the submenu options shown in Figure 13-4. The options are used to expand (display) cells that are hidden or collapse (hide) cells that are selected. These options work the same as the + and - buttons in front of each row.
Quick Explore	[See Using The Quick Explore Option]
Summarize Values By	Is used to change how the values displayed in the pivot table are calculated (summarized). (1)
Show Values As	Is used to select how values are displayed. [See Chapter 14, Using Percents] (1)
Show Details	[See Using The Show Details Option] (1)

Table 13-1 Pivot table shortcut menu options for fields in the Rows and Columns areas explained

(1) This option is only for cells created from a field in the Values area.

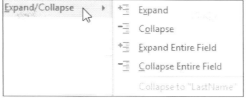

Figure 13-4 Expand/Collapse options

Figure 13-3 Filter options

 Data List Not Valid Message
It is possible that after you have created a pivot table and then import more data, you may see an error message that says that the data list is no longer valid. If that is the case, right-click on the pivot table and select the **REFRESH** option shown above in Figures 13-1 and 13-2.

Using The Quick Explore Option

This option displays the panel shown in Figure 13-5. The options are used to drill down (another way to filter data) in the hierarchy of data. To see how this option works, follow the steps below.

1. Open the E10.4 workbook.

2. Right-click on the "Adams" Row label (in Column A) and select **QUICK EXPLORE**. You will see the window shown in Figure 13-5.

    You can accept the default **DRILL TO** field or select a different field from one of the tables on the left side of the figure.

Figure 13-5 Explore panel

3. Click on the Drill To option.

    The data in the pivot table will be filtered, as shown in Figure 13-6.

    At the top of the figure, you will see the Last Name filter. It was created by the cell that you right-clicked on.

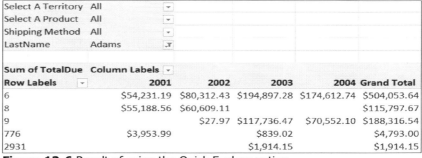

Figure 13-6 Result of using the Quick Explore option

The data displayed on the pivot table is contacts with the last name shown in the filter. If you look in the Filters area on the Pivot Table Fields list, you will see that the Last Name field was added to the Filters area. Compare this pivot table to the one shown in Chapter 10, Figure 10-46. The pivot table, now displays summary information for all contacts with the last name Adams.

Using The Show Details Option

Selecting this option displays up to the first 1,000 rows of data (on a new worksheet) that were used to create the value in the cell that this option was selected for. For example, I right-clicked in cell E6 (Sales amount for January 2007), in the pivot table created later in Exercise 13.3. Figure 13-7 shows portion of the table with rows of data from an aggregated value in a pivot table in cell E6. This is the same as using the Drill Down technique covered later in this chapter.

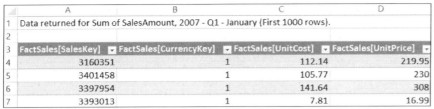

Figure 13-7 Show Details data

Exercise 13.1: Customize A Pivot Table

This exercise will show you how to customize a pivot table by changing the Row Labels name, add currency formatting and change the custom name of a measure. One of the best things that you can do for fields that are added to the Values area is to change the name. This will make it easier to understand the data in the pivot table or pivot chart.

1. Save the E10.1 workbook as E13.1 Row Labels and currency formatting modified.

If you look at the field in the Rows area, on the Pivot Table Fields list, you see that the field name is Ship Name. If you look at the pivot table, you don't see "Ship Name". Instead, you see the generic name, "Row Labels". I find it easier to understand the pivot table when it has row and column names that represent the data that is displayed.

2. Click in cell A1 ⇒ Type Ship To Name in the cell or formula bar ⇒ Press Enter.

3. Right-click on Column B ⇒
    Select Format Cells ⇒
    Select the Currency category.

    Figure 13-8 shows the options
    that should be selected.

    If these options are not selected,
    select them now.

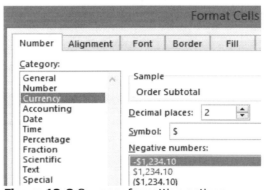

Figure 13-8 Currency formatting options

4. Click on the Sum of Subtotal field in
    the Values area ⇒ Select Value Field
    Settings.

    In the Custom Name field, type
    Order Subtotal ⇒ Click OK.

    The pivot table should look like the
    one shown in Figure 13-9.

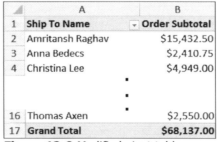

Figure 13-9 Modified pivot table

Named Sets

Named sets are used to define a group of columns or a group of rows to display in a pivot table. Because Power Pivot can use the Named sets feature in Excel, you can use MDX data without learning MDX.

Let me just fess up, right here and now. Currently, I only understand the basics of named sets and don't know a drop of MDX. I do plan to learn MDX down the road, way down the road <smile>. I have learned enough about named sets to create what I need. The two things that I do know about named sets though, are:

① They can be used as a filter, in a somewhat permanent way.

② Without writing code, you have to create a lot of filters or slicers (which can slow a pivot table down) to display specific rows or columns on a pivot table. This can get messy, if you know what I mean. Named sets allow you to pick and choose the row and column categories that appear on the pivot table without writing any code.

A Named set is a **MULTIDIMENSIONAL EXPRESSION (MDX)** that returns a set of dimension members. Named sets can also be used to create OLAP pivot tables that show different metrics for different areas of a business.

Named sets are created from the data in a pivot table, which makes it a subset of the data displayed in the pivot table. Named sets allow you to easily display a particular view of the data, like only displaying orders from two particular countries.

Use a named set when you know the data needs to be filtered or when there are specific rows or columns of data that you do not want to be displayed on the pivot table.

Named Sets Options

This section explains the Named Sets options and how to access them.

Pivot Table Tools Analyze tab ⇒ Calculations ⇒ **FIELDS, ITEMS & SETS** button, displays the options shown in Figure 13-10.

The options are explained in Table 13-2.

Named sets can be created before or after a pivot table has been created. The only requirement is to have a pivot table object on the worksheet.

Figure 13-10 Named Sets options

Option	Description
Create Set Based on Row Items	Is used to create a Named set for fields in the Rows area. (2)
Create Set Based on Column Items	Is used to create a Named set for fields in the Columns area. (2)
Manage Sets	Opens the dialog box shown in Figure 13-11. The options are used to create, edit and delete named sets.

Table 13-2 Named Sets options explained

(2) This option is only available after a pivot table has been created.

Figure 13-11 Set Manager dialog box

Selecting the **CREATE SET BASED ON ROW ITEMS** option, shown earlier in Figure 13-10, displays the dialog box shown in Figure 13-12.

To create a set, type in a name for it in the **SET NAME** field.

As you can see, there are two columns, which correspond to the number of fields in the Rows area at the bottom of the Pivot Table Fields list.

By default, if applicable, all of the named set combinations are displayed on the dialog box.

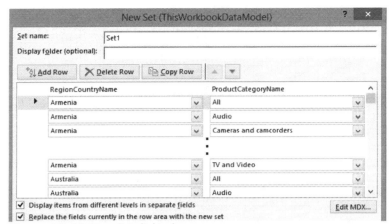

Figure 13-12 New Set dialog box

If you only wanted to include a few of the items, you would have to delete all of the combinations that you did not want to use. That can be time consuming. To maybe make it a little easier, you could open the drop-downs at the top of the list and select the values that you want to use. Then click on the row of the first value that you do not want to keep clicking the Delete Row button, until all other rows are deleted.

The **EDIT MDX** button, shown above in Figure 13-12, opens the Modify Set dialog box, shown later in Figure 13-17.

How The Display And Replace Named Set Options Work

If checked, the **DISPLAY ITEMS FROM DIFFERENT LEVELS IN SEPARATE FIELDS** option does not keep the current fields in the Row or Column area on the Pivot Table Fields list. Keeping this option checked, does not remove any rows or columns from the pivot table when the named set is applied to the pivot table. This kind of defeats the purpose of creating a named set.

If checked, the **REPLACE THE FIELDS CURRENTLY IN THE ROW (OR COLUMN) AREA WITH THE NEW SET** option, the fields in the corresponding area will be replaced with the options in the set. If this option is cleared, the set will be created, but not added to the corresponding area, until you add it.

I tested how these options work. Below is what I found out.

☑ If the Display option is not checked and the Replace option is checked or if both options are checked, what you delete on the dialog box is deleted from the pivot table.
☑ The Display option does nothing if the Replace option is checked.
☑ If the Display option is checked and the Replace option is not checked, what you delete on the dialog box is not deleted from the pivot table, but the set is created.

Sample Named Set

Based on the pivot table shown in Figure 13-13, you could define a set for computer sales in 2009 for Australia, audio sales in 2009 for Australia and Armenia and cell phone sales in 2007 for Armenia.

Figure 13-13 shows the E10.3 Yearly sales by country pivot table, without the Store Name and Products Subcategory fields in the Rows area.

Row Labels	2007	2008	2009	Grand Total
⊟ Armenia	$7,940,032.42	$8,662,141.74	$9,482,761.09	$26,084,935.24
Audio	$52,884.99	$180,801.20	$250,527.25	$484,213.44
Cameras and camcorders	$2,785,514.40	$2,727,453.28	$2,512,621.30	$8,025,588.97
Cell phones	$829,705.40	$899,327.86	$1,095,869.60	$2,824,902.87
Computers	$3,079,107.41	$3,203,311.88	$3,774,741.02	$10,057,160.30
Music, Movies and Audio Books	$178,498.46	$165,105.07	$132,000.27	$475,603.80
TV and Video	$1,014,321.76	$1,486,142.45	$1,717,001.65	$4,217,465.86
⊟ Australia	$23,168,631.98	$26,881,924.55	$29,116,033.12	$79,166,589.65
Audio	$237,934.94	$466,346.81	$902,949.84	$1,607,231.59
Cameras and camcorders	$7,846,918.33	$8,466,044.86	$8,260,609.52	$24,573,572.71

Figure 13-13 Yearly sales by country pivot table without some row labels

Figure 13-14 shows the items that would be used to create the named set, based on the criteria listed above. When you select a named set to be applied, the data in the pivot table will be changed accordingly. Figure 13-15 shows the pivot table with the named set options shown in Figure 13-14 applied.

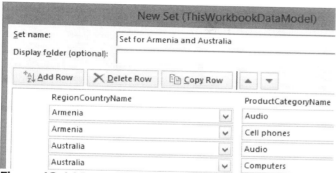

Figure 13-14 Items for a named set

Sum of SalesAmount	Column Labels			
Row Labels	2007	2008	2009	Grand Total
Armenia				
Audio	$52,884.99	$180,801.20	$250,527.25	$484,213.44
Cell phones	$829,705.40	$899,327.86	$1,095,869.60	$2,824,902.87
Australia				
Audio	$237,934.94	$466,346.81	$902,949.84	$1,607,231.59
Computers	$8,993,627.52	$10,054,059.38	$10,418,810.18	$29,466,497.08

Figure 13-15 Pivot table with the named set (for rows) shown above in Figure 13-14 applied

You will also notice changes in the Pivot Table Fields list, as shown in Figure 13-16. The changes are discussed below.

① A folder called **SETS** is automatically created and displayed above all of the tables, as illustrated in the figure, if the set contains fields from different tables. If you rename or don't rename a named set that only uses fields from one table, the set will appear with the table that the named set is based on, as shown later in Figure 13-20.

② The named sets that you create are automatically placed in the corresponding area on the Pivot Table Fields list, if both options at the bottom of Figure 13-12 shown earlier, are checked. Figure 13-16 shows the set placed in the Rows area.

If the named set was based on columns in the pivot table, the named set would be placed in the Columns area.

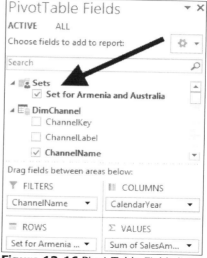

Figure 13-16 Pivot Table Fields list with a named set

 Named Set Warnings

What you will find after you create, apply a named set to a pivot table and save the changes, is that there is no built-in option to restore the pivot table to its original state. For example, Figure 13-15 shown earlier, has a named set applied to a pivot table. Figure 13-13 shown earlier, is the original pivot table.

There is no way to redisplay the pivot table shown earlier in Figure 13-13, without adding the rows (or columns) back to the set. The other work around that I came up with is that when the New Set dialog box is opened for the first time in the current pivot table, the items displayed are for the full pivot table. I save those options as a named set, then I create the named set that I really want and save that named set with a different name. That seemed easier then having to add the original fields back to the pivot table or modifying the set.

Named sets are available to all pivot tables in the workbook, even if the pivot tables are on different worksheets. If you delete a named set, it is removed from all pivot tables that it has been applied to.

The other piece of advice that I would give is that it may bring you some peace of mind if you save the workbook with a new name before creating a named set. That way, if you really get yourself into trouble and do not want to learn MDX to be able to make the changes on the dialog box shown in Figure 13-17, to restore the pivot table, you can open the original pivot table workbook, save it with a new name again and start over.

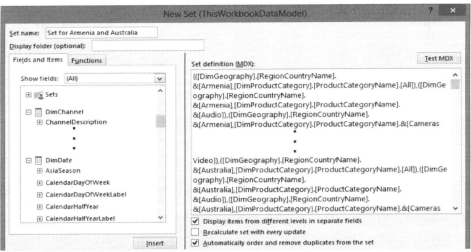

Figure 13-17 Modify Set dialog box (MDX)

Exercise 13.2: Create A Named Set And Apply It To A Pivot Table

This exercise will show you how to create a named set that filters out some of the columns in a pivot table. The goal is to display data for four regions in the US.

1. Save the E2.2 workbook as E13.2 Create a named set to filter columns of data.

2. Click in the pivot table ⇒ Analyze tab ⇒ Fields, Items & Sets button ⇒ Create Set Based on Column items.

3. In the **SET NAME** field, type 4 Regions.

4. In the Display folder field, type US Regions. This replaces the default "Sets" set folder name, illustrated earlier in Figure 13-16.

5. You should see an arrow next to Australia ⇒ Click the **DELETE ROW** button.

6. Except for the rows that start with "North" or "South", delete all of the other rows.

    You should have the options shown in Figure 13-18.

    Click OK. The pivot table will look like the one shown in Figure 13-19.

    Compare it to the pivot table shown in Chapter 2, Figure 2-26.

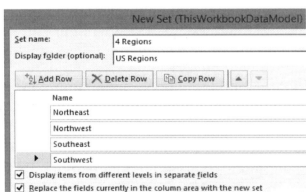

Figure 13-18 Options to display specific columns

At the top of the Pivot Table Fields list, you will see the set that you just created, as shown in Figure 13-20. Also notice that the set is in the Columns area of the Pivot Table Fields list, instead of the Name field.

Sum of SubTotal	Column Labels			
Row Labels ▼	Northeast	Northwest	Southeast	Southwest
(blank)	$6,532.47	$3,649,866.55	$12,238.85	$5,718,150.81
268	$100,165.04	$279,997.59	$181,804.21	$498,966.78
275	$3,547,034.40		$347,730.29	$4,230,221.05
276		$2,562,534.43		$7,859,324.25
277	$4,735,174.26		$309,496.80	$3,569,595.14
279			$8,714,865.97	
280		$4,029,938.36		
281		$936,689.47		$6,371,216.56
283		$4,551,897.66		
287		$2,814,958.89		
Grand Total	**$8,388,906.16**	**$18,825,882.96**	**$9,566,136.13**	**$28,247,474.59**

Figure 13-19 Pivot table with a named set applied to the columns

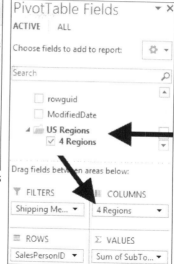

Figure 13-20 Named set illustrated

What Is OLAP?

OLAP stands for Online Analytical Processing. OLAP is used to perform multi-dimensional data analysis. By that I mean that OLAP is used to extract and view data in multi-dimensional databases.

The processing power needed to generate a sales report that displays sales figures for a specific year and month can take a long time when databases that contain millions of records are used. The server can take a performance hit (aka slow down), or even worse, become unstable and possibly crash.

Thus, OLAP was born, with the idea to compute all of the subtotals and totals for data (the millions and millions of records) and store these totals in a different type of database, as explained in the next section.

What Is An OLAP Cube?

An OLAP cube is a multi-dimensional array of data. The data in an OLAP cube is already summarized. This greatly improves the time it takes to perform queries. The data (known as measures) is categorized by dimensions.

A **MEASURE** is a value that has been totaled (summarized). Quantity on hand, quantity sold, price and order amount are examples of a measure.

A **DIMENSION** (formerly known as a member) is a field (or list), if you will, that a measure can be grouped or categorized by. Month, quarter, year, country, size, order date and sales rep name are examples of a dimension.

Guess What? MDX, which was briefly covered earlier in this chapter, is a query language that is used to create expressions that retrieve data from OLAP cubes. This means that the MDX language can be used to create calculations for pivot tables.

OLAP Tools

The options shown in Figure 13-21 are used with a pivot table that is connected to an OLAP data source, like a cube. Pivot Table Tools ⇒ Analyze tab ⇒ OLAP Tools, displays these options.

The **CONVERT TO FORMULAS** option displays the dialog box shown in Figure 13-22. It is used to convert a pivot table to a series of cube functions. Figure 13-23 shows the E10.3 Yearly sales by country pivot table after it was converted to cube functions. After the conversion, the **CUBEMEMBER FUNCTION** is used to retrieve an ordered list (aka dimension), from a cube.

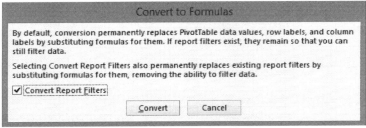

Figure 13-22 Convert to Formulas dialog box

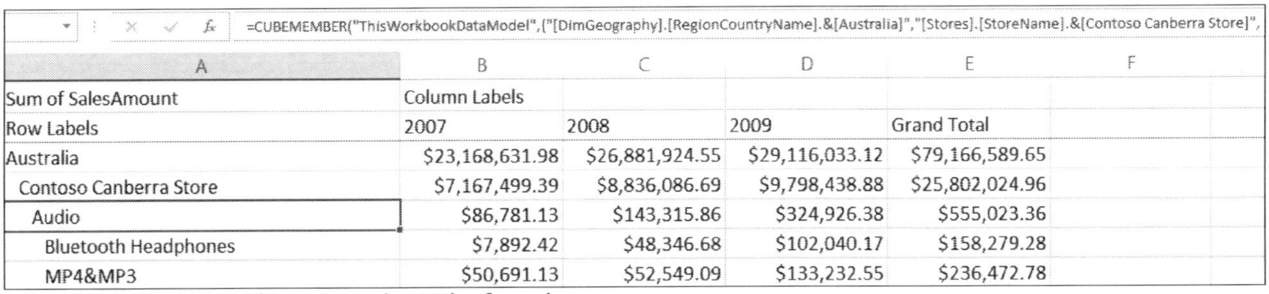

Figure 13-21 OLAP Tools button options

	A	B	C	D	E	F
	Sum of SalesAmount	Column Labels				
	Row Labels	2007	2008	2009	Grand Total	
	Australia	$23,168,631.98	$26,881,924.55	$29,116,033.12	$79,166,589.65	
	Contoso Canberra Store	$7,167,499.39	$8,836,086.69	$9,798,438.88	$25,802,024.96	
	Audio	$86,781.13	$143,315.86	$324,926.38	$555,023.36	
	Bluetooth Headphones	$7,892.42	$48,346.68	$102,040.17	$158,279.28	
	MP4&MP3	$50,691.13	$52,549.09	$133,232.55	$236,472.78	

Formula bar: =CUBEMEMBER("ThisWorkbookDataModel",{"[DimGeography].[RegionCountryName].&[Australia]","[Stores].[StoreName].&[Contoso Canberra Store]",

Figure 13-23 Pivot table converted to cube formulas

In the example shown above in Figure 13-23, the dimensions are in Column A. This is the equivalent of the "Rows" area on the Pivot Table Fields list. The formula to reference this column, is shown in Figure 13-24. It is the formula for the Audio dimension selected in Column A. This formula is in the formula bar at the top of Figure 13-23, but you cannot see it very well.

The first portion of the formula is the connection to the data model. The remainder of the formula is how the Audio member is referenced. If this sounds familiar, that is because it is like the named sets that was covered earlier in this chapter. What may not be obvious is that you can move these formulas around on the worksheet. If the sheet has slicers, they will still work.

=CUBEMEMBER("ThisWorkbookDataModel",{"[DimGeography].[RegionCountryName].&[Australia]","[Stores].[StoreName].&[Contoso Canberra Store]",

Figure 13-24 CubeMember formula

The **CUBEVALUE** formula shown in Figure 13-25 is used to get the 2007 value for the Audio member, that is selected in the spreadsheet, shown earlier in Figure 13-23. Aren't you happy to know that you did not have to type these formulas in? <smile>

=CUBEVALUE("ThisWorkbookDataModel",B1,A3,$A37,B$4)

Figure 13-25 CubeValue formula

Cube Functions

Figure 13-26 shows the Cube functions on the Formulas tab in Excel. Yes, I know that you are grumbling and making faces saying, "When would I need to use Cube functions?".

The short answer from a Power Pivot perspective, is when you cannot create what you need using DAX functions. An example would be to have the ability to add a column to a pivot table to create a custom calculation.

Cube functions are part of Excel and are used to connect straight to the data model, without having to use a pivot table to display the data.

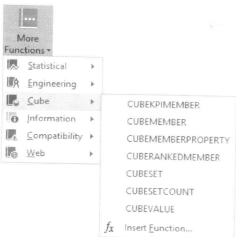

Figure 13-26 Cube functions

Exercise 13.3: Create A Summary Pivot Table

Exercise 10.3 covered creating a yearly sales pivot table. That pivot table contained a lot of data. In this exercise you will create a yearly sales pivot table. The difference is that in this exercise the totals will be displayed by year and by month. Slicers will also be created.

1. Save the E9.2 workbook as `E13.3 Sales summary by year and month pivot table`.

2. Add the fields in Table 13-3, to create the pivot table.

Table	Field	Add To Area
DimChannel	Channel Name	Filters
DimDate	Calendar Month Label	Rows
FactSales	Sales Amount	Values

Table 13-3 Fields to create the pivot table

 Why Not Add The Calendar Year Field Now?
As you can see, the months in the pivot table are not in the order that you want. If you added the Year field now, you would not be able to sort the months because the Row Labels sort options would be applied to the year field. The sort options only work for the first field in the Rows area. This means if you are going to add several fields to this area and need to sort one or all of them, add one field that needs to be sorted ⇒ Use the Rows sort options ⇒ Add the next field to the Rows area ⇒ Use the sort options for the next field, and so on.

3. The months need to be sorted in calendar month order. Follow the steps in Exercise 10.5, "How To Change The Sort Order Of The Month Names", to change the sort order of the months. In step 2, select Calendar Month Label field.

4. DimDate table ⇒
Add the Calendar Year field to the Rows area ⇒
Move it up, above the Calendar Month Label field.

The pivot table should look like the one shown in Figure 13-27.

Row Labels	Sum of SalesAmount
⊟ 2007	**$3,144,393,292.13**
January	$193,305,554.64
February	$209,439,067.93
March	$203,991,979.69
April	$276,891,048.16
May	$288,749,508.61
June	$283,186,644.54
July	$272,818,635.11
August	$263,780,279.28
September	$257,282,781.95
October	$288,853,903.92
November	$308,752,784.65
December	$297,341,103.65
⊟ 2008	**$2,642,413,217.03**
January	$183,970,020.28
February	$191,106,948.30

Figure 13-27 Sales summary pivot table, grouped by year

Add The Quarter Field To The Summary Pivot Table

In this part of the exercise you will add another dimension if you will, to the pivot table. To be able to see the differences with and without the new dimension, you will make a copy of the current pivot table on the same worksheet.

1. Select Columns A and B ⇒ Right-click on the column heading and select Copy.

2. Right-click on Column D ⇒ Select Paste.

3. Click in the second pivot table.

   Add the Calendar Quarter Label field in the DimDate table to the Rows area, below the Calendar Year field.

   The second pivot table should look like the one shown in Figure 13-28.

   As you can see, you can minimize a quarter (See 2007 Q3) or a year.

Row Labels	Sum of SalesAmount
⊟ 2007	**$3,144,393,292.13**
⊟ Q1	**$606,736,602.25**
January	$193,305,554.64
February	$209,439,067.93
March	$203,991,979.69
⊟ Q2	**$848,827,201.31**
April	$276,891,048.16
May	$288,749,508.61
June	$283,186,644.54
⊞ Q3	**$793,881,696.34**
⊟ Q4	**$894,947,792.23**
October	$288,853,903.92
November	$308,752,784.65
December	$297,341,103.65
⊟ 2008	**$2,642,413,217.03**
⊟ Q1	**$558,470,281.47**
January	$183,970,020.28
February	$191,106,948.30

Figure 13-28 Sales summary grouped by year, quarter and month

Create Slicers For The Summary Pivot Table

The pivot table shown above in Figure 13-28 basically displays all of the data in a table. It provides a high level overview of the sales. For some users, the pivot table would be more valuable if it had slicers that would allow the sales amount to be categorized more. In this part of the exercise, you will create slicers for the country and category name fields.

1. If necessary, add another sheet to the workbook ⇒ Rename the new sheet to Sales by Country & Category.

2. Copy and paste the pivot table shown above in Figure 13-28, to the new sheet.

3. Create a slicer for the Region Country Name field in the Dim Geography table ⇒ Change the Slicer Caption to Country.

4. Create a slicer for the Product Category Name field in the Dim Product Category table ⇒ Change the Slicer Caption to Product Category.

Now, the pivot table shown in Figure 13-29 allows the data to be filtered, so that more analysis can be done on the data.

For example, the new pivot table can show sale amounts by year, quarter and month, by country and/or product category.

Figure 13-29 Sales summary data filtered by country and product category

Exercise 13.4: Create A Named Set Using Multiple Rows

Exercise 13.2 covered creating a named set that used one column. Exercise 13.3 covered creating a pivot table that displayed the sale amount totals by year, quarter and month. As you saw, you could roll up the years and quarters, but not the month. What do you do if you only wanted to display random months in each year or quarter? I haven't tried, but it may be possible using filters.

Another option is to use a named set. Being able to select which months to display on the pivot table, you could just display the months where the same marketing campaign was run during the year. This would make it easy to be able to report on those months without having to figure out how to hide the months that are not needed.

In this exercise, you will create a named set that shows the quarters for each year and random months in each quarter. As you will see, each combination of year, quarter and month can be selected individually.

1. Save the E13.3 workbook as `E13.4 Named set with multiple rows`.

2. Delete the Sheet 1 tab ⇒ Rename the remaining tab to `Row level named set`.

3. Click on the pivot table ⇒ Analyze tab ⇒ Fields, Items & Sets button ⇒ Create Set Based on Row Items. As you see on the New Set dialog box, there is a row for each combination of values.

4. In the Set name field type `Months To Keep` ⇒ Enter a name for the Display folder.

5. Delete the rows in Table 13-4.

   When finished, you should have the rows for 2007 shown in Figure 13-30.

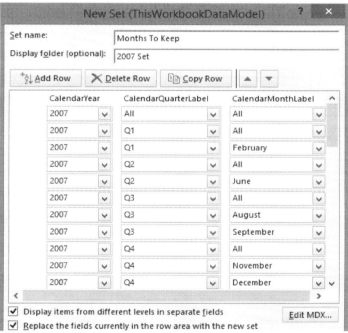

Year	Quarter	Month
2007	1	January
2007	1	March
2007	2	April
2007	2	May
2007	3	July
2007	4	October

Table 13-4 Rows to delete

 The **ALL** option in some of the drop-down lists on the dialog box, points to a summary value (data with bold formatting) in the pivot table.

Figure 13-30 Named set criteria

The pivot table should look like the one shown in Figure 13-31. Depending on the options selected on the slicers, you will see different sales amount totals. For this figure, I selected the United States and cleared the filter on the Product Category slicer. Notice that you can no longer roll up the data (like hide a year or quarter) on any level of the pivot table.

Figure 13-32 shows the Pivot Table Fields list. Notice that the set is at the top of the list. That is because the values in each row, come from different tables. If you wanted to edit the set, you could.

Row Labels	Sum of SalesAmount
2007	**$3,144,393,292.13**
Q1	**$606,736,602.25**
February	$209,439,067.93
Q2	**$848,827,201.31**
June	$283,186,644.54
Q3	**$793,881,696.34**
August	$263,780,279.28
September	$257,282,781.95
Q4	**$894,947,792.23**
November	$308,752,784.65
December	$297,341,103.65

Figure 13-31 Pivot table with specific rows (months) deleted in 2007

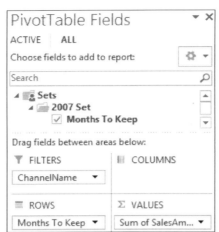

Figure 13-32 Pivot Table Fields list with a named set

What Does Drill Down Mean?

Drilling down refers to the process of initially viewing aggregated data at a high level (aka viewing data in summary format), then displaying the detail records for a portion of the high level summary. In some software, drilling down is executed by clicking on a plus sign button to see the next level down. In other software, double-clicking on a row of summary data displays the corresponding detail rows of data. Hierarchies can be created to add drill down functionality to a pivot table.

Drilling Down In A Pivot Table

If you have the need to see the rows of data that were used to create an aggregated value (a field in the Values area of the Pivot Table Fields list) in the pivot table, double-click on the cell that you want to see the rows of data for. A new sheet will be added to the workbook that displays up to 1,000 rows of data. [See Figure 13-7]

Summary

This chapter covered a way to customize currency values displayed on a pivot chart and two ways to drill down on the data in a pivot table. Named sets was introduced as a way to create a custom filter for a pivot table. My advice is to apply a named set to a copy of the pivot table in the workbook, just in case something goes wrong, as there is no undo for this feature. My goal of introducing named sets was to show that it is possible to "pick and choose" the rows or columns that are displayed on a pivot table, without writing code. Yes, you can thank me now <smile>.

ENHANCING PIVOT TABLES AND CHARTS PART 2

Overview

In this chapter you will learn about the following options that can be used to enhance pivot tables and charts.

- ☑ Key performance indicators
- ☑ Using percents
- ☑ Perspectives
- ☑ Date tables
- ☑ Hierarchies
- ☑ An option to automate refreshing data

CHAPTER 14

KPI's

(KPI stands for **KEY PERFORMANCE INDICATOR**). KPI's are a way to measure the performance of a process or objective. If you have seen or created a **SCORECARD**, you may already be familiar with KPI's. If you haven't seen a scorecard, it will remind you of a report card. It provides a summary of how the organization has performed during the last period. The goal of KPI's is to uncover performance that is not in the normal, acceptable range.

A KPI is an actual value that is measured against a target. This tool uses colored icons that indicate how a value compares to the target value. This array of colors depict the range of values that are considered, good (a value above the target value), acceptable (slightly above or below the target value) or poor (below the lowest acceptable target value).

Many dashboards are created around this concept because key performance indicators are one tool used to make business decisions, strategic or otherwise. KPI's are a measure of success, where you define what success is. A measure is needed to create a KPI. While some measures require DAX to be used to create the formula, the Auto Sum options can also be used to create a measure, if the calculation needed is not very complex. If that is the case, no DAX is required.

Chapter 3 briefly covered the Auto Sum and KPI options. KPI's are displayed visually, using icons (symbols). Traffic lights that use the colors, red, yellow and green, is a symbol that you may have already seen, to display the status of the metric. This allows the user to easily evaluate the value (usually per row) against the target value. KPI's are often used in dashboards because they make it easier to see trends, without having to read numbers.

KPI's are also used to alert the reader to values that are outside of the extended range. For example, if sales reps have a monthly goal of $50,000 worth of orders, it is easier to tell which reps did meet or exceed the expected goal, if there is a check mark icon, that indicates that goal was met, next to their name. This is easier then having to look at each reps total monthly order amount.

KPI Options On The Power Pivot Tab

The options shown in Figure 14-1 are used to create and edit KPI's. Keep in mind that KPI's cannot be created if the table does not have any measures.

The **NEW KPI** option opens the Key Performance Indicator (KPI) dialog box shown later in Figure 14-8.

The **MANAGE KPI'S** option opens the dialog box shown in Figure 14-2. The options on this dialog box are used to create, edit and delete KPI's.

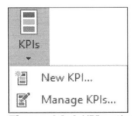

Figure 14-1 KPI options on the Power Pivot tab

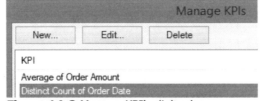

Figure 14-2 Manage KPI's dialog box

KPI Locations

The **KPI** measures illustrated in Figure 14-3, are displayed in the Pivot Table Fields list, at the button of the table, as illustrated in Figure 14-4.

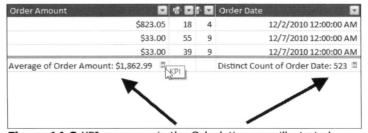

Figure 14-3 KPI measures in the Calculation area illustrated

When displayed in the Pivot Table Fields list, each KPI has three fields, as explained below.

The **VALUE** field displays the value of the calculation (measure).

The **GOAL** field contains the absolute value, which is set on the KPI dialog box. It is the same for every row of data.

The **STATUS** field contains the icon that represents the data in the Value field.

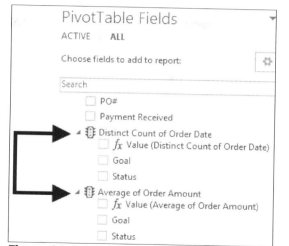

Figure 14-4 KPI's in the Pivot Table Fields list illustrated

Key Performance Indicator (KPI) Dialog Box

The three ways to open this dialog box, which is shown later in Figure 14-8, are explained below.

① Power Pivot tab ⇒ Select the **NEW KPI** option shown earlier in Figure 14-1.
② Power Pivot ⇒ Home tab ⇒ Click on the measure in the Calculation area ⇒ Click the **CREATE KPI** button.
③ In the Calculation area, right-click on the measure ⇒ Select Create KPI, as shown in Figure 14-5.

Deleting A KPI
Select the **DELETE** option shown in Figure 14-5 to delete the selected KPI. Deleting the KPI does not delete the measure that it was created from.

The **FORMAT** option opens the dialog box shown in Figure 14-6. The options are used to format a numeric field.

The **DESCRIPTION** option opens the dialog box shown in Figure 14-7. It is used to provide information about the KPI, like what pivot table uses it.

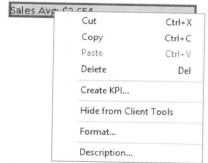

Figure 14-5 Measure shortcut menu

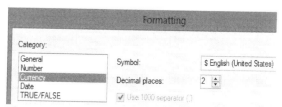

Figure 14-6 Formatting dialog box

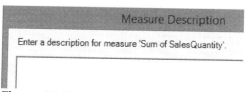

Figure 14-7 Measure Description dialog box

Figure 14-8 shows the dialog box used to create and edit KPI's. The options are explained below.

KPI BASE FIELD (VALUE) Defaults to the measure selected to open the dialog box. If this dialog box is opened from the Power Pivot tab and the workbook has more than one measure, you can select the measure that you want to use, from the drop-down list.

The measure selected in this field is known as the **BASE VALUE** because it is used as the comparison value for the target value.

DEFINE TARGET VALUE The options for selecting the target value are:

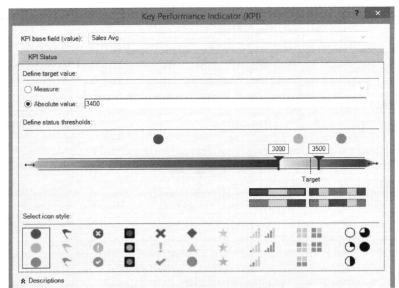

Figure 14-8 Key Performance Indicator (KPI) dialog box

① **MEASURE** Select this option if there is a measure other then the one being used as the base value, to use as the comparison. This target value option uses percents as the status thresholds.
② **ABSOLUTE VALUE** Select this option when you want to use a specific value in the comparison. For example, you need to track the daily sales of several stores and need to see how close each store is to meeting the $15,000 a day metric (goal). You would enter 15000 in this field. You can also use a percent in this field, by typing .10 for 10% or .25 for 25%.

One potential issue using the Absolute Value target value option with whole numbers, is if the Base Value changes a lot (it doesn't matter if the change is lower or higher). Data that initially met the criteria of being above average, may not be true anymore and the person using the dashboard may not know this unless the details of the KPI are displayed near the KPI on the worksheet or dashboard. The solution may be that the absolute value may need to be changed at some point.

DEFINE STATUS THRESHOLDS Is used to select the range and intervals that are acceptable. In theory, you are usually only selecting the middle range values. The arrows at the beginning and end of the bar slide to help select where the target value should be.

For example, the top bar shown in Figure 14-9, shows the Target market to the right of the bar. Dragging the right arrow to the left, moves the target value, as shown in the bottom bar.

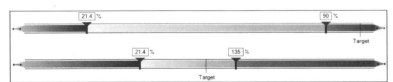

Figure 14-9 Target location before and after the move

There are two other ways to select the values or percents:

① Click in the left most box in this section of the dialog box and enter the lowest percent or value that is acceptable. Click in the other box and enter the largest percent or value that is acceptable. This translates into the lowest value that will be displayed as good.
② Click in the Define status thresholds section of the dialog box. The status markers will change to funnels. Drag each funnel marker to display the value or percent that you need.

Threshold Options

Below and to the right of the status thresholds are four sets of bars, as shown in Figure 14-10. Each represents a different way of displaying the data.

The first choice you have to make is if you want to display three or five status icons.

The options are explained below.

Figure 14-10 Threshold options

① This is the default option. It uses three icons. Red indicates a lower number (below the threshold). Yellow indicates that the value is in the acceptable range. Green indicates a higher number (above the threshold).
② The colors in this option work the opposite of option 1. Green represents low values and red represents high values.
③ This option uses five icons. Red, on both ends of the bar, indicates extreme values.
④ This option works the opposite of option 3. Red, in the middle, indicates that the value is closer to the base value.

SELECT ICON STYLE This is where you want to select the icons that will be displayed on the pivot table. The last three styles are for the five status threshold options. The icons in this section are the same style that the **ICON SETS** conditional formatting option uses. [See Chapter 15, Exercise 15.9]

DESCRIPTIONS Clicking on this option displays the screen shown in Figure 14-11.

This screen is used to document the options selected on the KPI Status screen. This is helpful because a few weeks or months from now, you may not remember why you selected the options that you did, to create the KPI. Don't act like I am the only one <smile>.

The KPI description field is also used as a tooltip in **POWER VIEW**.

To return to the other screen, click on the words **KPI STATUS**, at the top of the screen.

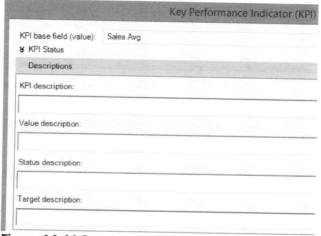

Figure 14-11 Description screen on the Key Performance Indicator (KPI) dialog box

Exercise 14.1: Create And Add A KPI To A Pivot Table

In this exercise you will create a measure that displays the average order amount. The first KPI field added will display the average sales amount per month. The second KPI field will display where the average sales amount falls in the range. The measures will be added to the first pivot table created in Exercise 13.3.

Create The Measure For The KPI

This measure is what the KPI will be based on.

1. Save the E13.3 workbook as `E14.1 Pivot Table With A KPI`.

2. Power Pivot window ⇒ Display the Fact Sales table ⇒ Display the **CALCULATION AREA**, if it is not already displayed ⇒ Click in an empty cell below the Sales Amount column.

3. Open the Auto Sum drop-down list and select Average.

If you look in the formula bar, you will see the DAX formula that was automatically created to calculate the average sales amount.

The first part of the formula is the column name, which is long, as shown in Figure 14-12.

f_x | Average of SalesAmount:=AVERAGE([SalesAmount])

Figure 14-12 Measure

4. Click in the formula bar and change the formula name to Sales Avg, as shown in Figure 14-13 ⇒ Click on a blank space, so that the formula name change will be updated.

Sales Avg:=AVERAGE([SalesAmount])

Figure 14-13 Modified measure field name

Create The KPI For The Sales Avg Measure

In this exercise, the calculated average sale amount is $3,654. The values below will be used to create the KPI. The criteria is listed below.

① The goal is $3,400.
② The acceptable range is $3,000 or higher. Anything above this is great.
③ Sale amounts less than $3,000 is not acceptable.

1. Right-click on the measure that you just created ⇒ Select Create KPI.

2. Select the Absolute value option ⇒ Type 3400 in the field.

3. Slide the first marker to 3000 or click in the marker label and type 3000.

4. In the second marker label, type 3500. You should have the options shown earlier in Figure 14-8.

5. Select an icon style that you like ⇒ Click OK.

Add The KPI Fields To The Pivot Table

The KPI that you just created, added a few values to the Fact Sales table. In addition to viewing these fields, you will also add some of them to the pivot table.

1. Display Sheet 1 ⇒ Delete the second pivot table.

2. In the Pivot Table Fields list, display the bottom of the Fact Sales table. You should see the KPI fields shown in Figure 14-14.

   To me, not seeing the value that the icon represents, makes it difficult to understand what the KPI icon means. Displaying the value field is optional.

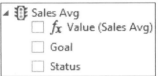

Figure 14-14 Sales Avg KPI fields

3. Check the Value and Status fields.

   The pivot table should look like the one shown in Figure 14-15.

Row Labels	Sum of SalesAmount	SalesAvg	SalesAvg Status
⊟2007	$3,144,393,292.13	$3,206.46	◯
January	$193,305,554.64	$2,616.91	⬤
February	$209,439,067.93	$2,982.95	⬤
March	$203,991,979.69	$2,771.78	⬤
April	$276,891,048.16	$3,031.50	◯
May	$288,749,508.61	$3,064.53	◯
June	$283,186,644.54	$3,059.72	◯
July	$272,818,635.11	$3,580.63	◯
August	$263,780,279.28	$3,466.92	◯
September	$257,282,781.95	$3,439.52	◯
October	$288,853,903.92	$2,959.02	⬤
November	$308,752,784.65	$3,951.53	◯
December	$297,341,103.65	$3,625.27	◯

Figure 14-15 KPI fields added to the pivot table

Using Percents

Calculated fields can be created to display percents in a pivot table.

If you want to see values as percents in the pivot table, but do not want to create calculated fields or formulas, you can right-click on a value in the pivot table and select **SHOW VALUES AS**, then select one of the options shown on the right of Figure 14-16.

Selecting one of the percent options displays the values in the pivot table as percents. It is not uncommon to have one pivot table display the values and another pivot table display the same values as percents, on the same worksheet.

Figure 14-17 displays the sales by country and by period. It shows the same data on both pivot tables.

The pivot table on the left displays the values. The pivot table on the right, displays the same values with the **% OF COLUMN TOTAL** percent option applied.

To create the table that displays the percents, I made a copy of the pivot table on the left, then applied the percent option to the pivot table on the right.

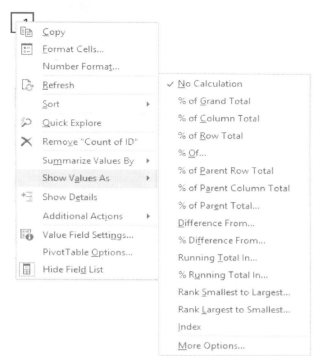

Figure 14-16 Percent options

Sales Period	Column Labels ▾			Sales Period	Column Labels ▾		
Row Labels ⊤	Current	MTD	YTD	Row Labels ⊤	Current	MTD	YTD
Armenia	$19,966.02	$575,832.63	$4,309,629.54	Armenia	0.28%	0.32%	0.37%
Australia	$60,751.65	$1,997,588.61	$13,617,449.14	Australia	0.84%	1.09%	1.16%
Bhutan	$19,016.94	$638,264.76	$4,168,192.06	Bhutan	0.26%	0.35%	0.35%
Canada	$134,287.70	$3,552,896.90	$21,331,141.77	Canada	1.86%	1.95%	1.82%
China	$1,035,643.68	$27,608,267.40	$177,671,551.46	China	14.33%	15.12%	15.13%
Denmark	$9,533.60	$217,565.80	$1,886,057.89	Denmark	0.13%	0.12%	0.16%
France	$379,196.10	$9,735,006.10	$62,678,377.33	France	5.25%	5.33%	5.34%

Figure 14-17 Same data displayed in percent format

Perspectives

Chapter 3 covered the Perspective options on the Advanced tab in Power Pivot. They are used to create a custom view of data in a workbook. By default, all of the data, unless hidden, can be viewed in the Pivot Table Fields list. There may be instances when all of the data does not need to be visible to create pivot tables.

Perspectives are used to select the columns of data from any table in the data model that you want to be displayed in Power Pivot and in the Pivot Table Fields list. Fields in a perspective are used as a data source and can be used to create reports in **POWER VIEW**. A feature that I like is that key fields (columns) do not have to be included in the perspective. This feature is helpful because rarely are key fields displayed in a pivot table. You can create as many perspectives as needed in the workbook.

While this sounds great, in order to use a perspective to create a pivot table or chart, the workbook has to be on a Share Point server. If you do not have access to this type of server, you can skip the demonstration below. It shows how to create a perspective, but not how to create a pivot table based on it. Don't feel bad, I do not have access to this type of server either <smile>.

Perspectives Dialog Box

Figure 14-18 shows the dialog box used to create and edit perspectives. It is easy to create a perspective. Check the fields you want to include or clear the check mark for fields that you want to remove from the perspective. Click the **NEW PERSPECTIVE** button to create another perspective.

When you hold the mouse pointer over a check box, the three icons illustrated above in Figure 14-18 appear.

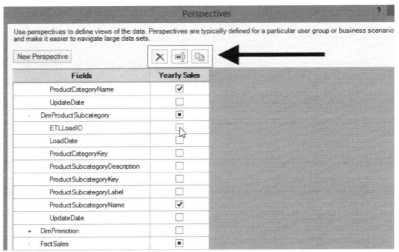

The buttons are used to delete the selected perspective, rename the perspective and copy the selected perspective to a new perspective.

The steps below demonstrate the basics of creating a perspective.

Figure 14-18 Perspectives dialog box

1. Save the E9.2 workbook as E14 Yearly Sales Perspective.

2. Power Pivot window ⇒ Advanced tab ⇒ Click the Create and Manage button.

3. New Perspective button ⇒ Type Yearly Sales as the Perspective Name. Ignore the message at the bottom of the dialog box, that says that there are no objects in the Perspective.

4. Check the fields in Table 14-1.

Table	Field
DimChannel	Channel Name
DimDate	Calendar Month Label
DimDate	Calendar Year
DimGeography	Region Country Name
DimProductCategory	Product Category Name
DimProductSubcategory	Product Subcategory Name
Fact Sales	Discount Amount
Fact Sales	Sales Amount
Fact Sales	Total Cost
Stores	Store Name

Table 14-1 Fields to create the Perspective

5. Figure 14-18 shown above, shows some of the fields that you just selected for the perspective. Click OK. The perspective will be created.

6. To view the fields and tables in the perspective, Power Pivot window ⇒ Advanced tab ⇒ **SELECT** button drop-down list ⇒ Select the Yearly Sales perspective.

   At the bottom of the workspace, you will only see the tables that were used to create a perspective. The reason that you only see one field for some tables is because that is what was selected to create the perspective.

Solving The Slicer Month Names In Calendar Order Problem

I have to admit that I am shocked that there is still no straight forward solution in Power Pivot for displaying months in calendar order, opposed to displaying them in alphabetical order. There is a solution (with several steps) in Excel, which you used in Chapter 10, Exercise 10.5, called Custom Lists, but you can't use it for slicers created from data in the data model.

There are solutions that require using DAX, but since that is beyond the scope of this book, I had to try and find a solution that did not require writing code. Chapter 3, Table 3-13, explained covered the **MARK AS DATE TABLE** and **DATE TABLE** options. Once I made the connection of having to force the months to appear in a specific order and looking at a date table that I had manually created, I knew this was a solution and one that did not require writing code.

Why Would I Need A Date Table?

In addition to the scenario discussed in the previous section, date tables are useful when there is a need to analyze data over time (forecasting). Date tables are required to use the time intelligence DAX functions. Displaying data in year to date or month to date format, requires a date table.

Date Table Requirements

To be used as a date table, the table must have all of the following:

① A date key field that has the Date data type.
② The date key field must have consecutive dates. No dates in the range can be skipped.
③ The table should have a matching date for the oldest and newest dates in the other tables in the data model that have dates.

Default Date Table Options

The default specifications for the date table that Power Pivot creates are listed below.

☑ Name of table created - Calendar
☑ Date range - 1/1/1996 - 12/31/2011
☑ Columns created [See Table 14-2]

Column Name	Format
Date	MM/DD/YYYY HH:MM:SS AM/PM
Year	YYYY
Month Number	1 to 12
Month	Month name spelled out like this January, February.
YYYY-MM	2015-09 (the dash is displayed as part of the date)
Day Of Week Number	1 to 7
Day Of Week	Monday, Tuesday

Table 14-2 Default columns created in date table

If you look in the Dim Date table [See Exercise 14.1], you will see a lot of other date related columns. They are all created from the date in the Date Key column. They were created using the Add Column (the last column in any table in the data model) to create a formula or DAX expression. After you create the date table using the built in functionality, you will be able to view the formulas that were used to create each of the columns, except the first one.

My Thoughts On Date Tables

Before creating this table, at the very least, you need to figure out the date range and what date formats are needed. The date range that you select should include dates as far back in time as you need to filter, slice and dice the data by. For example, if the order table has orders from 2000 to 2016, the minimum date range that you would select is 1/1/2000 to 12/31/2016.

It is not a requirement to create a date table that includes all of the dates in the table(s) in the data model. If you don't, when using the date table, records with dates outside of the date range of the date table will not be on any report.

While a date table can be created in Excel, I prefer to create it in Power Pivot because with a few mouse clicks, I can have the date range set up perfectly! And a few date columns are created without my intervention. When you create a calculated column in Power Pivot, the formula is automatically applied to every row in the table. This is easier for me, then creating formulas and dragging them down to the last row of the table, then setting the columns to be a table, so that I can link it to a table in the data model. Either way, if you don't create enough rows and columns in the date table, you will find yourself editing this table on a regular basis <smile>.

I went 10 years past the date that I created the table on, because I honestly do not want to be bothered updating the table any time soon. Doing this will also accommodate new records, in other tables that use this table, that will have dates beyond today. Yes, I know creating several extra years worth of data can slow the table down. Being who I am <smile>, I created the date table in its own workbook. This also allows me to create new date formats (new columns) as needed and test new date formats without having to worry about messing up live data. When I need a new workbook, I save the date workbook with a new name, so that I do not have to import the date table.

Date Table Button Options

Figure 14-19 shows the options for creating a new date table and updating an existing date table. The date table created, is similar to the one shown in Figure 14-20.

In addition to being able to select a different date range then the default range, formulas can be created to add additional date columns to the table.

The options on this button are explained below.

Figure 14-19 Date Table button options

When a date table that was created in Power Pivot is displayed and the Date Table button is clicked, the other options on the button are enabled.

NEW Creates a new date table.

SAVE CONFIGURATION Select this option if you want the default columns and new columns that you create, to be saved to the template (My Date Table) that is used to create a date table. Doing this means that the changes you make and save now, will appear in future date tables that you create on the computer that you are currently using.

SET DEFAULT Select this option if you made changes to the template that you no longer want. The original default date table settings will be restored.

UPDATE RANGE This option is used to change the date range in the table. The first date in this table should at least equal the oldest date in any of the other tables in the workbook. The last date in this table should at least equal the newest date in any of the other tables in the workbook. As I said earlier, in the date table that I created, the last date in the date table is 10 years after the date that I created the table on.

Exercise 14.2: Create A Date Table

In Chapter 12, Exercise 12.2, you created a dashboard that uses a month slicer. It needs to be modified to display the months in what I call "calendar month order". This exercise will show you how to create a date table, which will be used with the slicer that needs to display the month names in calendar month order.

Create The Date Table

1. Save the E12.2 workbook as `E14.2 Slicer month name resolution`.

2. Power Pivot window ⇒ Design tab ⇒ Date Table button ⇒ New, as shown above in Figure 14-19.

   The date table shown in Figure 14-20 will be created. Several thousand rows of data are created. One row for each date in the range. The Date column contains the full date.

	Date	Year	MonthNumber	Month	YYYY-MM	DayOfWeekNumber	DayOfWeek
1	1/1/1996 12:00:00 AM	1996	1	January	1996-01	2	Monday
2	1/2/1996 12:00:00 AM	1996	1	January	1996-01	3	Tuesday
3	1/3/1996 12:00:00 AM	1996	1	January	1996-01	4	Wednesday
4	1/4/1996 12:00:00 AM	1996	1	January	1996-01	5	Thursday
5	1/5/1996 12:00:00 AM	1996	1	January	1996-01	6	Friday

Figure 14-20 Default Date table

The other columns contain one or more pieces of the date in the Date column. For example, the YYYY-MM column contains the year and month of the date. Any of the data in these columns can be displayed on a pivot table. Did you notice the Month Number and Month columns? These are the columns that are needed to display the month names in calendar month order in a pivot table.

3. Rename the tab to `MyDatesTable`.

Viewing The Formulas Used To Create The Date Fields

Click on a column or cell to view the formula that created the data. All of the formulas use the Date column, which is the first column in the table. Figure 14-21 shows the formula used to create the Month column.

MMMM displays the month name spelled out. Changing the formula to only display three M's will display the month name abbreviated as three characters (Jan, Feb etc.).

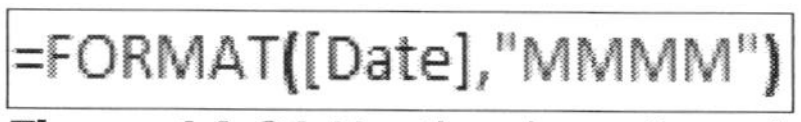

=FORMAT([Date],"MMMM")

Figure 14-21 Month column formula

If you had the need to display the month name abbreviated in some places, you would create another column in the table using the formula shown above in Figure 14-21, minus one "M".

Change The Date Range Of The Date Table

In this part of the exercise, you will learn how to modify the date range in the My Dates table. You will change the start date to 1/1/2005 and change the end date to five years from December 31st of this year. In the future, this is how you can add more dates to an existing date table.

1. Date Table button ⇒ Update Range.

   On the dialog box shown in Figure 14-22, you can type in the date range that you need or click the button at the end of the field and select the date on the calendar.

Figure 14-22 Date Table Range dialog box

2. Change the Start Date to 1/1/2005 ⇒ Change the End Date to five years from the end of this year. For example, if it is currently, 9/19/2015, change the date to 12/31/2020 ⇒ Click OK. The table will be updated.

Create The Relationship For The Date Table

To be able to use this date table with the other tables in the workbook, the date table needs to be linked to another table. In this workbook, it will be linked to the Dim Date table. The links will use the first column in each table.

1. Design tab ⇒ Create Relationship button.

2. Table 1 drop-down list ⇒ Select the Dim Date table ⇒ Click on the Date Key field.

3. Table 2 drop-down list ⇒ Select the MyDatesTable ⇒ Click on the Date field ⇒ Click OK.

4. To verify the relationship, click the Manage Relationships button. You should see the first relationship shown in Figure 14-23 ⇒ Close the Power Pivot window.

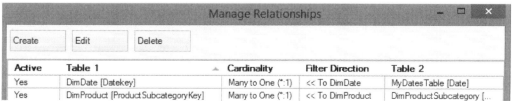

Active	Table 1		Cardinality	Filter Direction	Table 2
Yes	DimDate [Datekey]		Many to One (*:1)	<< To DimDate	MyDatesTable [Date]
Yes	DimProduct [ProductSubcategoryKey]		Many to One (*:1)	<< To DimProduct	DimProductSubcategory [...

Figure 14-23 Relationship for the new date table

Change The Month Slicer

In this part of the exercise you will delete the current month slicer and replace it with one that uses the new date table. I suspect that this is the moment that you have been waiting for.

1. In Excel, delete the Month slicer.

2. At the top of the Pivot Table Fields list, click on the **ALL** option ⇒ Scroll down the list and display the fields in the MyDatesTable, as shown in Figure 14-24.

   Notice that a hierarchy was automatically created in the date table. This is the same hierarchy that is covered in detail after this exercise.

   Right-click on the Month field ⇒ Select Add as Slicer.

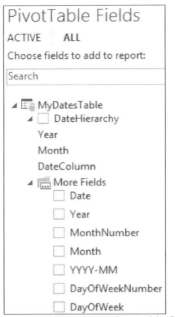

Figure 14-24 New date table fields

3. Click on the Slicer ⇒ On the Options tab, change the Columns option to 4 ⇒ Resize the slicer so that it fits next to the Year slicer.

   Notice that the months are in Calendar month order, as shown in Figure 14-25. Yeah!

Figure 14-25 Slicer in calendar month order

What Is A Hierarchy?

A hierarchy is two or more columns, in a table, that are used to group the rows of data in a nested format. Hierarchies are used to easily create a drill-down effect in a pivot table. If you have heard the term "Roll up the data", a hierarchy provides the functionality needed to roll up data (values) to a higher level.

The order that the columns are placed in a hierarchy is important. The column of data that is the broadest (also known as the top or highest level) is placed at the top of the hierarchy. The other columns that are added to the hierarchy, must represent a subset of the column above it. Fields in a hierarchy have what is known as a **PARENT-CHILD RELATIONSHIP**.

For example, a customer table usually has city, state and country fields. When viewing data in a pivot table, placing these three fields in the Filter area, in that order, would not produce the results that you are looking for. The correct order to place these fields in, is country, state and city. Each country has several states and each state has several cities.

When creating a pivot table that has these three fields in a hierarchy, you add the name of the hierarchy to the area (rows or columns) that you want the three fields displayed in. Once added to the pivot table, you will know quickly, whether or not you placed the fields in the right order, when you created the hierarchy. While hierarchies are not necessary, they can be useful, especially for people that are learning how to create pivot tables.

If you know that you have the need to create several pivot tables or charts that require the same fields in a table to be added to the same drop zone area, create a hierarchy for them. You can use as many fields as necessary to create the hierarchy. I vaguely remember reading somewhere that a hierarchy can have 64 levels maximum. Hopefully, that is enough for you <smile>.

If you are like me and cannot always remember the name of a field, using a hierarchy will help, because you can name the hierarchy whatever you want. Examples of groups of fields to create a hierarchy for, that come to mind are:

① Year, Quarter, Month
② Two fields that are consistently used to create filters for a pivot table, like sales rep name and orders
③ Country, State, City

How To Create A Hierarchy

Hierarchies are created in the Diagram View. Keep in mind that a table can have more than one hierarchy. There are three ways to create a hierarchy, as explained below.

Option 1

1. Click on the first field in the table that you want to add to the hierarchy.

2. Press the **CTRL KEY** ⇒ Click on the other fields to add to the hierarchy.

3. Right-click on one of the selected fields ⇒ Select **CREATE HIERARCHY**, as shown in Figure 14-26.

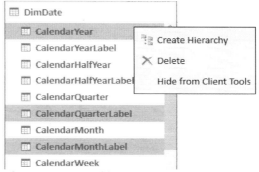

Figure 14-26 Field shortcut menu

4. At the bottom of the table, type in a name for the hierarchy.

Option 2

This is my favorite option because I can add the fields in order, usually without scrolling.

1. Click the **CREATE HIERARCHY** button at the top of the table.

2. Type in a name for the hierarchy in the highlighted field ⇒ Press Enter.

3. Right-click on the top level (the first) field that you want to add to the hierarchy ⇒ Add to Hierarchy ⇒ Select the hierarchy to add the field to, as shown in Figure 14-27.

   The only hierarchies that are displayed are ones that the field has not been added to.

   This prevents you from adding the same field twice to the same hierarchy.

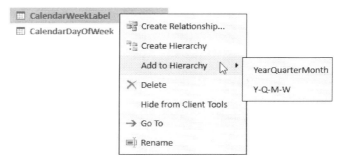

Figure 14-27 Multiple hierarchies to select from

The **DELETE** option deletes the field from the table.

4. In order, add the remaining fields needed to create the hierarchy.

Option 3

1. Click the **CREATE HIERARCHY** button at the top of the table.

2. Type in a name for the hierarchy in the highlighted field ⇒ Press Enter.

3. Drag the top level field down and place it below the hierarchy name. This can be time consuming if the table has a lot of fields. Making the table longer will help.

4. Drag the other fields to the hierarchy.

Exercise 14.3: Create A Date Field Hierarchy

Exercise 13.3 covered creating a summary pivot table. To create this pivot table, three date fields were added to the Rows area on the Pivot Table Fields list.

This exercise will show you how to create a hierarchy that has the year, quarter and month fields. If needed, the week field could also be added to the hierarchy.

Create The Hierarchy

1. Save the E9.2 workbook as E14.3 Date hierarchy.

2. Power Pivot window ⇒ Switch to the **DIAGRAM VIEW**.

3. Use one of the options outlined above to create a hierarchy with the following specifications. In the DimDate table, create a hierarchy named YearQuarterMonth, that has the following fields, in this order: Calendar Year, Calendar Quarter Label, Calendar Month Label.

View The Hierarchy In The Pivot Table Fields List

When hierarchies are created, they are stored at the bottom of the list of fields in the table (in the Design View).

In the Pivot Table Fields list, the hierarchies are displayed at the top of the table, as illustrated in Figure 14-28.

The **MORE FIELDS** section, shown at the bottom of the figure, contains all of the fields in the table. Instead of having to add each of the fields in the hierarchy individually, add the hierarchy name to the pivot table.

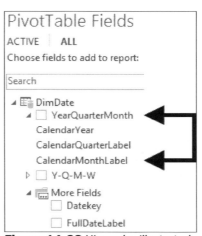

Figure 14-28 Hierarchy illustrated

Create A Pivot Table Using A Hierarchy

1. Add a pivot table to the existing sheet.

2. Display the fields in the DimDate table, shown above in Figure 14-28 ⇒ Add the YearQuarterMonth hierarchy to the Rows area.

3. Fact Sales table ⇒ Add the Sales Amount field to the Values area.

Another Way To Change The Sort Order Of Month Names

Chapter 10 covered applying the sort order changes directly to the pivot table. The same changes can be applied to the field in the Pivot Tables Fields list. If you viewed the months in the pivot table that you just created, you will see that the months are not displayed in order. This part of the exercise will show you how to change the sort order in the Pivot Table Fields list. For this to work, the pivot tables outline has to be expanded.

1. With the table collapsed (only shows the years and totals), right-click on the cell for the first year (cell A2) ⇒ Expand/Collapse option ⇒ Expand to Calendar Month Label, as illustrated in Figure 14-29 ⇒ Repeat this step for each year.

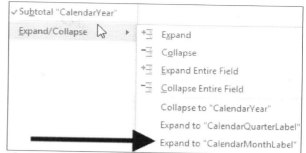

Figure 14-29 Expand/Collapse options

2. Click on any month name in the pivot table.

3. In the DimDate table, display the filter options for the Year Quarter Month hierarchy ⇒ At the top of the options, select the Calendar Month Label field, as illustrated in Figure 14-30 ⇒ Select **MORE SORT OPTIONS**.

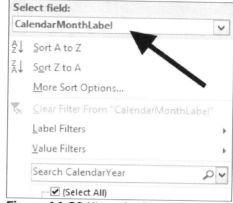

Figure 14-30 Hierarchy filter options

4. Starting with step 2, follow the steps in Exercise 10.5, "How To Change The Sort Order Of The Month Names", to change the sort order of the months. In step 2, select the Calendar Month Label field. All of the months, for all years in the pivot table, will be sorted. The pivot table should look like the one shown in Chapter 13, Figure 13-28.

Modifying Hierarchies

The options discussed below explain how to modify a hierarchy. Display the table that has the hierarchy that you want to modify in the Design View.

Adding A Level (Column) To A Hierarchy

After creating a hierarchy, you may decide that it needs another level. To add another level, display the hierarchy ⇒ Drag the field to the location in the hierarchy, where it is needed.

How To Change The Order Of The Fields In The Hierarchy

As you saw earlier, using Option 1 often means that the fields are not in the order that you need. The steps below show you how to put the fields in the right order.

1. Right-click on a field that you want to move ⇒ Select **MOVE UP** or **MOVE DOWN**, on the shortcut menu shown in Figure 14-31, depending on the direction that you want to move the field.

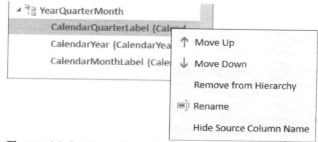

Figure 14-31 Hierarchy field shortcut menu

2. Repeat the step above until the fields are in the order that you need.

Renaming A Hierarchy Or Field In The Hierarchy

If you need to rename a hierarchy or field in the hierarchy, right-click on it ⇒ Select Rename.

When a field in a hierarchy is renamed, the original name is displayed in parenthesis and the new name is displayed after it. For example, the hierarchy on the left side of Figure 14-32, shows the **REGION** field name unchanged. If renamed, the Region field would be displayed like the one on the right side of the figure.

▲ CustomerList	▲ CustomerList
Country (Country)	Country (Country)
Region (Region)	State (Region)
City (City)	City (City)

Figure 14-32 Renamed field in a hierarchy

Hierarchies are also helpful when you need to display aggregated data by levels. A popular hierarchy that displays aggregated data (like order totals) is year, quarter and month levels.

Removing A Level (Column) From A Hierarchy

When you remove a column from the hierarchy, the column is not deleted from the table. To remove a column, display the hierarchy ⇒ Right-click on it and select Remove from Hierarchy.

Hiding A Hierarchy

[See Chapter 3, Diagram View]

Deleting A Hierarchy

Deleting a hierarchy does not delete the fields used in the hierarchy, from the table. To delete a hierarchy, right-click on the hierarchy name and select Delete.

 Hierarchies are not displayed in a table in the **DATA VIEW** (aka Grid view).

Hide Fields Used In A Hierarchy

Once a field is added to a hierarchy, there may not be a need to have the field displayed twice in the Pivot Table Fields list or in **POWER VIEW**. If that is the case, the field can be hidden. In the hierarchy, right-click on the field that you want to hide ⇒ Select **HIDE SOURCE COLUMN NAME**. This will hide the field in the table.

The Hide source option, on the shortcut menu (shown earlier in Figure 14-31), will change to **SHOW SOURCE**. This allows you to redisplay the field.

Exercise 14.4: Create A Pivot Table That Uses Two Hierarchies

This exercise will show you how to create a hierarchy that will group the Country, State (Region), City and Customer Name fields in a hierarchy. You will also learn how to create a hierarchy that groups the Year and Quarter fields in a date table. This will allow the order amounts to be displayed by year and quarter for each customer.

Import A Date Table And Mark It As A Date Table

To display data by quarter, a date table that has quarter values is needed. In this part of the exercise you will import a date table and mark it as a date table.

1. Save the E9.1 workbook as E14.4 Customer and date hierarchies.

2. Import the My Dates table from the MyDates workbook. This table is like the date table that you created in Exercise 14.2. I added the Quarter column to it.

3. Display the My Dates table ⇒ Design tab ⇒ Mark as Date Table button ⇒ Mark As Date Table option.

4. On the dialog box shown in Figure 14-33, select the Date field.

   Save the changes.

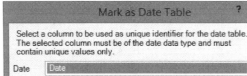

Mark as Date Table ?

Select a column to be used as unique identifier for the date table. The selected column must be of the date data type and must contain unique values only.

Date | Date

Figure 14-33 Mark as Date Table dialog box

5. Design tab ⇒ Click the Create Relationship button.

6. Table 1 drop-down list ⇒ Select the Orders table ⇒ Select the Order Date field.

7. Table 2 drop-down list ⇒ Select the My Dates table ⇒ Select the Date field.

Create The Customer List Hierarchy

This hierarchy will contain four fields in the Customer table.

1. Display the Diagram View.

2. In the Customer table, create the following hierarchy:
    ☑ Hierarchy name - Customer List
    ☑ Fields (in this order) - Country, Region, City, Customer Name

Create The Year Quarter Hierarchy

1. In the My Dates table, create the following hierarchy:
    ☑ Hierarchy name - YearQuarter
    ☑ Fields (in this order) - Year, Quarter

Create The Orders By Country Pivot Table

1. Add a pivot table to the sheet.

2. Rename the sheet to Orders By Country.

3. Customer table ⇒ Add the Customer List hierarchy to the Rows area.

4. Orders table ⇒ Add the Order Amount field to the Values area.

5. View tab ⇒ Freeze Panes button ⇒ Keep Top Row. This will keep the column headings visible when the sections are expanded in the pivot table.

6. Expand some of the sections.

    The pivot table should look like the one shown in Figure 14-34.

    This pivot table provides an overview of all of the orders.

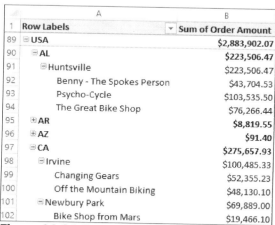

Row Labels	Sum of Order Amount
89 ⊟ USA	$2,883,902.07
90 ⊟ AL	$223,506.47
91 ⊟ Huntsville	$223,506.47
92 Benny - The Spokes Person	$43,704.53
93 Psycho-Cycle	$103,535.50
94 The Great Bike Shop	$76,266.44
95 ⊞ AR	$8,819.55
96 ⊞ AZ	$91.40
97 ⊟ CA	$275,657.93
98 ⊟ Irvine	$100,485.33
99 Changing Gears	$52,355.23
100 Off the Mountain Biking	$48,130.10
101 ⊟ Newbury Park	$69,889.00
102 Bike Shop from Mars	$19,466.10

Figure 14-34 Pivot table with four group levels

Create The Orders By Country And Year Pivot Table

The pivot table that you just created provides value, because it displays and totals the data on several levels. One thing that the pivot table does not show is a break down of the order amount by year. That is what you will add to the pivot table in this part of the exercise.

1. Copy the Orders by Country pivot table to a new sheet.

2. Rename the new sheet to Orders By Year.

3. Customer table ⇒ Add the Country field to the Filters area.

4. My Dates table ⇒ Add the YearQuarter hierarchy to the Columns area.

5. Click in cell B6 ⇒ View tab ⇒ Freeze Panes button ⇒ Freeze Panes.

Test The Pivot Table

1. Country filter ⇒ USA.

2. Expand the Year columns to display the totals by quarter.

3. Expand some of the states to display the cities and customers. The pivot table shown in Figure 14-35 displays the data at a more detail level, when needed.

As you scroll to the right to view data in other years, the country, state and customer name data is still visible in the left column. The pivot table shows totals by country, state, city and customer by year and quarter. I removed the Grand Total column from the figure to make it easier to see the rest of the pivot table.

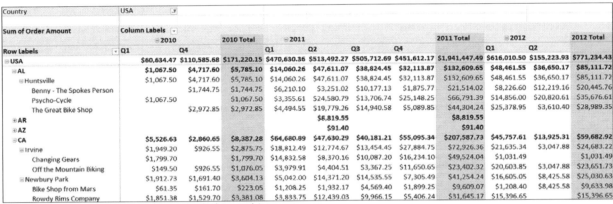

Figure 14-35 Pivot table with multiple hierarchies

Automating The Refresh Process

Refreshing data was covered in Chapter 3. All of the ways that data could be refreshed was also covered. One day it dawned on me that users that do not have an IT department to handle refreshing data could have some problems keeping the data current. I also thought that without instructions, users may not refresh the data at all and if they did, what if something went wrong?

With all of the options to refresh the data model, they all have two things in common, as explained below.

① You have to remember to do it.
② All of the options except "Refresh on open", are manual. Who said that every data source needs to be refreshed every time the workbook is opened? If the workbook has a lot of connections and/or several large data sources that have to be refreshed, it could take a while, waiting for the workbook to open.

As a consultant, I would create a script to refresh the data, that is run automatically, without user intervention. Then I thought what would someone do that cannot or does not want to write a script, but wants to automate the refresh process?

While typing changes for this book, it hit me. Why not create a macro? Then, I thought that I couldn't remember the last time that I used VBA (**VISUAL BASIC FOR APPLICATIONS**). Yes, I know that Power Pivot does not support VBA, but you can refresh Power Pivot data from the Excel window. And yes, I know that there is a Macro button on the View tab that is for creating macros, but additional functionality is needed to complete the task of automating the refresh process.

Exercise 14.5: Create A Macro To Automate The Refresh Process

This exercise will show you how to create a macro that will refresh all of the tables in one database connection and the data in an Excel spreadsheet connection, that are in the same workbook.

Enable The Developer Tab In Excel

The macro options are on the Developer tab in Excel, shown in Figure 14-36. If you do not see this tab in Excel, follow the steps in this section to enable the Developer tab. If you see the Developer tab, go to the next section.

Figure 14-36 Developer tab

1. Open the Excel Options dialog box ⇒ Customize Ribbon section.

 How To Display The Ribbon Shortcut Menu
Right-click on a blank space on any ribbon or right-click on any tab on the ribbon ⇒ Select **CUSTOMIZE THE RIBBON**, as shown in Figure 14-37.

Customize Quick Access Toolbar...

Show Quick Access Toolbar Below the Ribbon

Customize the Ribbon...

Collapse the Ribbon

Figure 14-37 Excel ribbon shortcut menu

2. In the list on the right side of the dialog box, if you see the Developer tab option, check it ⇒ Click OK and you're done ⇒ Go to the next section.

3. If you do not see the Developer tab, open the **CHOOSE COMMANDS FROM** drop-down list ⇒ Select **ALL TABS** ⇒ Click on the Developer option, illustrated in Figure 14-38 ⇒ Click the Add button ⇒ Click OK.

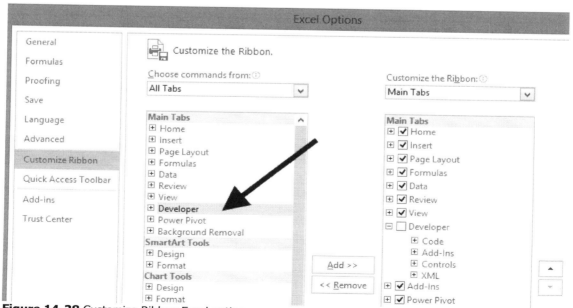
Figure 14-38 Customize Ribbon Excel options

Get Ready To Record The Macro

1. Save the E14.2 workbook as E14.5 Refresh Data Macro.

2. Developer tab ⇒ Record Macro button.

3. In the Macro Name field type RefreshData.

   The **STORE MACRO IN** option should have
   "This Workbook", as shown in Figure 14-39.

   Click OK.

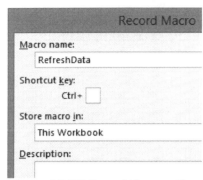

Figure 14-39 Record Macro options

 From this point on, every keystroke and click that you make will be recorded and saved in the macro.

Record The Macro

The macro that you will create will refresh the Product Category database and Store workbook. As you will see, there are other connections that could be refreshed.

On your own, if you wanted to refresh all of the tables in all of the connections, you would select the Refresh All option in the step 2, instead of selecting the Refresh option.

1. Data tab ⇒ Connections button.

2. Select the Product Categories connection ⇒ Refresh button ⇒ Refresh option. In the lower right corner of the Excel window, you will see the messages showing that the data is being refreshed. If the data actually changed, the data displayed in the pivot table and charts in the workbook, would also change.

3. Select the Stores workbook connection ⇒ Refresh button ⇒ Refresh option ⇒ When the Refresh is finished, click the Close button.

4. Developer tab ⇒ **STOP RECORDING** button.

View The Macro

The options discussed below are on the Developer tab.

① Clicking the **MACROS** button, displays the dialog box shown in Figure 14-40.
② The **VISUAL BASIC** button, displays the VBA code that was created from the steps recorded in the macro, as shown in Figure 14-41. If you do not see the code shown, right-click on the Module 1 option and select View Code.

View tab ⇒ Macros button ⇒ View Macros, also opens this dialog box.

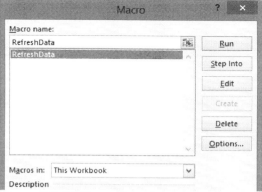

Figure 14-40 Macro dialog box

File ⇒ Close and Return to Microsoft Excel, closes the this window.

Figure 14-41 Visual Basic For Applications window

Attach The Macro To A Button Control

So far, so good. Unless you want to always have to run the macro from the dialog box shown earlier in Figure 14-40, the macro should be added to the worksheet. In this part of the exercise, you will add a button control to the worksheet and attach the macro to it.

1. Developer tab ⇒ Insert button ⇒ Select the **BUTTON** control, illustrated in Figure 14-42.

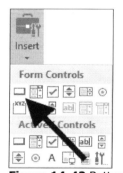

Figure 14-42 Button control illustrated

2. Draw a box to the right of the filters above the pivot table, then release the mouse button.

3. On the dialog box shown in Figure 14-43, click on the Refresh Data macro ⇒ Click OK.

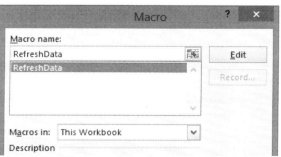

Figure 14-43 Macro dialog box

4. Right-click on the button ⇒
   Edit Text, as shown in Figure 14-44 ⇒
   Type `Refresh The Data` ⇒
   Click on an empty section of the worksheet.

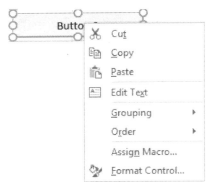

Figure 14-44 Button control shortcut menu

5. Right-click on the button ⇒ Format Control ⇒
   Change the Font Style to Bold ⇒
   Change the color to Red. The button should look like
   the one shown in Figure 14-45.

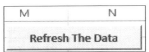

Figure 14-45 Button with macro attached

6. Click the button. You should see the Processing and Retrieving messages in the Status bar.

Save The Workbook

Workbooks that have macros cannot be saved with the **.xlsx** file extension.

1. Click the Save button ⇒
   On the message window
   shown in Figure 14-46,
   click No.

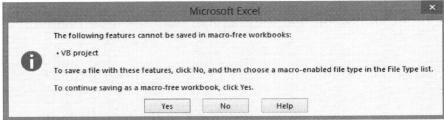

Figure 14-46 Save macro warning message

2. On the Save As dialog box ⇒ Change the Save as type option to Excel Macro-Enabled workbook (*.**xlsm**).
   The file name should still be the same ⇒ Click the Save button.

Refreshing Data Using VBA
The previous exercise demonstrated how to automate refreshing data. There are a few things to keep in mind when doing this on your own, as explained below.
① Excel processes connections in alphabetical order. If you need the connections processed in a specific order, the connections need to be renamed, in a way that makes them alphabetical, so that they are in the order that you need. The easy way to do this is to rename the connections by putting numbers in front of the existing connection name. For example, 01-Products connection, 02-Stores, etc.
② The macro would fail if it references an object (like a pivot table or chart) on the "Active Sheet", if the object is not on the sheet that you are running the macro from. The code shown earlier in Figure 14-41 does not reference anything specific to a sheet, so the macro can be run from any sheet in the workbook.

Summary

Like the previous chapter, this chapter presented options to enhance pivot tables. KPI's, which are a popular analysis and decision making tool, was covered to try and remove some of the mystery that often surrounds this tool. The all important date table was covered because most workbooks that you will create will need a date table. Hierarchies are useful when a workbook will contain several pivot tables that will need the same group of fields to be added to the Rows or Columns area. I covered creating a macro to automate refreshing data as a starting point to let you start to think outside the box on how to create solutions for functionality that Power Pivot does not have.

After completing the exercises in this chapter you will be able to:

☑ Use timelines
☑ Add links to display other pages in the workbook
☑ Add sparklines to a pivot table
☑ Apply conditional formatting to pivot tables

CHAPTER 15

Timelines

A timeline is another way to filter the data displayed on a pivot table or chart, similar to how slicers filter data. While slicers work with any field, timelines only work with a date field. When applied, the date range displayed on the timeline comes from the date field selected in the data source.

Truth be told, a timeline is easier to set up then a slicer. In Exercise 14.2, two slicers were needed to filter by year and month. Only one timeline object is needed to filter by year and month. Perhaps, even more important, by default, timelines display the months in calendar month order <smile>.

Timeline Tools Options Tab

The timeline object has its own tab, as shown in Figure 15-1. The options are explained in Table 15-1.

Figure 15-1 Timeline Tools Options tab

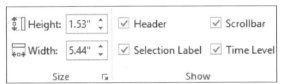

Figure 15-1 Timeline Tools Options tab (Continued)

Option	Description
Timeline Caption	This is the name displayed above the timeline. By default, the field name (the field that the slicer is attached to) is displayed. If you want to change the name, type over the name in this field.
Report Connections	Opens the dialog box shown in Figure 15-2. This dialog box is used to select which pivot tables and pivot charts to attach to the timeline.
Timeline Styles	[See Timeline Styles]
Bring Forward	Moves the selected object forward one level or to the front of all objects.
Send Backward	Moves the selected object back one level or all the way to the back.
Selection Pane	Displays the Selection panel. The feature is helpful if you have trouble selecting an object on the worksheet. [See Chapter 12, Selection Panel]
Align	Is used to line up the selected objects.
Group	Treats two or more objects as one. This is helpful when you need to apply the same formatting to several objects. If the objects are grouped, you only have to apply the formatting options once and they will be applied to all objects in the group.
Rotate	Is used to flip or rotate the selected object.
Height	Is used to change the height of the timeline. (1)
Width	Is used to change the width of the timeline. (1)
Header	Displays or hides the caption on the timeline.
Selection Label	Displays or hides the date or date range selected in the filter. **ALL PERIODS** indicates that no date or date range has been selected. [See Figure 15-4]
Scrollbar	Displays or hides the scrollbar at the bottom of the timeline.
Time Level	Displays or hides the time level options (years, quarters, months, days), shown later in Figure 15-5.

Table 15-1 Timeline Tools Options tab options explained

(1) This can also be done manually, by resizing the frame of the timeline.

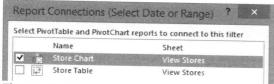

Figure 15-2 Report Connections dialog box

Timeline Styles

The options in this section of the toolbar are used to change the color scheme of the timeline.

If the styles shown earlier in Figure 15-1 do not meet your needs, open the Timeline Styles drop-down list and select **NEW TIMELINE STYLE**.

The options on the dialog box shown in Figure 15-3 are used to create a new style.

The **FORMAT** button opens the Format Timeline Element dialog box. It has the same options as the Format Slicer Element dialog box. [See Chapter 12, Figure 12-7]

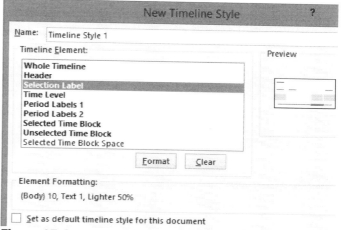

Figure 15-3 New Timeline Style dialog box

Timeline Options

Figure 15-4 shows the timeline that you will create in the first exercise. The options are explained below.

The **FILTER** button, in the upper right corner of the timeline object, works like the one on a slicer. It removes the selected filter options.

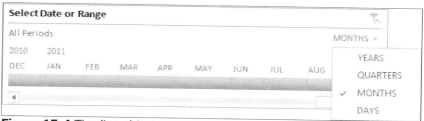

Figure 15-4 Timeline object

The **TIME LEVEL** drop-down list (below the Filter button) displays the options that are used to select how dates are displayed on the timeline. The default is months.

Changing this option to Quarters, changes the timeline to display dates, as shown in Figure 15-5. Compare this timeline to the one shown above in Figure 15-4.

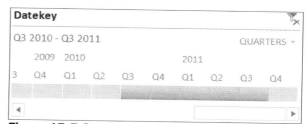

Figure 15-5 Quarters time level option selected

Insert Timeline Button And Dialog Box

The **INSERT TIMELINE** button, is used to create a timeline.
It is on the Analyze tab (next to the Insert Slicer button).
Clicking this button opens the dialog box shown in Figure 15-6.

The only fields displayed are date fields.

The **ACTIVE TAB** displays date fields in tables that were used
to create the pivot table or chart.

The **ALL TAB** displays all date fields in the workbook, whether
or not a date field in the table was used to create a pivot
table or chart.

Figure 15-6 Insert Timeslines dialog box

Format Timeline Panel

Once a timeline has been added to the sheet, the panel
shown in Figure 15-7 is accessed by right-clicking on the
timeline and selecting **SIZE AND PROPERTIES**.

The options are used to customize the timeline.

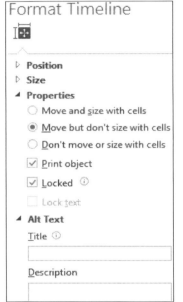

Figure 15-7 Format Timeline panel

Exercise 15.1: Add A Timeline To A Dashboard

This exercise will show you how to add a timeline that will filter data on a pivot table and chart.

1. Save the E12.2 workbook as `E15.1 Timeline`.

2. Make the following changes to the dashboard:
    ☑ Delete both slicers
    ☑ Rename the sheet to `View Stores`
    ☑ Change the chart name to `Store Chart`
    ☑ Change the pivot table name to `Store Table`

3. Click on the chart (or pivot table) and insert a timeline filter.

4. Insert Timelines dialog box ⇒ DimDate table, check the Date Key field, shown earlier in Figure 15-6.

5. Click OK ⇒ Move the timeline to the upper left corner of the sheet and resize it.

6. Change the Timeline Caption to `Select Date or Range`.

Connect The Timeline To Both Objects

If you used the timeline now, it would only filter data on the chart or table that it was created from. In some instances that may be what you want.

1. Select the timeline ⇒ On the Options tab, click the Report Connections button. As shown earlier in Figure 15-2, I created the timeline from the chart. It is the object that is checked on the dialog box, when I opened it.

2. Check the option that is not selected on your Report Connections dialog box ⇒ Click OK.

Use The Timeline

In this part of the exercise you will use the timeline to filter the data by year and month.

1. On the timeline, scroll until you see Jan 2009 ⇒ Click on the bar below Jan, as illustrated in Figure 15-8.

Notice that the Selection Label displays the month and year that you selected.

Also notice that the year that you selected is displayed at the top of the chart.

Figure 15-8 Bar to click on to select a month illustrated

2. Clear the filter.

Filter By A Date Range

1. Open the Time Level drop-down list ⇒ Select **DAYS**.

2. Scroll until you see Feb 1, 2007 ⇒ Click below Feb 1.

3. Place the mouse pointer on the right side of the selected square (the mouse pointer will change to an arrow) ⇒ Hold the mouse button down and drag the bar to the right. As you are scrolling, the Selection Label will change to include the time interval that is currently selected.

4. Continue dragging the bar to the right until Feb 15th is selected. You will see the range in the Selection Level. The data in the pivot table and chart only display data for records where the date in the Date Key field is between Feb 1-15th, 2007.

Exercise 15.2: Create A Line Chart And Add A Timeline

This exercise will show you how to apply a timeline to a chart.

Create The Pivot Chart

1. Save the New Orders workbook as E15.2 Line chart with a timeline.

2. Add a pivot chart to the existing sheet.

3. Add the fields in Table 15-2, to create the pivot chart.

Table	Field	Add To Area
MyDates	Year	Legend
New Orders	Order Amount	Values
New Orders	Sales Rep	Axis

Table 15-2 Fields to create the pivot chart

4. Change the chart type to Line with Markers.

5. Hide the Sales Rep button.

Add The Timeline

1. Analyze tab ⇒ Insert Timeline ⇒ On the Insert Timelines dialog box, select the Order Date field.

This chart style and timeline are helpful because you can easily see a years worth of data by itself, or with adjoining years, as shown in Figure 15-9.

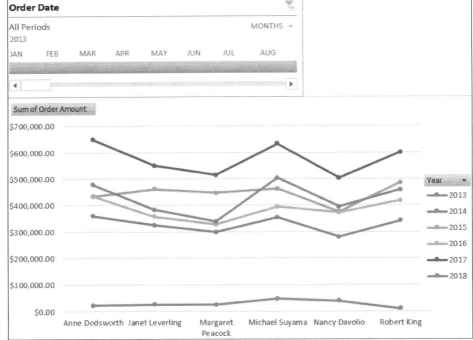

Figure 15-9 Line chart with a timeline that shows all of the orders

Using Hyperlinks

Hyperlinks, or links as they are commonly known, are used to display a different section of the same document, or a different document. Depending on how many tables and charts need to be created, it may be necessary to have them on more than one sheet in the workbook.

Another reason to have tables and charts on more than one sheet is to allow the main page to display data in a summary format and display the detail data for each summary on another sheet, which can be viewed when needed.

Exercise 15.3: Add A Link To A Dashboard

This exercise will show you how to create a link that will display another sheet in the same workbook.

Prep The Workbook

Before creating a link between sheets in the workbook, we need to add a second sheet with a chart to a workbook.

1. Save the E12.4 workbook as `E15.3 Link To Another Sheet`.

2. Copy and paste the Top 5 Stores chart to a new sheet.

3. Rename the new sheet to `Page 1` ⇒ Move the sheet before the Dashboard sheet.

Create The Link

1. On the Page 1 sheet ⇒ Click in an empty cell to the right of the chart ⇒ Insert tab ⇒ Hyperlink button.

2. Make the following changes on the dialog box shown in Figure 15-10.

    ☑ Select the Link to **PLACE IN THIS DOCUMENT** option.
    ☑ In the **TEXT TO DISPLAY FIELD**, type `View Dashboard`.
    ☑ Select the Dashboard **CELL REFERENCE**, illustrated in the figure.

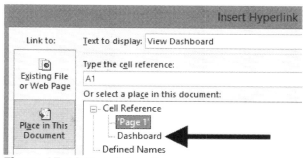

Figure 15-10 Hyperlink options

3. If you want, you can make the font size of the link larger or add a boarder to help make the link stand out on the sheet, as shown in Figure 15-11.

Figure 15-11 Link with a border

4. Click on the View Dashboard link. You should see the second page in the workbook.

What Is A Sparkline?

Simply put, a sparkline is a chart that is displayed in one cell on the worksheet. Usually it represents values to its left in the same row, but the sparkline can be placed before the data that it represents. Sparklines are used to show the trend of the data (some or all) in the row.

In my opinion, sparkline charts look better on tables that do not have groups, like the pivot table shown in Chapter 10, Figure 10-56, but as you will see, sparklines can be added to pivot tables that have groups. You can also select which rows a sparkline is created for.

Like the charts that you have created in this book, sparkline charts graphically represent data. They can be helpful when displaying large amounts of data in a pivot table. Minimum and maximum values are often displayed on a sparkline. In a way, sparkline charts remind me of a trendline chart because they present the numbers, if you will, in a way that shows the high and low values in the row of data. A good use of sparklines is to display economic cycles or stock opening and closing values.

The biggest difference between pivot charts and sparkline charts is that fields are not added to the sheet to create a sparkline chart. Sparkline charts are created from a range of data in each selected row, in the pivot table.

Sparkline Chart Types

The sparkline chart types are on the Insert tab in Excel. Sparklines for each row are created as a group. This means that changes that you make are automatically applied to all sparklines in the group. Being in a group, allows them to share formatting and scaling options. The three sparkline chart types are explained below.

LINE This chart type is used when there is a need to show trends in data over time. It works best when using sequential data, like months, years or the score at the end of each inning in a baseball game.

COLUMN Use this chart type when you need to compare values between categories. Examples of categories are products and countries.

WIN/LOSS This chart type is often used with stock data because it can display data whether the data in each cell is positive (a win) or negative (a loss). When used with data that has zero in a cell, the zero can be shown as a blank space in the sparkline.

Sparkline Tools Design Tab

The tab in Figure 15-12 shows the options that can be used to customize the sparkline. The options are explained in Table 15-3.

Figure 15-12 Sparkline Tools Design tab

Option	Description
Edit Data	[See Edit Data options] (2)
Line	Changes the selected sparkline to a Line chart sparkline.
Column	Changes the selected sparkline to a Column chart sparkline.
Win/Loss	Changes the selected sparkline to a Win/Loss chart sparkline.
Show	The options in this section are used to add markers to the sparkline to emphasize values that meet the condition.
Style	Is used to change the color of the sparkline.
Sparkline Color	Is used to change the color and weight of the sparkline, with the options shown in Figure 15-13.
Marker Color	The options shown in Figure 15-14 are used to change the color of the marker options in the **SHOW SECTION** of the Design tab, shown above in Figure 15-12.
Axis	[See Axis Options]
Group	Is used to put the selected cells into a group. (2)
Ungroup	Removes the group feature. This means that different formatting can be applied to each sparkline, that was in the group, individually. (2)
Clear	Is used to delete the sparkline group or selected cells in the sparkline group. (2)

Table 15-3 Sparkline Tools Design tab options explained

(2) This option is also available on the Sparkline shortcut menu shown later in Figure 15-18.

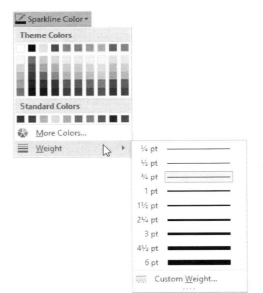

By default, all of the marker options shown in Figure 15-14 use the same color, which means that when you look at the sparkline chart, you don't know what point each marker represents.

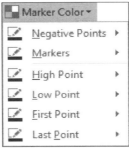

Figure 15-14 Marker color options

Figure 15-13 Sparkline color and weight options

Edit Data Options

The first two options shown in Figure 15-15 are used to change the data source location of a sparkline group or an individual sparkline (one cell). These two options are explained in the Sparkline Shortcut Menu section. The other options are explained below.

The **HIDDEN & EMPTY CELLS** option opens the dialog box shown in Figure 15-16. The options are used to select how to handle empty sparkline cells and whether or not the data in the hidden rows and columns should be displayed in the sparkline.

The **SWITCH ROW/COLUMN** option is only enabled when the data source has the same number of rows and columns. It is used to select whether the sparkline data should be displayed by row or by column.

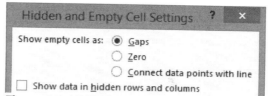

Figure 15-16 Hidden and Empty Cell Settings dialog box

Figure 15-15 Edit Data options

Axis Options

The options shown in Figure 15-17 are used to change the scaling of each axis of the sparkline in the group.

The **SAME FOR ALL SPARKLINES** option is helpful when the sparkline displays the values in a misleading way.

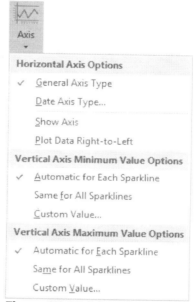

Figure 15-17 Axis options

Sparkline Shortcut Menu

Figure 15-18 shows the shortcut menu. (Right-click on the sparkline on the worksheet ⇒ Sparklines)

The **EDIT GROUP LOCATION & DATA** option opens the Edit Sparklines dialog box. It is used to change the range of data for the entire sparkline group or where the sparkline group will be placed. It has the same options as the Create Sparkline dialog box, shown later in Figure 15-20.

The **EDIT SINGLE SPARKLINE'S DATA** option uses the dialog box shown in Figure 15-19, to change the range of data for the selected cell in the sparkline.

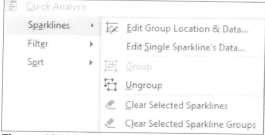

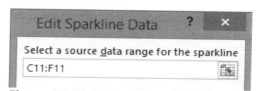

Figure 15-19 Edit Sparkline Data dialog box

Figure 15-18 Sparklines shortcut menu options

Exercise 15.4: Create Sparklines

This exercise will show you how to create sparklines using each of the chart types.

Create A Line Sparkline

This sparkline will be added to a pivot table that has groups. The sparkline will be created for one year of data, by quarter, for customers in one city.

1. Save the E14.4 workbook as E15.4 Line Sparkline.

2. Delete the Orders By Country tab.

3. On the Orders by Year tab, display the data for customers in Huntsville, AL.

4. Close the quarters for 2010 and 2012.

 Selecting The Range Of Data To Create The Sparkline For
To save a step, you can select the range of data before selecting the sparkline chart type.

5. Select the range C9:F11. This is the data for the 2011 quarters, for the three customers in Huntsville. If your data is indifferent cells, select the 2011 quarters range, for your data.

6. Insert tab ⇒ Line sparkline button. You should see the range that you selected in the Date Range field.

7. Click the button at the end of the Location Range field on the dialog box.

   Select the range J9:J11, or the corresponding cells in a different empty column, if your pivot table is using any of these columns.

   Click the button on the Create Sparklines dialog box. You should have the ranges shown in Figure 15-20 or something similar.

Figure 15-20 Create Sparklines dialog box

8. Click OK. You should see the sparkline shown in Figure 15-21. I added the 2011 Data heading, to know what data the sparklines represent. I changed the width of the sparkline, so that it would appear darker in the figure.

Sum of Order Amount	Column Labels								
	⊞2010	⊟2011				2011 Total	⊞2012	Grand Total	
Row Labels		Q1	Q2	Q3	Q4				2011 Data
⊟USA	$171,220.15	$470,630.36	$513,492.27	$505,712.69	$451,612.17	$1,941,447.49	$771,234.43	$2,883,902.07	
⊟AL	$5,785.10	$14,060.26	$47,611.07	$38,824.45	$32,113.87	$132,609.65	$85,111.72	$223,506.47	
⊟Huntsville	$5,785.10	$14,060.26	$47,611.07	$38,824.45	$32,113.87	$132,609.65	$85,111.72	$223,506.47	
Benny - The Spokes Person	$1,744.75	$6,210.10	$3,251.02	$10,177.13	$1,875.77	$21,514.02	$20,445.76	$43,704.53	
Psycho-Cycle	$1,067.50	$3,355.61	$24,580.79	$13,706.74	$25,148.25	$66,791.39	$35,676.61	$103,535.50	
The Great Bike Shop	$2,972.85	$4,494.55	$19,779.26	$14,940.58	$5,089.85	$44,304.24	$28,989.35	$76,266.44	

Figure 15-21 Line sparkline

Create A Column Sparkline

Often, the Grand total column in a pivot table is removed when using sparklines, so that the sparkline is right next to the data that it represents.

1. Save the E10.6 workbook as E15.4 Column Sparkline.

2. Click in the pivot table ⇒ Design tab ⇒ Grand Totals ⇒ On for Columns Only.

3. Select the range B5:D14 ⇒ Insert tab ⇒ Column sparkline button.

4. Select or type in the range E5:E14.

5. Make the sparkline column wider. The pivot table should look like the one shown in Figure 15-22.

. . . .

	A	B	C	D	E
3	**Sum of SalesAmount**	**Column Labels** ▾			
4	**Row Labels** ▾	**2007**	**2008**	**2009**	
5	Contoso Asia Online Store	$156,883,859.58	$188,427,344.54	$212,850,715.76	
6	Contoso Asia Reseller	$114,185,396.49	$122,563,956.44	$125,585,967.89	
7	Contoso Catalog Store	$273,924,905.90	$211,973,099.70	$210,006,950.16	
8	Contoso Europe Online Store	$167,679,516.43	$170,444,136.21	$175,239,722.44	
9	Contoso Europe Reseller	$122,337,430.46	$111,492,926.96	$104,077,933.71	
10	Contoso North America Online Store	$189,940,381.44	$208,983,212.70	$215,622,220.78	
11	Contoso North America Reseller	$139,379,974.11	$135,938,379.30	$128,986,735.50	
12	Contoso Sydney No.2 Store	$8,306,886.65	$8,920,073.26	$9,487,219.85	
13	Contoso Sydney No.1 Store	$7,694,245.94	$9,125,764.60	$9,830,374.39	
14	Contoso Taipei Store	$7,728,609.19	$9,090,492.56	$9,621,821.55	
15	**Grand Total**	**$1,188,061,206.20**	**$1,176,959,386.27**	**$1,201,309,662.04**	

Figure 15-22 Column sparkline

Analyzing Color Sparklines

Basing decisions on the height of the bars can be misleading, as explained with examples from Figure 15-22.

① The totals on row 10 are very close in value, yet the column sparkline displays columns in different sizes. On a regular column chart, the columns for the three columns would be close in height.

② There is almost a $100,000 difference between the 2009 total in rows 5 and 6, yet the height of the columns appear to be identical.

Why Does This Happen?

The height of the columns in the sparkline do not represent the actual data values. The column height is based on the values in each row being ranked from low to high. The lowest value is always displayed with a short column. The next value is displayed with the middle height column and the largest value is displayed with the tallest column.

The number of values selected for the sparkline doesn't seem to matter, as the same thing happens, even when four or more columns of data are used to create the sparkline. I know because I changed the Line sparkline created earlier in this exercise, to a Column sparkline.

Can This Be Fixed?

Earlier in this chapter, the options on the Sparkline Tools Design tab were covered. So, the answer is yes, this can be fixed, by using the same minimum and maximum values for all of the Column sparklines in the group. The steps below show you how.

1. Click on any sparkline in Column E. All of the sparklines should be selected.

2. Design tab ⇒ Axis button ⇒ Vertical Axis Minimum Value options ⇒ Same for All Sparklines.

3. Design tab ⇒ Axis button ⇒ Vertical Axis Maximum Value options ⇒ Same for All Sparklines. The sparklines should look like the ones shown in Figure 15-23. Now, the size of the sparkline columns are based on all of the values, in all rows that the sparkline is created for.

Sum of SalesAmount	**Column Labels** ▾			
Row Labels ▾	**2007**	**2008**	**2009**	
Contoso Asia Online Store	$156,883,859.58	$188,427,344.54	$212,850,715.76	
Contoso Asia Reseller	$114,185,396.49	$122,563,956.44	$125,585,967.89	
Contoso Catalog Store	$273,924,905.90	$211,973,099.70	$210,006,950.16	
Contoso Europe Online Store	$167,679,516.43	$170,444,136.21	$175,239,722.44	
Contoso Europe Reseller	$122,337,430.46	$111,492,926.96	$104,077,933.71	
Contoso North America Online Store	$189,940,381.44	$208,983,212.70	$215,622,220.78	
Contoso North America Reseller	$139,379,974.11	$135,938,379.30	$128,986,735.50	
Contoso Sydney No.2 Store	$8,306,886.65	$8,920,073.26	$9,487,219.85	
Contoso Sydney No.1 Store	$7,694,245.94	$9,125,764.60	$9,830,374.39	
Contoso Taipei Store	$7,728,609.19	$9,090,492.56	$9,621,821.55	

Figure 15-23 Minimum and maximum axis value options applied to the sparkline

Create A Win/Loss Sparkline

1. Save the E10.5 workbook as E15.4 Win Loss Sparkline.

2. Select the range B7:E18 ⇒ Insert tab ⇒ Win/Loss sparkline button.

3. Select the column after the Grand total column as the Location Range. The sparkline should look like the one shown in Figure 15-24. Notice that nothing is displayed in the sparkline when the corresponding cell is empty.

Sum of TotalDue	Column Labels ▾					
Row Labels ▾	2001	2002	2003	2004	Grand Total	
January		$1,605,782.19	$2,233,575.11	$3,691,013.22	$7,530,370.53	▬ ▬ ▬
February		$3,130,823.04	$3,705,635.50	$5,207,182.51	$12,043,641.05	▬ ▬ ▬
March		$2,643,081.08	$2,611,621.26	$5,272,786.81	$10,527,489.15	▬ ▬ ▬
April		$1,905,833.91	$3,041,865.44	$4,722,890.74	$9,670,590.09	▬ ▬ ▬
May		$3,758,329.29	$4,449,886.23	$6,518,825.23	$14,727,040.75	▬ ▬ ▬
June		$2,546,121.96	$3,257,517.70	$6,728,034.99	$12,531,674.65	▬ ▬ ▬
July	$1,172,359.43	$3,781,879.07	$4,681,520.64	$56,178.92	$9,691,938.06	▬ ▬ ▬ ▬
August	$2,605,514.98	$5,433,609.34	$6,775,857.07		$14,814,981.40	▬ ▬ ▬
September	$2,073,058.54	$4,242,717.72	$6,762,753.81		$13,078,530.07	▬ ▬ ▬
October	$1,688,963.27	$2,854,206.75	$4,243,366.59		$8,786,536.62	▬ ▬ ▬
November	$3,690,018.67	$4,427,598.00	$5,961,182.68		$14,078,799.34	▬ ▬ ▬
December	$3,097,637.34	$3,545,522.74	$6,582,833.04		$13,225,993.12	▬ ▬ ▬
Grand Total	$14,327,552.23	$39,875,505.10	$54,307,615.09	$32,196,912.42	$140,707,584.82	

Figure 15-24 Win/Loss sparkline

Handling A Non Consecutive Date Range

Keep in mind that sparklines work on the premise <aka "assumes", smile> that data that is based on dates have equal intervals, like daily (every day for seven consecutive days, opposed to every other day) or monthly (consecutive months). When the date range is not consecutive, the sparkline does not display the columns as expected.

I think that it may be better for the date gaps to appear in the sparkline, to indicate that the date range is not consecutive.

The pivot table shown in Figure 15-25 shows a date range. Notice that there is no data for 9/21 or 9/23.

	A	B	C	D	E	F
2	Row Labels ▾	9/19/2015	9/20/2015	9/22/2015	9/24/2015	9/25/2015
3	Alley Cat Cycles	$505.26	$1,154.00	$3,479.70	$19.00	$5,219.55
4	Bike-A-Holics Anonymous	$5,219.55	$29.00	$789.51	$178.20	$1,100.00
5	Bikes, Bikes, and More Bikes	$2,447.34	$458.00	$8,819.55	$1,010.10	$1,961.00
6	Changing Gears	$16.50	$628.00	$624.00	$1,799.70	$2,007.56
7	Cycle City Rome	$227.27	$148.00	$329.85	$222.00	$3,545.10

Figure 15-25 Pivot table with a non consecutive date range

1. Save the Sparkline workbook as E15.4 Date Range Sparkline.

2. Create a Column sparkline for the range B3:F7.

3. Make the sparkline column wider. The sparkline should look like the one shown in Figure 15-26.

	A	B	C	D	E	F	G
2	Row Labels ▾	9/19/2015	9/20/2015	9/22/2015	9/24/2015	9/25/2015	
3	Alley Cat Cycles	$505.26	$1,154.00	$3,479.70	$19.00	$5,219.55	▬ ▬ ▬ ▬ ▬
4	Bike-A-Holics Anonymous	$5,219.55	$29.00	$789.51	$178.20	$1,100.00	▬ ▬ ▬ ▬ ▬
5	Bikes, Bikes, and More Bikes	$2,447.34	$458.00	$8,819.55	$1,010.10	$1,961.00	▬ ▬ ▬ ▬ ▬
6	Changing Gears	$16.50	$628.00	$624.00	$1,799.70	$2,007.56	▬ ▬ ▬ ▬ ▬
7	Cycle City Rome	$227.27	$148.00	$329.85	$222.00	$3,545.10	▬ ▬ ▬ ▬ ▬

Figure 15-26 Column sparkline created using a non consecutive date range

The way that the sparkline is displayed, you cannot tell that the dates are not consecutive. If there was a blank space in the sparkline where the dates are not consecutive, it would hopefully alert the person viewing the sparkline. The way to do that is with the Axis minimum and maximum options and selecting the date range of the sparkline data.

4. Select the sparkline ⇒ Design tab ⇒ Axis button ⇒ Select both Same for All Sparklines options.

5. With the sparkline still selected ⇒ Design tab ⇒ Axis button ⇒ Data Axis Type.

6. Select the range B2:F2, as shown in Figure 15-27. The modified sparkline should look like the one shown in Figure 15-28. Notice the space after the second and third columns. The spaces indicate that there is a break, if you will, in the date range.

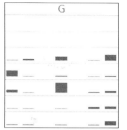

Figure 15-27 Sparkline Date Range dialog box

Figure 15-28 Revised column sparkline

Conditional Formatting

In the previous chapter, KPI's were covered. When you think about it, KPI's are a type of conditional formatting. Perhaps I am getting lazy, but setting up a KPI can be time consuming. I don't know what it is about an icon on every row in a pivot table, that makes the pivot table seem busy, but to me, it is harder to "see" the important data with all of the icons. It goes without saying though, if you are designing the dashboard for someone else and they want the traffic light icons to represent KPI values, add them and just think about the money you are being paid <smile>.

If you are not a fan of KPI's, don't worry because there are other ways to bring attention to certain cells in a pivot table. Collectively, the other options are known as conditional formatting. In addition to conditional formatting bringing attention to specific cells, it also helps break up the monotony of columns and columns and rows and rows of data.

What Are Rules?

Rules are the criteria that you create to select which cells in the pivot table, formatting should or should not be applied to. Rules are similar to filters. Don't worry, you do not have to write any code to create conditional formatting rules.

Conditional Formatting Button

This button is on the Home tab in Excel. It displays the options shown in Figure 15-29. The items on the button provide options to format cells in the pivot table.

They may or may not be what you need. If the options are not enough, you can edit the rule on the New Formatting Rule dialog box.

The first five options on the button are explained in Table 15-4. The other options are covered later in this chapter.

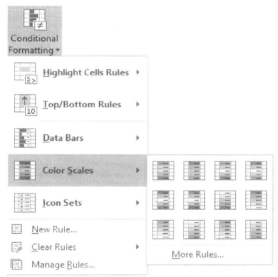

Figure 15-29 Conditional Formatting options

Option	Is Used To Create A Rule That . . .
Highlight Cells Rules	Adds color to the background of cells whose values meet the criteria.
Top/Bottom Rules	Adds color to the background of the top (largest) or bottom (lowest) N cells of data, by rank. Unlike the Top/Bottom N filter option, that filters all of the rows in the pivot table, the Top/Bottom Rules conditional formatting option does not. It finds the top or bottom N values in the selected cell range to apply formatting to. Rules for formatting the cell background of data that is above or below the average value of selected cells can also be created.

Table 15-4 Conditional Formatting options explained

Option	Is Used To Create A Rule That . . .
Data Bars	Displays a bar in each cell that represents the value in the cell. Conditions can be set to select which cells the bars are placed in. (3)
Color Scales	Displays a gradient color background to every cell in the selected range. The color represents where the value in the cell falls in the range that is selected. Lighter colors usually represent lower values and the darkest color is used to represent the highest values, but the opposite color scheme can also be applied.
Icon Sets	Displays icons in all cells or only cells that meet the criteria. This option will remind you of KPI's. (3)

Table 15-4 Conditional Formatting options explained (Continued)

(3) The formatting can be applied with or without displaying the value in the cell.

New Formatting Rule Dialog Box

Select the **NEW RULE** or the **MORE RULES** option, shown above in Figure 15-29 to open this dialog box. The options on this dialog box are used to create conditional formatting. Many of the options on this dialog box provide more functionality and customizations for the options on the Conditional Formatting button, shown above in Figure 15-29.

For example, the options shown on the right side of Figure 15-30 are used to create data bar rules. Figure 15-31 also shows options that are used to create data bar rules. As you can see, the dialog box has a lot more options, then the options on the Conditional Formatting button.

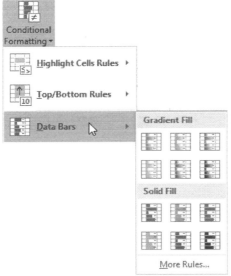

Figure 15-30 Conditional Formatting Data Bars rule options

Figure 15-31 New Formatting Rule dialog box

Clearing Rules

The options shown in Figure 15-32 are used to remove some or all of the rules that have been applied to the pivot table.

Figure 15-32 Clear Rules options

Managing Rules

Selecting the **MANAGE RULES** option shown above in Figure 15-32 opens the dialog box shown in Figure 15-33. As explained below, the options are used to view, create, edit, delete and reorder the rules.

The **NEW RULE** button opens the New Formatting Rule dialog box shown earlier in Figure 15-31.

The **EDIT RULE** button opens the **EDIT FORMATTING RULE** dialog box. It is used to change an existing rule and has the same options as the New Formatting Rule dialog box.

Figure 15-33 Conditional Formatting Rules Manager dialog box

The **DELETE RULE** button deletes the selected rule at the bottom of the dialog box.

The **MOVE UP** and **MOVE DOWN** buttons (next to the Delete button) are used to change the order of the rules. The order that the rules are listed in, are the order that they are applied in.

The **STOP IF TRUE** option is helpful when there are two or more rules applied to the same cells. You may have the need to only process some of the rules for the same cells, based on whether or not one of the conditions is met. If so, check this option for the last rule that you want processed.

Letting The User Know About The Conditional Formatting
The conditional formatting exercises in this chapter show you how to create a variety of conditional formatting. While you know what the formatting is designed to do because you created it, it is a good idea to put something on the worksheet that briefly explains what the formatting means.

Conditional Formatting Exercise Tips
① The Conditional Formatting button is on the Home tab.
② The **CELL RANGES** listed in the exercises are the range in my workbooks, based on the previous exercises. If your pivot tables are in a slightly different location, use the range based on the location of your pivot table.
③ I select the cell range for the formatting before opening the New Formatting Rule dialog box because I find it easier. Doing this is optional.
④ I use the **MORE RULES** option (opposed to the New Rule option) on the shortcut menu of the formatting type (shown earlier in Figure 15-30) because it selects the **RULE TYPE** for me. The New Rule option on the Conditional Formatting button does not.
⑤ Many of the values that you have to type in for the criteria (in the exercises in this chapter) are large and have a lot of zeros. I put spaces between some of the numbers to make them easier to read. When you type the number in, do not use spaces.

Exercise 15.5: Create Highlight Cells Conditional Formatting

This exercise will show you how to create highlight cell rules, which will change the background color of cells that meet the criteria.

Create A Rule For Store Sale Amount Totals Over $7.1 Million

1. Save the E12.2 workbook as E15.5 Highlight cells conditional formatting.

2. Delete the slicers and chart.

3. Select the range L6:N61 ⇒ Home tab ⇒ Conditional Formatting button ⇒ Highlight Cells Rules ⇒ More Rules.

4. In the second drop-down list, select **GREATER THAN** ⇒ Type 710 0000.

   Figure 15-34 shows the formatting rule.

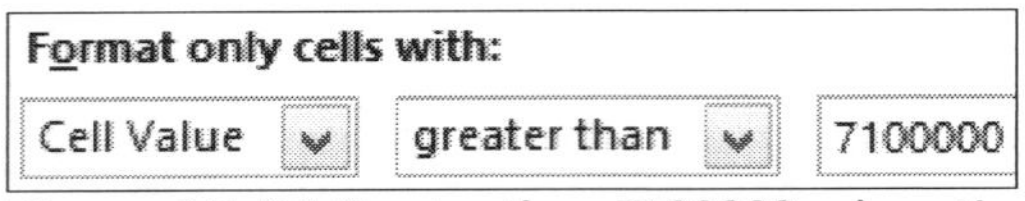

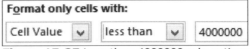

Figure 15-34 Greater than 7100000 rule options

5. Click the Format button ⇒ Fill tab ⇒ Select the color Green ⇒ Click OK twice, to close both dialog boxes.

Create A Rule For Store Sale Amount Totals Less Than $4 Million

1. Select the range L6:N61 ⇒ Conditional Formatting button ⇒ Highlight Cells Rules ⇒ More Rules.

2. In the second drop-down list, select **LESS THAN** ⇒ Type 400 0000.

3. Click the Format button ⇒ Fill tab ⇒ Select the color Red.

   Figure 15-35 shows the formatting rule.

Figure 15-35 Less than 4000000 rule options

Figure 15-36 shows the formatting applied to the pivot table.

Row Labels	2007	2008	2009
Contoso Arlington Store	$6,915,310.31	$5,158,464.82	$3,952,938.88
Contoso Aurora Store	$7,144,291.33	$4,789,827.08	$4,083,439.36
Contoso Austin Store	$6,737,409.74	$5,013,923.07	$4,081,586.18
Contoso Bacliff Store	$7,268,854.81	$4,942,836.30	$4,129,717.62
Contoso Baytown Store	$7,314,056.39	$4,482,648.01	$3,926,343.38

Figure 15-36 Highlight cell formatting applied to the pivot table

The **A DATE OCCURRING** highlighting cell rule, shown in Figure 15-37, is used to create a rule for date comparison. This option (on the shortcut menu) is only enabled when cells with dates have been selected. It will highlight cells that fall into a category, like last week, last month, this month or the last 7 days, as shown in Figure 15-38.

Selecting the More Rules option, shown in Figure 15-37, displays the New Formatting Rule dialog box, with the Highlighting Cell formatting rules displayed.

Open the Format only cells with drop-down list and select the **DATES OCCURRING** option, illustrated in Figure 15-39, to create the rule.

When a date occurring rule is created, it is automatically updated by the system clock on the computer. For example, if it is currently September 2015 and you create a rule to highlight cells with data from last month, cells that have a date in August 2015 will be highlighted. If you view the same data in December 2015, cells with a date in November 2015 will be highlighted.

Figure 15-37 Highlight Cells Rules options

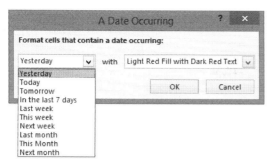

Figure 15-38 A Date Occurring dialog box

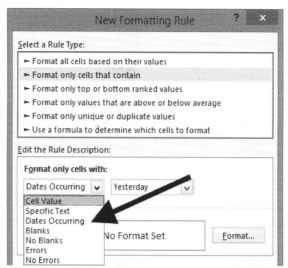

Figure 15-39 Date Occurring options on the New Formatting Rule dialog box

 Using The Format Painter With Conditional Formatting
Once you create conditional formatting, you can apply it to other cells by using the Format Painter.

Exercise 15.6: Create Top/Bottom Conditional Formatting

This exercise will show you how to apply Top N conditional formatting to cells. The formatting will be applied to a pivot table that displays the top 10 rows of data. The conditional formatting created in this exercise will be applied to the 10 cells with the largest values displayed in the pivot table.

1. Save the E10.6 workbook as `E15.6 Top 10 Conditional Formatting`.

2. You should see three years of data. If not, display all of the years now.

3. Select the range B5:D14 ⇒ Conditional Formatting button ⇒ Top/Bottom Rules ⇒ More Rules.

4. Select the color Yellow.
   Figure 15-40 shows the formatting rule.
   Figure 15-41 shows the formatting rule applied to the pivot table.

Figure 15-40 Top 10 formatting rule options

The Top 10 conditional formatting rules, shown above in Figure 15-40, has nothing to do with the Top 10 filter that was created for the pivot table. Keep in mind that conditional formatting is applied to cells, not rows.

4	Row Labels		2007	2008	2009
5	Contoso Asia Online Store		$156,883,859.58	$188,427,344.54	$212,850,715.76
6	Contoso Asia Reseller		$114,185,396.49	$122,563,956.44	$125,585,967.89
7	Contoso Catalog Store		$273,924,905.90	$211,973,099.70	$210,006,950.16
8	Contoso Europe Online Store		$167,679,516.43	$170,444,136.21	$175,239,722.44
9	Contoso Europe Reseller		$122,337,430.46	$111,492,926.96	$104,077,933.71
10	Contoso North America Online Store		$189,940,381.44	$208,983,212.70	$215,622,220.78
11	Contoso North America Reseller		$139,379,974.11	$135,938,379.30	$128,986,735.50
12	Contoso Sydney No.2 Store		$8,306,886.65	$8,920,073.26	$9,487,219.85

Figure 15-41 Top 10 conditional formatting rule options applied to the pivot table

Data Bars

Data bars are similar to sparklines, in that they display a graphic of the data, on a cell by cell basis. Data bars start on the right or left side of the cell and extend out towards the center of the cell. The length of the bar is controlled by the size of the value in the cell that it represents. By default, larger values are displayed with more color and smaller values are displayed with less color.

Keep in mind that if the value in the cell is zero, a bar will not be displayed. Negative values can be represented by a data bar. They are displayed with a different color. Totals should not be included in the cell range that the data bars will be applied to.

Exercise 15.7: Create Data Bar Conditional Formatting

This exercise will show you how to display data bars in a column of data.

1. Save the E10.1 workbook as E15.7 Data Bars Conditional Formatting.

2. Select the range B2:B16 ⇒ Conditional Formatting button ⇒ Data Bars ⇒ More Rules.

3. Change the **FILL** option to Gradient Fill ⇒ Select a color that you like.

4. Change the **BAR DIRECTION** option to **LEFT-TO-RIGHT**. You should have the options shown in Figure 15-42.

    The pivot table should look like the one shown in Figure 15-43.

    If you sorted the Sum of Total values in descending order, the pivot table would look like the one shown in Figure 15-44.

Figure 15-42 Data Bar formatting options

The **TYPE** and **VALUE** options shown above in Figure 15-42, are used if you need to select a range of values that each cell must meet, to have a data bar displayed in the cell.

The **BAR DIRECTION** Context option is the default. It displays the bars from left to right.

The **NEGATIVE VALUES AND AXIS** button displays the dialog box shown in Figure 15-45. The dialog box displays more color options for the bar, border and axis settings of negative values.

Row Labels	Sum of Subtotal
Amritansh Raghav	$15,432.50
Anna Bedecs	$2,410.75
Christina Lee	$4,949.00
Elizabeth Andersen	$4,683.00
Francisco Pérez-Olaeta	$8,007.50
John Edwards	$1,190.00
John Rodman	$860.00
Karen Toh	$1,505.00
Ming-Yang Xie	$13,800.00
Peter Krschne	$1,019.50
Roland Wacker	$1,412.50
Run Liu	$3,625.25
Soo Jung Lee	$2,905.50
Sven Mortensen	$3,786.50
Thomas Axen	$2,550.00

Figure 15-43 Pivot table with data bar formatting applied

Row Labels	Sum of Subtotal
Amritansh Raghav	$15,432.50
Ming-Yang Xie	$13,800.00
Francisco Pérez-Olaeta	$8,007.50
Christina Lee	$4,949.00
Elizabeth Andersen	$4,683.00
Sven Mortensen	$3,786.50
Run Liu	$3,625.25
Soo Jung Lee	$2,905.50
Thomas Axen	$2,550.00
Anna Bedecs	$2,410.75
Karen Toh	$1,505.00
Roland Wacker	$1,412.50
John Edwards	$1,190.00
Peter Krschne	$1,019.50
John Rodman	$860.00

Figure 15-44 Pivot table with data bar formatting sorted

Negative Value Options

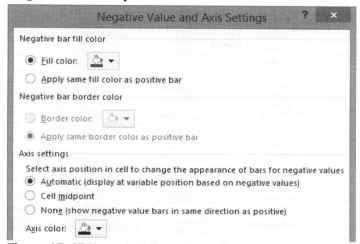

Figure 15-45 Negative Value and Axis Settings dialog box

 Icon Sets can also be used as data bars. Select this option in the **FORMAT STYLE** drop-down list, shown earlier in Figure 15-42. If the Icon Sets option was selected and the default options shown in Figure 15-46 were used, the pivot table shown earlier in Figure 15-43 would look like the one shown in Figure 15-47. Yes, this is another way to create a **KPI**.

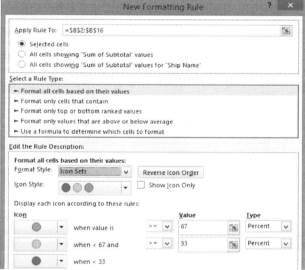

Figure 15-46 Icon Sets options

Row Labels		Sum of Subtotal
Amritansh Raghav	●	$15,432.50
Anna Bedecs	●	$2,410.75
Christina Lee	●	$4,949.00
Elizabeth Andersen	●	$4,683.00
Francisco Pérez-Olaeta	○	$8,007.50
John Edwards	●	$1,190.00
John Rodman	●	$860.00
Karen Toh	●	$1,505.00
Ming-Yang Xie	○	$13,800.00
Peter Krschne	●	$1,019.50
Roland Wacker	●	$1,412.50
Run Liu	●	$3,625.25
Soo Jung Lee	●	$2,905.50
Sven Mortensen	●	$3,786.50
Thomas Axen	●	$2,550.00
Grand Total		**$68,137.00**

Figure 15-47 Icon Sets options applied to a pivot table

Exercise 15.8: Create Nested Conditional Formatting

The previous exercise showed you how to create data bar formatting. There may be times when you only need data bars, or any conditional cell formatting for that matter, to be displayed in some cells and not others. I'm thinking about only displaying a data bar in cells that have one of the top 10 values. This exercise will show you how to select when data bars are displayed.

1. Save the E10.6 workbook as E15.8 Nested Conditional Formatting.

2. Change the Row Labels Top 10 filter to the Top 20. Doing this just displays more data in the pivot table.

Create Data Bar Conditional Formatting For The Top 10 Values

This formatting will be applied to the 10 cells in the pivot table that have the largest values.

1.   Select the range B5:D24.

2.   Create data bar formatting using the following criteria:
      ☑ Fill - Gradient Fill
      ☑ Color - Select a color that you like

Create Conditional Formatting To Not Display Data Bars

To only display data bar formatting for the top 10 values means that the bottom 50 values cannot have the data bar formatting applied. Yes, to complete this exercise, a little math is involved <smile>.

The range B5:D24, displays 20 values per column. There are three columns. 20 values per column x 3 columns = 60 values. This means that 50 values have to be hidden, if you only want the top 10 values (cells) to have the formatting and yes, it took me a while to figure this out.

1.   Select the range B5:D24 ⇒ Conditional Formatting button ⇒ Top/Bottom Rules ⇒ More Rules.

2.   Select Bottom in the first drop-down list.

3.   Type 50 in the next field, as shown in Figure 15-48.

     Click OK.

     The reason that a color is not selected is because the 50 cells with the lowest values should not have data bars applied.

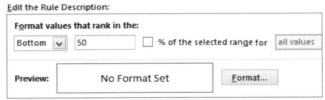

Figure 15-48 Formatting options to not format the 50 cells with the lowest values

Modify The Formatting Rules

To force only displaying 10 cells with data bars, the other 50 cells have to be formatted first. This rule has to be applied first. In addition to that, the **STOP IF TRUE** option must be enabled for this rule.

1.   Open the Rules Manager.

2.   Check the Stop if True option for the Bottom 50 rule.

     The rules should be in the order shown in Figure 15-49.

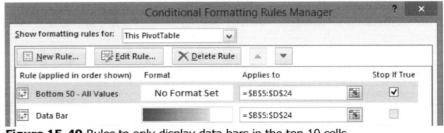

Figure 15-49 Rules to only display data bars in the top 10 cells

3.   Click Apply ⇒ Click OK.

     Only 10 cells, as shown in Figure 15-50, should have data bars.

Figure 15-50 Conditional top 10 data bar formatting applied to the pivot table

Exercise 15.9: Create Conditional Formatting With Icons

This exercise will show you how to display an icon in each cell, based on which condition the value in the cell meets. If you have created **IF-THEN-ELSE** formulas, you already know how to use this option. This exercise will also show you how to remove conditional formatting.

1. Save the E13.3 workbook as `E15.9 Icon Sets Conditional Formatting`.

2. On Sheet 1 ⇒ Delete the second pivot table ⇒ Delete the other tab.

3. Select the range B5:B16 ⇒ Conditional Formatting button ⇒ Icon Sets ⇒ More Rules.

4. Select an **ICON STYLE** that you like.

5. Change the **WHEN VALUE IS** operator to >= ⇒ Change the **TYPE** to Number ⇒ In the Value field type `275 000 000`.

6. Change the next operator to > ⇒ Change the Type to Number ⇒ In the Value field type `200 000 000`.

7. Click in another field. This will update the rules.

Figure 15-51 shows the options that should be selected. Make sure that the **WHEN CLAUSES** (illustrated in the figure) match exactly, before clicking OK. The first year of data should look like the year shown in Figure 15-52.

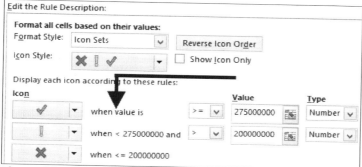

Figure 15-51 Icon Sets conditional formatting options

Row Labels ⌄		Sum of SalesAmount
⊟2007		**$3,144,393,292.13**
January	✖	$193,305,554.64
February	⫿	$209,439,067.93
March	⫿	$203,991,979.69
April	✓	$276,891,048.16
May	✓	$288,749,508.61
June	✓	$283,186,644.54
July	⫿	$272,818,635.11
August	⫿	$263,780,279.28
September	⫿	$257,282,781.95
October	✓	$288,853,903.92
November	✓	$308,752,784.65
December	✓	$297,341,103.65

Figure 15-52 Icon Sets conditional formatting applied to the pivot table

Modify The Conditional Formatting

The pivot table that you just added conditional formatting to would look better if all of the years had the icon set conditional formatting applied. In this part of the exercise, you will modify the existing conditional formatting options to apply them to all of the month rows, in the pivot table.

1. Click on a data cell in Column B ⇒ Conditional Formatting button ⇒ Manage Rules.

2. Click the **EDIT RULE** button.

3. On the Edit Formatting Rule dialog box, change the **APPLY RULE TO** field to the range B5:B42, as shown in Figure 15-53.

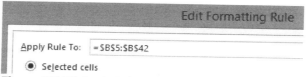

Figure 15-53 Apply Rule To field modified

You can type the change or click the button at the end of the field and select the range. When finished, click OK.

The **APPLIES TO** field, on the Conditional Formatting Rules Manager dialog box, contains all of the cells that the formatting will be applied to. In this exercise, the formatting does not need to be applied to each years total cell (Cells B17 and B30). There are two ways to remove the conditional formatting from these cells, as explained below.

① Select the cells in the pivot table that need to have the conditional formatting removed, then select the **CLEAR RULES FROM SELECTED CELLS** option, shown earlier in Figure 15-32. This removes the cells from the Conditional Formatting Rules Manager dialog box.

② Remove the cells from the **APPLIES TO** field, on the Conditional Formatting Rules Manager dialog box, illustrated in Figure 15-54. To remove a cell, select the $ before the cell, the cell and the comma after it, then press the Delete key. Click the Apply button, then click OK. If you mess up, close the dialog box and try again.

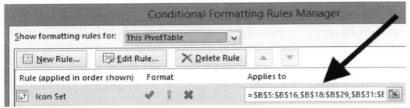

Figure 15-54 Applies to field illustrated

4. Select one of the options discussed above to remove the conditional formatting from cells B17 and B30. When finished, you should not see icons in these two cells.

Adjusting The Space Between The Icons And Data

There is a sizeable amount of space between the icons and data in the pivot table. By default, the icons are left aligned. Changing the icons or data alignment won't work well all of the time, because some data values could be large and others small. This would only allow the data to be aligned on the right. Using the **INCREASE INDENT** option would move the data to the left and keep it aligned on the right.

1. Select the range B17:B29.

2. Home tab ⇒ Alignment section ⇒ Click the Increase Indent button once.

   Figure 15-55 shows the 2008 data indented.

	A	B
3	**Row Labels** ⏷	**Sum of SalesAmount**
4	⊟ **2007**	**$3,144,393,292.13**
5	January ✖	$193,305,554.64
6	February ❚	$209,439,067.93
7	March ❚	$203,991,979.69
8	April ✔	$276,891,048.16
9	May ✔	$288,749,508.61
10	June ✔	$283,186,644.54
11	July ❚	$272,818,635.11
12	August ❚	$263,780,279.28
13	September ❚	$257,282,781.95
14	October ✔	$288,853,903.92
15	November ✔	$308,752,784.65
16	December ✔	$297,341,103.65
17	⊟ **2008**	**$2,642,413,217.03**
18	January ✖	$183,970,020.28
19	February ✖	$191,106,948.30
20	March ✖	$183,393,312.89
21	April ❚	$223,849,292.33

Figure 15-55 Indented data

Color Scales

Figure 15-29 shown earlier, shows the Color Scales options. The options on the sub menu have three or six colors.

The **MORE RULES** option displays similar options as the data bars. Color scales display a gradient background color based on the value in the scale. It is not a requirement to apply the color scale to the entire pivot table.

Exercise 15.10: Create Color Scale Conditional Formatting

This exercise will show you how to apply three color scale formatting. On your own, you can experiment with the options to see what works best with your data.

1. Save the E10.6 workbook as E15.10 Color Scale Conditional Formatting.

2. Remove the Row Labels Top 10 Value filter.

3. Select the range B5:D25 ⇒ Conditional Formatting button ⇒ Color Scales ⇒ More Rules.

4. Change the Format Style option to **3-COLOR SCALE**.

5. Select a color for the Minimum, Midpoint and Maximum options. I prefer using three colors in the same color family, but you can select colors that you want.

    Selecting the **MORE COLORS** option on the Color drop-down list is used to create custom colors. You should have the options shown in Figure 15-56. Figure 15-57 shows the pivot table with the color scale applied.

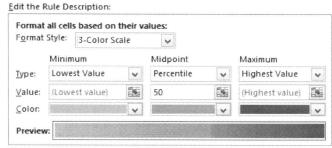

Figure 15-56 Color scale options

4	Row Labels	2007	2008	2009
5	Contoso Albany Store	$7,081,978.89	$4,727,609.36	$4,169,224.12
6	Contoso Alexandria Store	$6,612,399.40	$4,769,138.38	$3,980,032.68
7	Contoso Amsterdam Store	$7,526,105.22	$4,001,770.02	$3,336,812.99
8	Contoso Anchorage Store	$7,041,007.77	$4,707,612.73	$4,420,011.73
9	Contoso Annapolis Store	$6,950,230.55	$4,878,354.56	$4,291,001.64
10	Contoso Appleton Store	$7,091,570.75	$4,822,593.83	$3,899,074.31
11	Contoso Arlington Store	$6,915,310.31	$5,158,464.82	$3,952,938.88
12	Contoso Ashgabat No.2 Store	$7,832,371.46	$8,487,774.60	$9,444,449.58
13	Contoso Ashgabat No.1 Store	$7,374,074.43	$8,733,429.42	$9,664,197.70
14	Contoso Asia Online Store	$156,883,859.58	$188,427,344.54	$212,850,715.76
15	Contoso Asia Reseller	$114,185,396.49	$122,563,956.44	$125,585,967.89
16	Contoso Athens Store	$7,695,648.26	$3,833,526.54	$3,865,558.31
17	Contoso Atlantic City Store	$6,609,523.72	$5,057,540.21	$3,896,191.77
18	Contoso Attleboro Store	$6,659,981.24	$4,791,315.44	$4,033,578.97
19	Contoso Aurora Store	$7,144,291.33	$4,789,827.08	$4,083,439.36
20	Contoso Austin Store	$6,737,409.74	$5,013,923.07	$4,081,586.18
21	Contoso Back River Store	$6,558,714.62	$4,911,027.11	$4,236,970.10
22	Contoso Bacliff Store	$7,268,854.81	$4,942,836.30	$4,129,717.62
23	Contoso Baildon Store	$7,571,069.41	$4,152,973.26	$3,594,493.66
24	Contoso Baltimore Store	$6,847,989.64	$5,088,960.84	$3,829,400.35
25	Contoso Bangkok No.1 Store	$786,515.33	$1,508,081.39	$8,118,519.53

Figure 15-57 Pivot table with a color scale applied

Using The Conditional Formatting Button Options

The conditional formatting exercises in this chapter used the More Rules option. As shown earlier in Figure 15-29, each type of conditional formatting has options on the button that you can use. This section will show you how to create conditional formatting using the options on the sub menus.

Use The Data Bars Menu Options

The steps below show you how to display data bars on a pivot table, like the ones applied earlier in Exercise 15.7. If you want to follow along, save a copy of the E10.1 workbook.

1. Click in a cell, in the column, in the pivot table that you want to apply the conditional formatting to.

2. Conditional Formatting button ⇒ Data Bars ⇒ On the sub menu, select one of the Gradient Fill color options.

3. Click on the button at the end of the cell that you selected, to display the options shown in Figure 15-58. The options are explained below.

Figure 15-58 Formatting rule options

Select the **SELECTED CELLS** option if you only want to apply the formatting to the selected cell in the pivot table. You can select a range of cells before selecting the type of conditional formatting that you want to apply.

The **ALL CELLS SHOWING . . .VALUES** option will apply the conditional formatting to every row in the pivot table and to the grand total column. I am not sure that I understand the point of including the grand total values in the conditional formatting range, as they are usually much larger then the values in the cells.

The **ALL CELLS SHOWING . . . VALUES FOR . . .** option is the one that has the most value in my opinion because it only applies the conditional formatting to the rows, not the grand total amounts.

4. Select the last formatting option.

    The top of the pivot table should look like the one shown in Figure 15-59.

Row Labels ▾	Sum of Subtotal
Amritansh Raghav	$15,432.50
Anna Bedecs	$2,410.75
Christina Lee	$4,949.00
Elizabeth Andersen	$4,683.00
Francisco Pérez-Olaeta	$8,007.50

Figure 15-59 Conditional formatting using the sub menu options

Use The Top/Bottom Rules Menu Options

The steps below will show you how to use the Top/Bottom Rules menu options. If you want to follow along, make a copy of the E10.6 workbook.

1. Select the range in the pivot table, that you want to apply the conditional formatting to.

2. Conditional Formatting button ⇒ Top/Bottom Rules ⇒ On the sub menu, select the **TOP 10 ITEMS** option ⇒ On the dialog box shown in Figure 15-60, if you want, you can select a different color from the second drop-down list ⇒ Click OK.

Figure 15-60 Top 10 Items dialog box

3. On the Formatting Options drop-down list (See Figure 15-58 above), if you select the second option. You will see that the top 10 values are grand totals. This is why I said earlier, that I did not see the point of this option.

Summary

This chapter covered Excel features that can be used to enhance pivot tables. Conditional formatting can help make understanding the data easier. Keep in mind that the formatting is usually applied to the table. While not demonstrated in the exercises, the formatting updates when the data used to create the pivot table changes. For example, Exercise 15.7, displays customers and their subtotal amounts. As more customers are added to the table, the conditional formatting will automatically be applied.

If you are planning to use Power Query, Power View, Power BI Desktop or any tool that can access the data model, you not will have to back track to learn the capabilities of the data model. I hope that this book has provided you with a foundation of Power Pivot that you can use to import your own data and create the pivot tables and charts that you need.

INDEX